LATIN AMERICAN STUDIES
VOL. 4

READERS AND
LABYRINTHS

GARLAND REFERENCE LIBRARY
OF THE HUMANITIES
VOL. 1810

LATIN AMERICAN STUDIES

DAVID WILLIAM FOSTER
Series Editor

READERS AND LABYRINTHS

Detective Fiction in Borges, Bustos Domecq, and Eco

Jorge Hernández Martín

GARLAND PUBLISHING, Inc.
New York & London / 1995

Library of Congress Cataloging-in-Publication Data

Hernández Martín, Jorge, 1956–
    Readers and labyrinths : detective fiction in Borges,
Bustos Domecq, and Eco / by Jorge Hernández Martín.
        p.   cm. — (Garland reference library of the human-
ities ; vol. 1810. Latin American studies ; vol. 4)
    Includes bibliographical references.
    ISBN 0-8153-1515-5 (alk. paper)
    1. Borges, Jorge Luis, 1899–   —Criticism and interpreta-
tion.   2. Bustos Domecq, H. (Honorio)—Criticism and
interpretation.   3. Eco, Umberto. Nome della rosa.
4. Borges, Jorge Luis, 1899—Influence.   5. Detective
and mystery stories—History and criticism.   I. Title.
II. Series: Garland reference library of the humanities ;
vol. 1810.   III. Series: Garland reference library of the
humanities. Latin American studies ; vol. 4.
PQ7797.B635Z734   1995
863—dc20   94-38652
                                                            CIP

Printed on acid-free, 250-year-life paper
Manufactured in the United States of America

¿Eres tú acaso al sopesar estas inquietudes algo más que una indiferencia resbalante sobre la argumentación que señalo, o un juicio acerca de las opiniones que muestro? Yo, al escribirlas, sólo soy una certidumbre que sugiere las palabras más aptas para persuadir tu atención.

[Are you, when considering these restless thoughts, anything more than a passing indifference over the arguments that I am indicating, or a judgment on the opinions that I present? I, when writing them, am only a certainty that suggests the words more apt to persuade your attention.]

Jorge Luis Borges, *Inquisiciones 85*

Contents

Part Three:

THE READERS WRITE: BUSTOS DOMECQ AND *SIX PROBLEMS FOR DON ISIDRO PARODI*

Part Four:

THE TEXT AS WEB: A CASE FOR CONJECTURE IN *THE NAME OF THE ROSE*

Preface

Detective fiction places great emphasis on interpretation, both within the story and in relation to the reader. It uses the reader's involvement with the text as a means to an end: The reader must make conjectures about motives and outcomes in the textual design, and the text anticipates and uses these guesses to arrive at the revelation at the end of the story. The reader, in other words, is an essential part of the story.

The characteristic conventions of the genre make up what I would like to call "the detectory schema." We see it operating in texts as diverse as *Oedipus Rex* and Poe's imaginative Dupin stories. Other works, however, take this conventional schema and problematize it: They change the rules—the formulas of composition—that we have come to expect from detective fiction. Examples are "Death and the Compass" by Jorge Luis Borges, "The Twelve Figures of the World" by Honorio Bustos Domecq, and *The Name of the Rose* by Umberto Eco.

Borges was very interested in the activity of interpretation and conjecture. For him, the great lesson of detective fiction is that we read the story as if the whole truth of the matter were not presented. That manner of reading, he believed, had been created by Poe. Honorio Bustos Domecq is partly his creation: He is the product of a collaboration between Borges and Adolfo Bioy Casares. In the figure of Bustos Domecq, two different experiences of reading have come together to form a writing self on the shared ground of detective fiction. Eco's novel, *The Name of the Rose*, is a veritable Borges museum, with its labyrinth, its library, its mirrors, its menaced detective plot, and, owing something to the wax museum, its aged librarian. In it, he takes Borges's concerns and inscribes them into his text, which becomes a site for transformations and exchanges wrought by the detectory schema.

When one first examines the role of the detective reader, one sees an isolated interpreter who becomes progressively more entangled in the text. The detective reader becomes involved in the interpretation of signs, a process prone to error and imprecision. It is in relation to this process that I develop the idea of the "conjectural," or detectory, reader. When we look at the works of Borges, Bustos Domecq, and Eco, we see in all of them a clear reference to the codes of detective fiction but also a manipulation of the detectory schema for unusual ends. They resist the detective reader and interfere with the single-minded quest that such a reader by definition pursues. How can a critic of these fictions account for such textual strategies?

These issues make up the subject of this book. I begin by exploring the peculiarities of conventional detective fiction and propose that a detectory schema is at work in the texts of this genre; I examine the transformations wrought by Borges, Bustos Domecq, and Eco, and the strategies enacted by the reading and writing selves on the site of the text. In following these threads, we come, in the best detective fiction style, to a revelation: that the answer to the mysterious, enduring appeal of detective fiction lies, for casual readers as well as academic critics, in the semiotic foundations of detective narrative discourse.

Jorge Hernández Martín
Dartmouth College

Foreword

The story of the twentieth century is one of detection. Science and technology have made the modern world into the very image of complexity where we, the readers of a text that is the world (and in which we are also written), are confronted with an overload of signs on whose decipherment depends our sense of who we are. As the Cabbala was to Borges, detective fiction is to us, seeking a metaphor for the process we need to evoke significance in an unsettling world. The investigation of the psyche and its expressions is another instance of clue hunting for patterns of order and confusion.[1] Freud and Jung showed that we ourselves are a mystery, and that the surface of things is not to be trusted, but interpreted in search of hidden meanings. The work of Freud took place in a time when archaeologists were searching for clues of Europe's past. Heinrich Schliemann had unearthed Troy; Arthur Evans was excavating the palace of Minos at Knossos. With their discoveries, myth became palpable history and the image of the labyrinth, a maze of chambers from which escape was nearly if not completely impossible, became a modern symbol for complexity—the complexity of the mind, of intellectual work, of the world. Another name for the thread that leads one out of the maze is "clue"; the detective (archeological and otherwise) following that clue became the modern hero in what also became the typical twentieth-century story.

The first of the three stories that set the standards of what would be known as detective fiction sprung from the mind of Edgar Allan Poe in his Dupin tales of the early 1840s. It is not entirely coincidental that these works were written in the age of science. In science, the term "paradigm" refers to principles that provide models for scientific activity by specifying the problems and setting up methods for their solutions. Poe's tales, also, are paradigms in the discourse of literature. Given their emphasis on scientific method and discovery they may also have influenced the development of scientists. Consider Thomas S. Kuhn's remarks in *The Structure of Scientific Revolutions* on scientific problems as "enigmas" and scientists as "solvers of enigmas": "Enigmas are . . . that special category of problems that may serve to put to the test ingenuity and the ability to solve them" (70). Kuhn's words carry an echo of the detective genre, as if they came from fiction and not from a text intent on explaining the development of science. Detective fiction, broadly defined, clearly has influence and plays a central role in our times. Whether Kuhn meant his utterance to connect to the genre or not, the connection between enigma, inquiry and resolution, and detective fiction exists.

In science, paradigms become worn out as they lose their explanatory power or come at odds with the body of discovery. A similar process occurs in fiction, when the rules guiding a genre become automatic, obvious, and too easily anticipated by the reader, and the yarn fails to entertain. The perpetual and unerring problem solving of the classic detective story eventually fails to amaze, and it is at that point that readers, whose perceptions have been shaped by the form and who have learned to look at certain things in light of the reiterated development of the stories, begin to focus their attention, skeptically, on the pattern of inquiry and resolution itself. Renovation and novelty can be expected from readers who, knowing full well what to expect, read the pattern differently, against itself, and give rise to a change, let us say, in what has become the paradigm of the detective story. This has been the achievement of Borges in detective fiction. The anomalies of his story "Death and the Compass" are the transformations performed by a reader on the paradigm of the classic or English mystery story. Borges's story represents a modest revolution, a brief exploration into new possibilities, an end and a beginning.

Jorge Luis Borges, the labyrinth maker, was both a reader and the author of stories that use the detective theme. In Borges we find an author who has recognized the detective story as a genre at the center of our modernity and who has used it to comment on that modernity. He is not alone in this enterprise; many other writers have found the detective story a means to exemplify many of our present-day concerns, ranging from the limits of rationality and the problems of reading to the limits of interpretation. Borges, of course, has his place in Latin American letters as one of the most influential writers of this century. Some critics, however, consider his affinity for detective fiction to be a quirk of his controversial intellectual persona and of the conditions at that time in Latin America. In a personal interview, Paco Ignacio Taibo II, a prolific representative of the new Mexican detective novel who cultivates the far grittier branch of the detective story developed by the likes of Chandler and Hammett, referred to the work on the genre by Borges and the generation of the 1930s and 1940s in Latin America as the "prehistory" of detective fiction, if not a downright prehistoric expression of the detective story. He was suggesting that the tradition advocated by Borges, who introduced the genre to Latin America, was the "puzzle" type of detective story, the kind depending on the sedentary reasoner detective and the quaint piece of deduction. Given the social conditions of Latin America, Taibo argued, to expect the kind of stability that would allow for a detective to arrive at a solution through methodology, or to assume a degree of operative stability to be present in the detective's investigation, is an unrealistic, even ludicrous, presupposition. Current international practice of the genre has favored the "hard-boiled" tradition established by Hammett, Chandler, and Ross Macdonald, with the detectives at odds with the culture and administrative corruption, and in direct and painful confrontation with the agents of the law—and it has been popular. This implies that by standards of popularity and the proper depiction of social reality, Taibo was right.

Modalities of detective stories are forks in the paths of literature; in contrast to the story that accentuates the social context and reduces the role of logic in the resolution of the mystery, what Borges admires in the work of Poe, Wilkie Collins, G.K. Chesterton, and Agatha Christie is the intellectual labor required to resolve a mystery. The labor of the intellect is something shared by the reader, who anticipates the outcome, and the author, who delays the resolution. The detective story represents for Borges intellectual play and the active practice of doubt in the face of deception; it functions in Borges's work as a metaphor for the process of interpretation and discovery that is closely associated to the act of reading. Borges takes into consideration an instability that is not the instability of social systems but that of language, which reflects the social systems. Of course, both the "hard-boiled" and the older modalities of detective fiction are skeptical of social practice, if social practice includes the act of reading and the development of beliefs. But the skepticism proposed by Borges when he endorses suspicion as reading practice is, perhaps surprisingly, much more radical than the one practiced by the writers of the "hard" school. What the Borges reader is asked to scrutinize is narrative discourse itself and its ability to represent reality. Borges considers the process of resolution of a mystery analogous to an act of reading that is taking place in the instability of language, where inference has no recourse to other criteria for truth but interpretation and further interpretation of "facts," whose veracity is always in question. Borges thus deplores the violence that is found in the "hard" examples of the genre, its sinister characters, and the emphasis on what pretends to be a realistic setting over the problem of reasoning, because it forgets "the intellectual origin of the detective story" [el origen intelectual del relato policial (*Oral* 79)]. With his endorsement of the classic detective story, Borges was making a choice in line with his conception of literacy and the act of reading, which he considered to be the most important and, paradoxically, most anonymous act in literature.

According to Borges, the compositional rigor of the detective story represents for a writer "an obligation to invent," (Rodríguez Monegal and Reid 148), given the restrictions that result from the imposition of rules in composition. The direct result of these rules of composition is the creation of certain expectations in the reader of how the text will work. How well the book meets those expectations it has helped to create becomes a shared criterion on the basis of which reader and author can engage in an intellectual game where textual truth is at stake. The fundamental point in this exchange is that the reader questions the text in a manner that is appropriate to the detective text and to no other; that is, the reader has internalized an approach or way of reading from repeated contact with the form. The writer, bound to invent for a demanding and informed reader, strives for novelty. Faced with deceit, the reader grows suspicious of the author's intentions: "How is the text trying to hide its truth this time?" could be the suspicious reader's query. Borges, in a discussion of detective fiction, proposes that the coming together of the book and a reader is what produces the "aesthetic fact." Perhaps that is a way of saying that at that moment, and at no other, literature happens. His proposition leads him to consider that literary genres depend more on the way they are read than on the texts themselves (*Oral* 67). For Borges, rather than being a set of texts bearing some traits in common, detective fiction represents the creation of a reader.

NOTES

Unless otherwise noted, all English translations are by the author.

1. For the conjunction of the detective and the psychoanalyst, see John P. Muller and William J. Richardson, eds., *The Purloined Poe: Lacan, Derrida, and Psychoanalytic Reading*. See also Michael Sheperd's *Sherlock Holmes and the Case of Dr. Freud* and Nicholas Meyer's *The Seven Per Cent Solution*, a best-selling novel and winner of the Crime Writer's Golden Dagger Award.

PART ONE

*The Obligation to Invent: Readers,
Writers, and the Detectory Schema*

A Model of Competence
The Reader That Detective Fiction Has Made

Detective fiction has made a reader; that is, detective fiction has defined a way of reading that could, in the absence of a detective story text, generate a reading *as if* the text before the reader were a detective story, hiding some specificity such as a name, a place, a motive, a fact. We can conceive of a "specialized" reader who is the product of a process of learning and cognition stemming from a relationship with a certain kind of text. Jorge Luis Borges identifies the reader of detective fiction as one who practices a state of readerly suspicion that has developed from familiarity with this kind of fiction (*Oral* 67). Borges describes it as a way of approaching a story and performing with it certain operations that are intended to dispel a mystery. The presence of a mystery in the text constitutes this reader, and any text can be held suspect of telling only a partial truth. Competence in this role is intertextual and built from recurring features of similar texts, but it can be transposed as a set of cognitive operations to other, generically different texts, transforming them in curious ways.

The Formalist concept of parody is useful for understanding certain developments of the detective story, especially in respect to the way certain aspects of a genre become "automatized," or overly familiar to the reader, and are then used for an effect different from the one initially intended in the work of art.[1] Parody entails an understanding of the prior model that is later interpreted in a way different from the model. The interpretive strategy used in reading a detective novel is the renovating function of the reader, who arises as a critical concept

3

from the detectory schema. In detective fiction (fiction characterized by the detectory schema), the way in which the interpretation takes place (the rules that must be postulated in order to arrive at an answer) is what reveals the nature of the reader who must be "there" for the message to be understood as a message and not as a random series of facts or "noise."

How the reader's "little gray cells" (to quote Christie's Hercule Poirot) will arrange the facts to arrive at an answer is not predictable and remains in the domain of probability, but every text read in the context of generic expectations will be interpreted by what are recognized to be the norms governing that genre. The range of generic expectations becomes a stabilizing factor in the interpretation of texts. This "principle of stability" (in reading) is intertextual currency, transferable to other "raw materials" (texts) as a set of rules that specify a reading strategy used to arrive at an answer through the logic of the question. The result is a different conception of what constitutes a genre: "Genres can be seen not only in the traditional ways as patterns or models that writers follow in constructing texts, but also from the other direction, as different packages of rules that readers apply in construing them, as ready-made strategies for reading" (Rabinowitz, 177). The application of the particular "package" of detective rules can result in misreading, but an examination of the misreading will reveal the composition of the reader created by detective fiction.

In "The Macbeth Murder Mystery," James Thurber presents the following example of a misreading based on the rules of the game established by detective fiction. An American woman on vacation in England, "all ready to read a good mystery story" in her hotel room, finds that chance has provided her with a William Shakespeare paperback tragedy instead of her customary fare. That night the woman becomes convinced that Macbeth is not guilty because "Shakespeare was too smart for that." Macbeth is too clearly a suspect and so is Lady Macbeth. "You suspect them the most, of course, but those are the ones who are never guilty," says the American woman, and she is right, of course. A writer of detective fiction would anticipate the reader's suspicions and, by letting the clues point in one obvious direction, obscure the agent of crime who lurks under a more innocuous disguise. Also notable is the woman's appraisal of the mystery's author. Deviousness is the mystery author's stock in trade, and reputations are made on the cleverness with which the author is able to throw the reader off the scent and have him or her suspect the wrong person. Only the second- and third-rate crafter of detective stories would allow his or her reader see through the plot and anticipate, without much ado, the resolution of the crime. With Macbeth and his Lady thus disqualified by generic practice, the reader's suspicion falls on Banquo, but he soon turns up as the second victim.

The flight of the king's sons is too suspicious for the American woman intent on identifying the ruse designed to throw her off the scent: "When they flee, they are never guilty." Fleeing the scene of the crime is one way of casting instant suspicion on a character; so much so that a detective story reader will discount fleeing characters as too obvious to suspect. Usually, the reader finds out that the character has left for some other reason, perhaps related to some subplot, but not to the central mystery. The reader's concern is with the central criminal, who, incidentally, is usually one person. In one stroke, the American woman makes her discovery and dispels the mystery that has baffled Shakespearian scholars for three hundred years; the American woman names the elusive third murderer. "It was Macduff, I'm certain. You couldn't have one of the victims murdered by two ordinary thugs—the murderer has to be somebody important"; therefore it must be Macduff, who discovers the body and announces the tragedy in such stilted fashion that his intervention seems quite rehearsed.

The last conjecture performed by the American woman upon Shakespeare's text fails to take into account that *all* Shakespearian characters adopt the stylization of speech evident in Macduff. The unhistorical and ungeneric reading that Thurber produces can be explained in terms of the conjectural, or detective, reader, who is responsible for reading *Macbeth* as a detective story. The concern of the detective reader is with the identity of the murderer, and in pursuing this concern the reader foregrounds textual features (facts) by rules that might be quite alien to the text at hand at the expense of a number of factors that resist full appropriation into a detectory schema. In Thurber's example, the rules that "comprise" this reader became apparent in the parodic treatment of the reading experience.

The rule that most constrains the conjectural reader is the proposition "the most obvious suspect is not the murderer." The central issue is the identity of the murderer, and Macbeth is the most obvious person. The conjectural reader proposes a hypothesis that while aiming, for example, to define who is guilty or not guilty, must also explain tentatively *why* it is such as it is (Eco, "Horns" 202). This overcoded process of definition can be traced in a syllogistic mode. ("To define," writes Umberto Eco, "means to isolate the middle term [the cause] and to choose the middle term means to decide what has to be explained" ["Horns" 203]):

> Macbeth is the obvious suspect.
> In a detective story, the obvious suspect is innocent.
> Macbeth is innocent.

The parodic handling of reason in Thurber's story is apparent in the oversight of the reader. "The definition cannot be demonstrated as the conclusion of a syllogism (since it is merely postulated), yet it is a further syllogism that can enable one to see whether there is a corresponding relation among *facts*" ("Horns" 203). This is the role of deduction in scientific reasoning for Charles Sanders Peirce (if the rule is right, every result will prove that the thing is). Nothing, however, ensures that the crucial second term (a framing device) proposed by the reader of detective stories in Thurber's tale is universally true. At best, it is an opinion based on the observation of a number of cases.

The role created for the reader by detective fiction amounts to a strategy of questioning texts. The strategy mirrors the interpretive acts of the detective engaged in the resolution of a case. Eco writes that "a well organized text presupposes a model of competence coming . . . from outside the text, but on the other hand works to build up, by merely textual means, such competence" (*Role* 7–8). The reader that detective fiction has created makes conjectures about the facts presented in the story and formulates questions about the relation between the signs of the text, what they express and what they do not, in order to generate from appearances the explanation that best accounts for the traces of mystery that this reader presupposes to be at work in the text. The role of the reader, as created by detective fiction, is to conduct an "independent" investigation that attempts to anticipate the outcome of each new twist of the story. The clues or signs encountered in the narrative provide the basis on which the pattern of the mysterious event can be postulated as a hypothesis. The outcome of the investigation represents the codification in time of the narrated event; that is to say, the investigator seeks the revelation of guiding principles or motives, sees the sequence of actions in light of some guiding principles that he or she has brought about through imagination, and ultimately, discovers the name of a perpetrator. The reader of detective stories has in common with the student of semiotics a fundamental concern for everything that precedes the sign and is presupposed by it. This isolation of optimal guiding principles in the act of reading is explained by the critic Jonathan Culler in terms of "literary competence":

> When one wonders whether a particular line of thought will work out, whether one will succeed in elucidating an obscure passage, one posits norms of successful interpretations, adequate clarity, sufficient coherence. These norms may remain vague and they may vary from one interpretive community to another, but the process of interpretation is incomprehensible without them, and one is usefully reminded of this by the allusion to norms implicit in the concept of "literary competence." (Culler, *Pursuit* 51)

Conjectural thinking enables the reader to postulate the code at work in the text that best accounts for its composition; it mediates the encounter between reader and text. Conjecture is the fundamental act performed by the reader that permits the codification of the clues hidden among the many facts reported by the detective text.

"Retroduction," as Peirce called it, is one feature of conjectural thinking that is concerned with the elucidation of past events and is therefore of special value to the detective. One of the most famous practitioners of this divinatory art comments to his colleague, Watson: "In the everyday affairs of life it is more useful to reason forward, and so the other comes to be neglected. . . . Most people, if you describe a train of events to them, would tell you what the result would be. . . . There are few people, however, who, if you told them a result, would be able to evolve from their own inner consciousness what the steps were that led to that result. This power is what I mean when I talk of reasoning backward or analytically" (Doyle, 100). In the process of investigation, it is this type of reasoning, frequently expressed as the tracing of effects to causes, that allows sense to be made from obscure circumstances and enables the reader to assemble the tracks that he or she follows in a pattern of order. The importance of this type of reasoning to the sign-based disciplines such as medicine and law is evident, yet seldom has retroduction been recognized as different from deduction and induction, though closely associated with them. Charles Sanders Peirce brought retroduction into its own by recognizing its singular power. The value of "abduction" (another, more general term for the act, which Peirce codified) is that, as he has noted, it is the start of a new idea (*Collected Papers* 2.97). Abduction is the rational process by which a phenomenon, linguistic or otherwise, can be codified and thereby rendered comprehensible. The representation of conjectural, abductive thinking has been a central—if critically neglected—feature of detective fiction from its inception.

The strategies of a conjectural reader can be applied to other texts, not just in detective stories, with the result that story is construed in terms of a detectory schema regulating its composition. The existence of this reader can and very often has been anticipated in the composition of fiction. "To read," writes Jonathan Culler, "is to play the role of a reader and to interpret is to posit an experience of reading . . . it is to imagine what 'a reader' would feel and understand. To read is to operate in the hypothesis of a reader" (*On Deconstruction* 67). Certainly the conjectural reader role is a method of decomposition that can construe a story (any story) as a suspicious reader would: as if the truth was not what was being revealed at any one moment.

A person who chooses to read a work from the genre of detective fiction chooses to read that work because he or she desires a specific effect or gratification which can only be obtained by reading a work of detective fiction. There is a certain thrill involved in reading detective fiction that involves the active pursuit of a line of reasoning, the discarding of one or several hypotheses, and the formulation of new ones with every twist of the story. The ability to play along and against an author's intentions is best understood as a form of competence, but it is important to note that the main motivation to become the model reader—the informed and subtle reader—of a detective story is enjoyment. The enjoyment offered by the detective story is an intellectual one. In Wilkie Collins's *The Moonstone*, the initial narrator Gabriel Betteredge speaks of catching "detective fever," and in the case of the proper Betteredge, it is against his better judgment that he is caught up in the plot and the suspense of the mystery. He is driven by the need to know.

The suspense created by the detective story is—to use an internal combustion metaphor—the fuel for the reader's curiosity, though at this level of engagement the experience of reading detective fiction appears to be rather passive. For the creation of suspense, the author gives the reader enough information to keep him or her thinking and guessing in anticipation of the climactic resolution of the story. It is through engagement with this information that the reader attains an active role in the fiction. One may wait and follow along to find out what the end might be, but the game of detective fiction involves guessing ahead and isolating significant figures on which to base one's hypothesis. There is a margin of error in this process, but the risk taken by the reader is where the gratification lies: The challenge is in being able to remember a certain fact and "abduct" its importance to the solution before that solution is given by the author.

Reasoning is at the center of the detective story. The mental record of facts that readers retain as they travel towards a probable end is one aspect of this process of reasoning. They collect the data into an "encyclopedia" of facts, keeping this information gleaned from the text (some relevant, some irrelevant) suspended, as it were, ready to bring it into play as the case develops. The image of the labyrinth, which appears in the work of Borges and Eco, is related to this "specialized," active reader, the reader who is the product of a process of learning and cognition stemming from a relationship with a certain kind of text. Eco has theorized about Borges's signature metaphor in terms of labyrinthine inferential relations (*Semiotics and Philosophy* 80–84), and the association is fair. Closely related to the mental gathering and recording of information, which produces an encyclopedic collection of facts, is the process of theory formation that accompanies it. One can perceive the almost visual configuration of sense proposed by the hypothesis in terms of a labyrinth where each fact is connected with another (sometimes temporarily) while others lie idle until they are also brought into play by some twist of the plot.

The proposition of hypotheses is another source of enjoyment for the reader of the detective story. The reader may create a scenario for the resolution of the mystery early on and allow the facts encountered in the temporal sequence of the reading to modify it. Again, becoming engaged with the game of detective fiction is a matter of choice. One may choose to be or not to be the model reader proposed by the text. The reader may opt to allow a perception to develop as facts are encountered, reserving the hypothesis for a time when a pattern is well-developed, or the encyclopedia of facts reaches a certain volume. Or he or she may choose to withhold judgment and be passively surprised by the final revelation. Each option represents a step down in the ladder of diminishing returns. The proposal of conjectures is related to the act of gambling, with the stakes at their highest with the earliest hypothesis, when fewer facts are at the reader's disposal. Being correct at this early point in the journey is a triumph of competence and represents the modest risks and intellectual rewards that the genre has to offer for the reasoning reader.

Whether or not one's initial conjecture is correct, the prompt elaboration of a theory for the events narrated has an added value for the detective story reader. This value should be understood in terms of thinking flexibility. The process toward resolution involves a continuous evaluation of the data and sometimes momentous modifications of the "structure" of sense that had been formulated up to the moment of the encounter with the conflicting data. We might recall the American lady's case built against Banquo. She buttresses suspicion with a series of arguments and orders the fictional world in terms of who is most and least likely to have committed the crime at a point in the story. In terms of the detective story, the American lady has built her labyrinth of culpability on the issues of means, motives, and opportunity available to the characters. With the death of Banquo, the process must begin anew, and a fresh arrangement of sense must be produced that, while it may keep some elements in place, must rearrange significantly the playing field in order to produce a new culprit.

Such constant shifts of perspective based on new evidence and, perhaps more interestingly, based on seeing evidence in a new light is another of detective fiction's charms. One may fault the form for its many oversights and shortcomings, but a first-rate detective mystery delivers intellectual stimulation, and it is this stimulation that is sought by the reader who chooses the engagement with the fiction. The transposition of the detective reader from the detective genre to other genres is not of course limited to the case of the American lady. A conjectural reader, the product of detective fiction, questions and anticipates fictional discourse in any of its manifestations. The detective story reader is a conscious reader who questions his or her own intuitions and provides tentative evidence for the feeling of suspicion on the way to a conclusion. In some rational manner, the reader must account for feelings and impressions in terms of facts and argument. The act makes a critic out of the reader for the purposes of fiction.

One other peculiarity of detective readers makes them unique: They seek a solution to a textual enigma. The solution is satisfactory if it answers all the questions raised within the text. This is the expectation of the reader, and the most conspicuous feature of that expectation is a drive toward order and completion.

NOTES

1. For the important Formalist groundwork on parody, see Boris Tomachevsky's "Thematics" (Lemon and Reis, 61–95).

The Detectory Schema
The Case against Oedipus Wrecks

The textual dimension of the detective story, or the detectory schema, allows us to recognize the genre from its formal features. The schema formally defines detective fiction as a set of coded operations that the conjectural reader must perform in order to resolve a mystery. Not only the detective but the reader as well produces hypotheses to account for mysterious circumstances: This is the central effect of the detectory schema. One could imagine the detectory schema as a machine whose sole purpose is to elicit hypotheses from the activating reader, and so the schema works to move the action forward by building expectations and dashing them by turns, heading inexorably toward some resolution. This seemingly infallible abductive process relates back to the textual model that Poe introduced. In the composition of short stories, Poe was a practicing advocate for the Aristotelian conception of plot with a clear beginning, middle, and end. It is toward this end, which should produce "a single effect," that Poe's short stories are geared, and that is certainly the case with his Dupin stories, in which the detectory schema plays an important part. Poe's narrative disposition defines one of the important presuppositions constituting the conjectural reader. This reader is formed by the knowledge that not only is there a mystery to be solved in the story, but the mystery has a unique and unifying solution.

From the Greeks came the imperative to pursue research wherever it may lead; isn't Oedipus the man who had to know the truth, whatever the cost? The critic Bernard Knox has written, "Oedipus's heroic achievement is the discovery of the truth and that discovery is the most thoroughgoing and dreadful catastrophe the stage has ever presented" (132). Oedipus followed the clues, questioned the witnesses, and sought out the metaphorical Minotaur in a maze of his own making. The irony of Sophocles' play *Oedipus Rex* is that Oedipus finds his own image at the center of the maze. Much has been written about this prototypical tragedy, which was the model used by Aristotle for his *Poetics*.[1] The three main elements of the detectory schema—a mystery, an inquiry, the concealed facts made known—are the central feature of the four acts that comprise the body of the work. This is not to say, however, that the play is a "whodunnit" in the traditional sense that one associates with the stories of the detective genre; the detectory schema apparent in the play is only one aspect of the tragedy.[2] In fact, as I will show, if read in terms of the detectory schema and the problem of cognition that the schema implies, the play loses the tragic necessity at its heart.

When Poe adapted poetic logic to the ends of crime detection, he established a set of laws governing the mechanics of text production's, structure and logical conventions. This adherence to norm in the creation of generic fiction has a parallel in the reader's expectations. The reader anticipates the elements that comprise a mystery: It should originate with a crime that will find its solution in the course of the investigation. The investigation will proceed by the rational means available to a detective for the deciphering of clues and will ultimately reveal a criminal along with a summary of the means used in attaining the solution (Todorov 44). The mystery schema consists of a cause (usually associated with the solution, a series of effects or clues) and a methodology, which allows for the reduction of possibilities in the text to a single formulation. This duality, described by Tzvetan Todorov in "Typology of the Detective Story" in *The Poetics of Prose*, is the basis of the Oedipus story.

Sophocles' tragedy also has a temporal structure that is characteristic of detective fiction. Tzvetan Todorov identifies two such structures in the traditional form. The generic text consists of a narrative that proceeds chronologically as the investigation unfolds in a process of reconstructing an earlier narrative, the story of the crime that made the investigation necessary (44). Todorov's claim is that there are always two stories in the single instance of the detective story. The investigation is an attempt at presenting an ordered account of an initial story from traces that persist in the present. The reordering that takes place in the detective mystery amounts to reducing the excesses of the past (its *outré* features revealed in details) into the linear, singular chronicle that is the account of an investigation culminating with discovery. For the reader, the set of laws governing this second story exist as a ready-made text that can be superimposed on any subject matter (or plot) to constitute the binary relation that Todorov identifies in the detective story.

If read as detective fiction, *Oedipus Rex* will reveal an unusual conclusion. This conclusion is less dramatic than the discovery made by Oedipus, but it is startling in its own right: If all the evidence found in the play is evaluated on the terms of the detective reader, one will come to the conclusion that Oedipus did not necessarily murder his father Laius. The reader must leave by the wayside all preconceived notions about the case in order to evaluate the facts properly. The key is to disregard prophecy and supernatural agencies, which, given the conventions of the detective genre, are ways to obscure the truth and delay or misdirect the investigation. Oedipus, in fact, does this at the early stages of his inquiry into the case of the murdered king. In his inquiry into the forgotten murder of Laius, Oedipus pits his method of rational investigation against the method of divine prophecy that he mocks in his address to the soothsayer Tiresias: "With no help from the birds, the flight of my own intelligence hit the mark" (161). Oedipus's approach to the investigation of the king's death defines him and his role. Oedipus, Knox writes, "is a questioner, a researcher, a discoverer—the Greek words are those of the sophistic vocabulary" (125). The real interest of the play lies in how Oedipus goes about finding the truth, dispelling the darkness of ignorance. "I'll bring it all to light myself," Oedipus says (147), and he is then "the investigator, prosecutor and judge of a murderer" (124). Oedipus's retroductive rationalism holds center stage. Knox explains:

> Prophecy was one of the great controversial questions of the day. It was in fact the key question, for the rationalist critique of the whole archaic tradition had concentrated its

fire on this particular sector. . . . If the case for divine
foreknowledge could be successfully demolished, the
whole traditional edifice went down with it. If the gods
did not know the future, they did not know any more than
man. These are exactly the issues of the Sophoclean play.
(120)

Like the classic mystery, *Oedipus Rex* begins with a crime *ante res*.
Oedipus's decision to consult the oracle of Delphi is arrived at
through "groping, laboring over many paths of thought" (142).
The actions of Oedipus are guided by reason and, progressively,
by observation and conjecture. When Creon returns from the
oracle with news of a defilement that has resulted from the death
of the king, Oedipus the investigator asks, "Where to find it now,
the trail of ancient guilt so hard to trace?" (145). He seeks to find
the clue that will lead him to other clues, which will lead to a
name. In this, the most purely detectory feature of Sophocles'
play is revealed: Oedipus's quandary is a quest for "who did it?"

How is Oedipus going to discover the guilty party after so
many years? He is soberly assessing the limits of the possible in
dramatically charged conditions. After determining where the
crime is committed, he asks about the existence of witnesses to the deed: "No messenger, no fellow traveller saw what
happened? Someone to cross-examine?" (145). Oedipus concentrates on the mechanics of the crime. Analyzing the available
data is of paramount importance. The search that engages both
Oedipus and the reader is for information that will allow a
rational explanation, and that they can use to solve the mystery.
How relevant the information gathered may be to the plot is
equally important for the resolution; hence, the initial resistance
of Oedipus and Iocasta to the words of Tiresias. If the
information Tiresias has to give is a product of incantations and
the interpretation of omens, it may not serve to bring the
investigation any closer to the truth. In the prologue of the play,
Oedipus has solved the riddle of the Sphinx; he is full of
intellectual pride. To Tiresias, Oedipus says: "There was a riddle,
not for some passer-by to solve—it cried out for a prophet.
Where were you? Did you rise to the crisis? Not a word, you and
your birds, your gods—nothing. No, but I came by; Oedipus the
ignorant, I stopped the Sphinx!" (161). Oedipus exults over the

power of his intellect and his ability to reason.[3] The role of Oedipus occurs in all detective narrative: the investigator who becomes manifest by his decision to investigate. Oedipus thus reveals one aspect of the principles of the detectory schema.

The reader who must work with or against the turns of Oedipus's inquiry, like the detective at the onset of the investigation, will ignore possibly misleading preconceptions, mystical explanations for events, and foreshadowing while observing the events, speeches, and facts presented within the story as possible evidence for the correct interpretation of the mystery. Evidence that contradicts other evidence is particularly important because it indicates that someone may be lying or lacks information that the reader has, which places the reader at an advantage over that character and allows the reader to judge the degree of a character's participation in the events. Contradiction might also indicate two conflicting interpretations of the truth in the fictional world that will have to be evaluated by the reader. It is the reader's task to produce a potential explanation for the state of things in the face of, and very often using, contrasting pieces of evidence.

Equally important for the reader is the absence of relevant evidence, for the absence of facts also casts a light on the resolution of an enigma. If evidence is missing from the text, the reader can tentatively rule out certain actions, since, if they had happened, the evidence would necessarily be displayed in the text. Finally, the reader must constantly ask the question that organizes every configuration of sense produced in the reading: Is a particular conclusion arrived at from evidence consistent with the rest of the evidence presented in the story? Or, placing the evidence in relation to the conclusion, is the evidence presented in the story consistent with a particular conclusion? Both the reader and any interpreting agency within the text must answer this fundamental detectory question, since it is from the correspondence between evidence and hypothesis that a conclusion that accurately describes the events that have taken place will be developed.

In a detectory reading of *Oedipus Rex*, the first and most important thing for the reader to do is suppress any preconceived ideas about Oedipus's doings and presumed guilt and to proceed with the investigation on the basis of what is found in the text. If the reader comes to the story with a preconceived notion of who Oedipus is or what he has done, he or she will enter the story looking for evidence that confirms the preconceived idea. Of these preconceptions, the most pernicious is that Oedipus is guilty of the death of his father. The death of the king is undeniable; it is outside the action and unchangeable. The determination of *who* killed him was not likely to have been the true interest of the play to an Athenian audience. Lore had already made that aspect of the plot common knowledge. The tension of the play, for the Greek audience, would have centered on *how* Oedipus would find out the name of the murderer. While Oedipus might be guilty of his father's death in the myth, Sophocles' play does not follow the myth to the letter. In his commentary on the play, James Hogan points out that according to legend, the plague in Thebes occurs immediately after Oedipus's triumphs over the Sphinx, whereas Sophocles allows a significant amount of time to pass for "the dramatic gain to be had from the fall of a king happy and secure in throne and family" (23). At the same time, the expansion of the interim blurs the clues of the murder case in the memory of witnesses and in the physical evidence that can be produced to arrive at a clear conclusion. Also, if an inconsistency with the Greek myth is apparent in Sophocles' rendering of the events, a detectory reader may conclude that other inconsistencies are equally possible, throwing the case against Oedipus open for investigation.

    A second preconception that compromises Oedipus, but is untenable for a detective reader, is that in fulfilling part of the crimes imputed to him, he has fulfilled all of them. It is evident that Iocasta is Oedipus's mother and that Oedipus has had carnal relations with her. The time that Sophocles has let pass in his representation of the events has allowed the couple to produce offspring that are mentioned in the play and one, a daughter, appears in the play in order to accompany the blinded Oedipus into exile. But just because Oedipus has carnal knowledge of his mother does not imply that he killed his father (except in an important metaphoric sense). Oedipus admits guilt for the murder of Laius because he accepts the truth of the whole prophecy when he finds out that Iocasta is his mother. Culturally, Oedipus is a Theban, and as a Theban he is predisposed to believe in prophecy, though he resists the lure of supernatural agents long enough to assert his being a man of reason. But it is unacceptable to a detective reader that Oedipus's actions be predetermined, since these predeterminations do not follow the laws of nature, which are the natural domain of the inductive process of discovery; predetermination is not valid as detectory proof.

In the eyes of the detective reader, Oedipus wavers in one shining moment between the rational and thorough path of investigation and the lure of the occult. If Oedipus had not had a propensity to believe in prophecies, reportedly from before the beginning of the play when he fled Corinth to escape the words of a soothsayer, he would not have been so apt to believe his own and total guilt after a cursory evaluation of evidence that was, in fact, insufficient to convict him. The initial report of the death of Laius is delivered by Creon, who cites the surviving witness to the king's murder. Creon describes the scene as reported by the witness in the following way: "He said thieves attacked them—a whole band, not single-handed, cut King Laius down" (146). Previously, Creon had entreated Oedipus to take up the cause of the king's death by order of Apollo saying that the oracle had commanded, "Pay the killers back—whoever is responsible" (144). The key point to be gathered from Creon's report of the events, which includes the command of Apollo, is that Laius was killed by a group of men, not by a single agent.

Oedipus does notice the implications of the witness's testimony. While waiting for the witness to appear in court, he says to Iocasta, who recalls that Laius had been killed by robbers at a crossroads, "You said *thieves*—[the witness] told you a whole band of them murdered Laius. So, if he still holds to the same number, I cannot be the killer. One can't equal many. But if he refers to one man, one alone, clearly the scales come down on me: I am guilty" (188). The survivor's testimony that Laius was killed by a group of robbers creates a discrepancy with the story of Oedipus's single-handed killing that must be resolved. Oedipus does recall his encounter with a party at a crossroads and tells of having killed everyone in the entourage, "every mother's son" (186). However, no witness is reported in his version of the events, which could therefore be an account of a different encounter and another murder. In regard to the witness's testimony, the persistent question is why, if it were Laius's entourage that Oedipus encountered on the road, has he mistaken Oedipus, a royal prince from Corinth, for a band of robbers?[4]

At this point, before the witness of Laius's murder is brought to the Theban court, a detectory reader, finding the erstwhile detective under investigation, will have examined Oedipus's entanglement along the lines laid out above and will be willing to suspend any verdict until new evidence is produced on the case. As the story continues, Oedipus's conclusions as well as the conclusions of most readers of the play diverge from the interpretation of the detectory reader. One can understand how the shock of having committed an incestuous act (when in fact he thought he had been trying to avoid it) could make Oedipus believe he was a murderer. Overwhelmed by the force of fate in the prophecy, and against his better judgment—as he showed at the onset, before he himself was accused by Tiresias—Oedipus jumps to the conclusion that since he has committed incest, he must also be guilty of murder. What is harder to understand is why so many readers have jumped along with him to this feeble conclusion.

The witness to Laius's murder, a shepherd, confirms that he received an infant from the queen to dispose of and proceeds to give further evidence for the possibility of Oedipus' innocence in relation to the murder of the king. The Corinthian messenger who later gave the infant to the foster parents Polybus and Merope is present at the inquest and points out to the shepherd that the man who stands before them is the very infant that the shepherd had given him so many years before: "Look, here he is, my fine old friend—the same man who was just a baby then" (209). One translator of and commentator on the play, Thomas Gould, notes that "it probably should be inferred . . . that the herdsman does not know that Oedipus and the foundling are the same person until the [messenger] tells him" (132). The shepherd's ignorance also implies that he also does not recognize Oedipus as the man who assaulted the king's retinue. Though made aware of the identity of Oedipus in relation to his abandonment, the shepherd goes on to say that "if you are the man he says you are, believe me, you were born for pain" (213). The shepherd does not, in other words, make a connection between Oedipus and parricide. When he relates how the queen relinquished the child, he explains that the reason given was that the child *would* kill his parent (213). The verb form is irresolute: The shepherd does not know that this man has killed—or even that he will kill—his parent. Equally important is the fact that the shepherd is never asked whether this man before him is the murderer of the king. That connection is an inference barely supported by the exchange that seals Oedipus's fate.

At the end of the passage of the shepherd's testimony, Oedipus declares his own guilt: "I stand revealed at last—cursed in my birth, cursed in marriage, cursed in the lives I cut down with these hands!" (213). Later, Oedipus sentences himself to death: "[The god's] command was clear, every word: death for the father-killer, the curse—he said destroy me!" (227). The detectory reader finds this sentence rather hasty. First, the shepherd does not express any recognition of Oedipus as the man who killed his master, and neither does he establish whether the crime was committed by one man or many, which was the point of bringing the witness into court; second, Oedipus does not recognize the shepherd to be a man in the party that he attacked at the crossroads. For the detectory reader, the tragedy of Oedipus's case is Oedipus's failure to carry out his investigation in the manner he set out to do, and his further failure to decisively determine his guilt from the questioning of the facts and the unearthing of evidence. Oedipus's example is a case of a detective mystified in the face of overwhelming odds, and the pity felt is pity for a man who, once having established his qualifications as a reasoner, falls prey to his belief in the supernatural and the power of fate. In the face of the evidence (or the lack of it) in the text, the detective reader must come to the conclusion that Oedipus is innocent of parricide, and that the play is a cautionary tale about the dangers of unquestioned evidence, since the particular conclusion arrived at by Oedipus is not consistent with the evidence presented in the story.

The critic Jonathan Culler concurs with the detectory reader's conclusion by noting that "Oedipus himself and all his readers are convinced of his guilt but our conviction does not come from the revelation of the deed . . . . His conclusion is based not on new evidence concerning a past deed but on the force of meaning, the interweaving of prophesies and the demands of narrative coherence" (*Pursuit* 174). Oedipus's discovery is the discovery of his fundamental ignorance that yields to "the force of meaning." The detectory reader, using a method which critically analyzes the evidence and separates the processes of reason from superstition and false associations, reaches a conclusion about the case of Oedipus that deviates significantly from the mainstream interpretation of the work. It is important to note that what such reading brings into question is the necessity of meaning of the narrative. In the case of *Oedipus Rex*, meaning evidently precedes the events narrated. Culler explains that "if [Oedipus] were to resist the logic of signification, arguing that 'the fact that he's my father doesn't mean that I killed him,' demanding more evidence about the past event, [he] would not acquire the necessary tragic stature" (175). *Oedipus Rex* is a tragedy of cognition, and recognition is at the very center of the work. Oedipus recognizes that "he is not the measure of all things but the thing measured and found wanting" (Knox, 126). To the detective reader, Oedipus (whose name resembles the Greek word *oida*, "I know" [134]), has been involved in a quest for a culprit's identity and has been undone because he is unaware of his own actions and unable to maintain the detectory frame of mind during his investigation, which might have cleared him of at least one of the heinous crimes with which he is faced. Recognition is a feature that the play shares with the detectory schema and its drive toward identifying either the murderer or the means by which the crime was committed. Discovery is equally at the center of the detectory story, where "the final discovery that two characters of the plot are only one," as Borges reminds his reader, "can be pleasurable" (Rodríguez Monegal and Reid, 71).

NOTES

1. A survey is provided in *Twentieth-Century Interpretations of Oedipus Rex*, edited by M.J. O'Brien. For the sources of Sophocles' play, see J.P. Vernant and P. Vidal-Naquet's *Tragedy and Myth in Ancient Greece*. Also, a valuable discussion of Sophocles' play as mystery is to be found in David I. Grossvogel's *Mystery and Its Fictions* (22–38).

2. In regard to the relation between the detective and drama, Ionesco makes a rather extreme, but challenging assertion: "All the plays that have ever been written, from Ancient Greece to the present day, have never been anything but thrillers. Drama has always been realistic and there has always been a detective about. Every play is an investigation brought to a successful conclusion. There is a riddle and it is solved in the final scene" (*Plays* 2.119).

3. Vernant and Detienne discuss the social context of Oedipus' power of intellect in *Cunning Intelligence in Greek Culture and Society*; they identify one particular type of intelligence known to the Greeks as *metis*, "an intelligence which, instead of contemplating unchanging essences, is directly involved in the difficulties of practical life with all its risks, confronted with a world of hostile forces which are disturbing because they are always changing and ambiguous" (44). The etymology of *metis* relates its expression to "very ancient techniques that use the pliability and torsion of plant fibres to make knots, ropes, meshes and nets to surprise, trap and bind and that exploit the fact that many pieces can be fitted together to produce a well-articulated whole" (46). The solving of enigmas and riddles is one level of operation of *metis* (2).

4. For further discussion of this aspect of the tragedy, see Sandor Goodhart's "Oedipus and Laius' Many Murderers."

In Poe's Image
The Reader That Poe Has Created

Edgar Allan Poe's story "The Murders in the Rue Morgue" (1841) refines the detectory schema by introducing the figure of the reasoning detective to the composition of the narrative. Similarly, by means of the acumen of Auguste Dupin, in both "The Mystery of Marie Rogêt" (1842) and "The Purloined Letter" (1845) the process of investigation ends with a revelation of the truth arrived through an intellectual process. This emphasis on coming to the end point where something is revealed is a teleological conception of composition, one that relates closely to Aristotle's definition of plot as something with a beginning, middle, and end. As Poe himself said, an author should seek a single effect by means of the aesthetic manipulation of the reader.[1] The concision of his compositional method is clearly evident in "murders," the first of the stories that establish Poe as the inventor and "undisputed master" of the detective genre, according to Borges (Alifano, 45).

In "The Murders in the Rue Morgue," Poe begins to formalize the detectory schema into the literary generic conventions that would define detective fiction for years to come. He establishes a number of devices still useful today in the game of delay and misdirection that characterizes the genre: "The wrongly suspected man, to whom all the superficial evidence (motive, access, etc.) points; the hermetically-sealed death chamber . . . ; the solution by the unexpected means" (Sayers, *Omnibus* 17). There are still other contributions to be found in that and the other stories mentioned, a list of which constitute a veritable catalogue: "The transcendent and eccentric detective; the admiring and slightly stupid fool; the well-intentioned blundering and unimaginativeness of the official guardians of the law . . . deduction by putting one's self in another's position . . . concealing by means of the ultra-obvious; the staged ruse to force the culprit's hand; even the expansive and condescending explanation when the chase is done" (Haycraft, *Art* 12).

Poe's emphasis on methodology in the resolution of his detective stories has led some readers to consider him not so much the inventor of a type of fiction, but rather the proponent of a rational method for which his fiction provides a structural model (Harrowitz, 180–81). That argument does justice to the "ratiocinative" accent of Poe's stories, which is the display of abductive reasoning on the part of Dupin, the detective in "The Murders in the Rue Morgue." It is the character of Chevalier Auguste Dupin that gives us the first clues about the nature of the reader that Poe is creating by his fiction. Borges points out Dupin's "decent voluntary impersonality": "We know nothing even of the face of this individual who dates from the year 1841; he has no more visible features than infinite night or libraries" (*Tri Quarterly* 364). As Poe says himself, his hero seems to resemble a mode of mind or a set of mental features: "As the strong man exults in his physical ability, delighting in such exercises as call his muscles into action, so glories the analyst in that moral activity which *disentangles*" (*Complete* 2). With "moral," Poe implies "mental." "Mental" is the general character of Dupin's interests: "He is fond of enigmas, of conundrums, of hieroglyphics; exhibiting in his solutions of each a degree of *acumen* which appears to the ordinary apprehension pre-ternatural. His results brought about by the very same essence of method, have, in truth, the whole air of intuition" (2). The central goal of "The Murders in the Rue Morgue" is the celebration of Dupin's use of analytical detection to solve murder.

The story is built around Dupin's unique detection abilities, making them the focus of the reader's attention. The concept of analytical detection is presented in a brief introduc-tion, followed by an episode in which Dupin is able to "read" the narrator's thoughts. Then Poe utilizes various techniques to keep the reader's attention focused on Dupin's singular ability. The murders are gruesome, yet the reporting is detached because the details are gathered from newspaper reports and couched in the medical style of the professional inquest. The emotional ramifications are kept in check by this approach. Personal information about the victims is kept to a minimum, so that sympathy is not felt for the characters; rather, the mechanics of the event, dryly reported, become the focus of attention for the reader.

The plight of the wrongly accused man, Le Bon, is also downplayed. Dupin expresses his concern for the case in the following terms: "An inquiry will afford us amusement . . . and besides, Le Bon once rendered me a service for which I am not ungrateful" (120): a slight acquaintance between the two men and merely hinted at, with the result that personal interest is not seen as Dupin's motivation in the case. Instead, Dupin claims to be lured by what Peirce, in defining the process of imaginative hypotheses-making, called "the play of musement." Dupin's claim implies no emotional considerations to sidetrack either the detective's or the reader's attention from the analytical activity that is the hallmark of the story. Another concern that becomes evident in Dupin's handling of the stories' elements is the character of the investigator himself: Poe distances the character of the investigator from his reader.

One reason for this might be that character development would detract from a full appreciation of the character's acumen, his most distinguishing feature. The idiosyncrasies of Dupin's character do not upstage his deductive powers. Dupin is a recluse, a friend of darkness, and yet his life is never presented with the kind of detailed development that would allow the reader to dwell on it. This aspect of the investigator's life is left purposely vague. Our knowledge of Dupin's doings is mediated by the narrator, who can manipulate our perception of the detective. The critic Leroy Day notes that Dupin is full of contradictions that never allow the reader to fully understand his character. Without a full understanding of the character, the reader cannot form an attachment to some imagined sense of person: "Dupin turns out to be the precise bundle of contradictions which render him immune to psychological analysis" (38). Dupin is both mysterious and revelatory in the stories, in keeping with the creative and resolvent aspects of his personality that account for his acumen.

Borges, taking exception to Dorothy Sayers's preference for the more developed character of Sherlock Holmes, comes to the defense of Dupin with the following observation: "Sherlock is inferior to Auguste, not only because a decipherer of ashes and a hunter of bicycle tracks is inferior to a reasoner but above all because he is not an 'ingenious automaton'" (*TriQuarterly* 364). "Ingenious automaton" is a label that Borges borrows from George Bernard Shaw, and it is an appropriate, humorous, and oddly flattering tag for Dupin, who is appreciated by Borges precisely for his lack of psychological appeal. Dupin is a character whose self-professed method to discover the ways of the criminal mind is mental identification with his opponent. Dupin is a dehumanized consciousness whose approach to interpretation reminds one of Eco's Model Reader, who, as Lubomir Dolezel says, "becomes a metonym for the set of interpretive norms which have to be applied to resolve the case" (182). The reader that Poe has modeled with Dupin is a proficient reader, or rather, the reader who represents the degree of proficiency demanded by the text.

Borges's criticism of Holmes as "a decipherer of ashes and a hunter of bicycle tracks" means that Holmes relies too often on observation and thus short-changes the reasoner he is capable of being to the detriment of the detective story (*TriQuarterly* 364). Holmes's reliance on classification systems to interpret ashes, for example, has been criticized from other quarters. Pierre Nordon notes that "Holmes gets much more conclusive results from observation than from logical processes" (Nordon in Sebeok and Umiker-Sebeok, 24). Determining a man's height from the length of his steps, Sebeok Thomas argues, is a feat of much less intellectual caliber than, say, reasoning that the nail fastening a window *must* be broken because the turn of events dictate that fact by logical imperative. The central issue of the detectory schema is the use of reason.[2] The reader has to choose an interpretive approach that accounts for the context of the problem and that is appropriate to its composition. The approach he or she chooses will foreground certain aspects of the problem and neglect others. The solution of the mystery depends on this motivated choice.

The process of proper analytic detection is introduced by Poe in "The Murders in the Rue Morgue." Poe describes it as a form of proficiency that means "capacity for success" in undertakings "where mind struggles with mind" (*Complete* 3). Through the unidentified narrator of the story, Poe likens the process to a game of draughts, which he then contrasts to a game of chess. In reference to chess, Poe comments that "what is complex is mistaken for what is profound." Chess is usually considered the more difficult of the two games, but only because of the combinatory number of possible moves. In contrast, draughts is really a greater test of skill. Chess can be lost or won depending on which opponent concentrates the hardest, while draughts is won by the player with the keenest sense of strategy and perception.

Using this comparison, Poe then differentiates between the analyst (draughts player) and the ingenuous man (chess player): "The analytical power should not be confounded with simple ingenuity; for while the analyst is necessarily ingenious, the ingenious man is often remarkably incapable of analysis" (*Complete* 4). Poe admires analytical skills, for they include "a comprehension of all the sources whence legitimate advantage may be found" (3). In other words, the ingenious man is brilliant only in a certain context, while the analyst is capable of thinking outside the boundaries and observing everything that is relevant to the game. An analytic draughts player observes not only what is on the board in front of him, but reads the face and actions of his opponent for further advantage. In the same respect, Poe's detective will not look for "what has occurred," but "what has not occurred before." He is not confined by the conventional order of investigation (the boundaries of the board game) but thinks outside the routine of investigation. It is this ability that comprises true acumen.

In a semiotic framework, Poe's discussion of a game of draughts is analogous to a communicative act that "presupposes a signification system as its necessary condition" (Eco, *Theory* 9) but is not limited to a singular signification system in order to take place. On the contrary, the exchange described by Poe gives a specific orientation to the movement of the pieces on the board, for example, but it also involves the knowledge of many other codes or rules organizing meaning, such as gestures and the calculation of probabilities as sources of advantage. Proficiency is fully realized in the act of recovering (or producing) meaning. It comes from knowledge attained through attention and acumen and constitutes "that perfection in the game which includes a comprehension of *all* the sources whence legitimate advantage may be derived" (*Complete* 3). In "The Murders in the Rue Morgue," Poe's theorizing is rudimentary (it will be more developed in "The Purloined Letter"). Still, the story sets many of the precedents for understanding this reader that Poe has made.

When Poe writes that "the analyst throws himself into the spirit of his opponent, identifies himself therewith," (*Complete* 3) he writes certainly about empathy between minds in a vein of psychologistic understanding typical of Romantic hermeneutics,[3] but the context of his discussion makes it clear that this empathy takes place in a field of relations that are largely codified as game. It is helpful, then, to recover Poe's insight on acumen as an evaluational skill in which the other's presence is understood as part of a semiotic construct that is propitiated by the encounter and by whose rules the analyst, to use Poe's terms, "may seduce into error or hurry into miscalculation" (3). Both reader and writer are bound and identified so inextricably with the compositional rules of the detectory schema that it is difficult to assert where the role of one ends and the other begins.

In her essay on Poe, Dorothy Sayers emphasizes that all the clues needed for the resolution of the mystery are given to the reader in Poe's detective stories. Sayers notes that this element of "fair play" is most interesting for the connoisseur, because it allows for a higher degree of involvement in the resolution of the mystery ("Introduction" 18). The reader can anticipate the answer to the clues by formulating conjectures on the basis of facts that are made equally available to the detective and the reader. The aspect of the intellectual game that takes place between the detective and the criminal who covers his tracks and tries to outwit his pursuer is amplified in an analogous (and parallel) operation that takes place between reader and narrator.

Emphasis on the "fair play" rule (which is mainly concerned with the regulation of facts made available to the reader) enables the development of a competence in guessing along with the detective, the agent of reason in the text. Competence in detective fiction also involves recognizing the compositional regularities of the genre and anticipating them in the story. At this stage, the true conflict is between author and reader: "After reading half a dozen stories by one author," writes Sayers, the reader "is sufficiently advanced in Dupin's psychological method . . . to see with the author's eyes. . . . Instead of detecting the murderer, he is engaged in detecting the writer" ("Introduction" 43). In order to understand a detective story, the reader begins with an orientation toward the conceptual horizon of the narration, which in the case of the detective story necessitates attention also to its rules of composition, which form part of the conceptual horizon of the author who sets out to render the mystery. The detective story represents the articulation of these two compositional principles by means of recognizable, shared conventions. The author and the reader are both encoded in the genre as equivalent interpretive strategies composing the narrative. It is, therefore, not surprising to find the double a recurrent feature in detective fiction.

"The Murders in the Rue Morgue" is not a story of empathy between minds. The facts of the case do not allow it, since the perpetrator of the crime is an ape. Dupin has to think, rather, on the means necessary to lure the owner of the ape into revealing himself. The case serves as an exposition of Dupin's method. It is because of this emphasis that the story does not play as fair with the reader as Sayers would believe, since some of the evidence that is found near the scene of the crime and that identifies the sailor who owns the ape is not produced until Dupin explains the mystery, making it impossible for the reader to anticipate this identification. Similarly, the inhuman hair found in the victim's hand is produced as evidence at the end, making this part of Dupin's solution doubly baffling for the reader, who has not been informed up to this point of its existence, and who cannot quite accept that the police, no matter how inept, would have missed such a piece of evidence. But it is precisely Poe's focus on Dupin's reasoning powers in this, the first detective story, that explains the sleight of hand that makes his solution all the more surprising in its effect. Poe makes clear that the quality of Dupin's observations is crucial and contingent on knowing what constitutes an important element in the particular case. The story began with a theoretical discussion of the method of inquiry needed for detection. This method is systematic in its application, not merely intuitive. It is also not Cartesian, that is, not a formalized series of steps to be applied to every problem. Poe stresses the importance of the particular, and Dupin's investigation is the exemplary case of the detective's duty to knowing what particulars to look for.

The similarity between Dupin's method and Peircian abduction could not be more marked. Both rely on observation in the determination of possible causes and on intuition in the formulation of hypotheses. The detective story from Poe to the present relies on prominent displays of abductive reasoning as the groundwork for what is known and how it is known. Dupin's method shares with Peirce's pragmatism the belief that the meaning of signs depends on the activity of those signs within inquiry. Peirce was, in fact, familiar with at least one of Poe's ratiocination stories. In a commentary on "The Murders in the Rue Morgue," Peirce echoes Dupin's pronouncement that the *outré* character of that grisly crime is the very reason for its easy solution. Peirce writes: "Those problems that at first blush appear utterly insoluble receive, in that very circum-stance . . . their smoothly-fitting keys" (*Collected Papers* 6.460). One of the seemingly insurmountable challenges to Dupin's acumen is the locked-room setting of the crime in the Rue Morgue. The critic John Irwin notes that faced with the circumstances, Dupin searches for a "clew," a particular fact that will allow him to start the elaboration of a hypothesis. Irwin's clever suggestion is that the search for a "clew" leads him to the "clou," which is the French word for nail (Irwin 50–51): A broken window nail is the solution to the mystery of the locked room. What is significant about Dupin's discovery is that the detective concludes that the window must be the only means of egress from the room. It is then that Dupin examines the window and discovers that the fastening nail is in fact broken. Dupin discovers the window and solves the mystery by means of reason, combined with the belief that there is a rational explanation to everything.

Similarly, the exaggerated nature of the crime leads Dupin to doubt a human agent: "It is not our part, as reasoners, to reject [this conclusion] on account of apparent impossibilities. It is only left for us to prove that these apparent 'impossibilities' are, in reality, not such" (*Complete* 16). "The Murders in the Rue Morgue" enunciates for the first time the key features of the detectory reader: "When you have eliminated all the impossibilities, then, whatever remains, *however improbable*, must be the truth" and, also, that the *outré* features of a mystery are precisely what makes it easy to solve (Sayers, "Introduction" 17). To comprehend the matter as a whole, the detective must form a configuration of the facts to account for the event. The most important quality of this configuration must be that its features fit the crime. Whereas the police see in the crime a statistical whole requiring a preestablished application of method to all cases, Dupin argues for evaluation in context, with the content providing the norms of inquiry.

In contrast, "The Man of the Crowd" is another of Poe's stories that shows traces of the detectory schema, but it does so without the characteristic focus of the investigation, or the neat closure that functions to tie the story together into a whole by resolving the questions posed by the mysterious circumstances. The anonymous first-person chronicler (wearing "caoutchouc overshoes") is charged with detective curiosity as he speculates about his surroundings:

> At first my observations took an abstract and generalizing turn. I looked at the passengers in masses, and thought of them in their aggregate relatives. Soon, however, I descended to details, and regarded with minute interest the innumerable varieties of figure, dress, air, gait, visage, and expression of countenance. (*Complete* 216)

He singles out one countenance from the others as belonging to "the type and the genius of deep crime" (221) and narrates the suspect's actions in the streets of London, all the while conjecturing as to the motives for the man's actions, as well as the possible significance of his gestures, pauses, and visits. He arrives at a revelation about the unreadability of "the man of the crowd." The individual history of crime anticipated in the narrator's pursuit remains an inscrutable mystery: "I was at a loss to comprehend the waywardness of his actions" (220).

"The Man of the Crowd" is a story that dwells on the negativity that is part of the detectory schema on the way to resolution. The critic John Cawelti has noted that feature of the narrative, describing it as "the dark confusion and uncertainty reached after the examination of clues and witnesses" (86). The narrator's failure to define the motives and specifics of the criminal deed has constructed a tale of detection, with the negation of the process's denouement. His inability to solve the mystery anticipates the antidetective story, in which a mystery cannot be dispelled by rational means. In "The Man of the Crowd," Poe handles the detectory schema in the very anti-rationalist terms that characterize his other, more sensationalist stories of undispelled mystery and horror. His detective stories, in contrast, can be understood as an imposition of rational will on circumstances that are always to some degree beyond the reasoner's understanding.

The cognitive dimension of detective fiction, then, articulates the question-generating mechanism of the detective schema and formulates possible explanations for the events represented. This cognitive dimension, so characteristic of detective fiction, is constituted primarily by abductive reasoning. Causality in detective stories is determined by an assessment of the evidence and, in a crucial first step, by the determination or choice of what constitutes evidence. The guesses of the detective represent a range of abductions that the codes of the genre (and other cultural codes) validate and make possible. Once competence is built regarding what these codes are about, the way is clear for a parallel intelligence to join in the detective's game (as long as the evidence is all there and has not been elided from the text). The conjectural reader can be understood as a strategy in the face of a text that is suspected of withholding an answer, that is (or is suspected to be) reticent about providing certain information, or whose very composition constitutes an enigma.[4]

NOTES

1. See "The Philosophy of Composition" and the article on "The Twice-Told Tales" in *Selected Writings of Edgar Allan Poe*.

2. Accusations of withholding information notwithstanding, Arthur Conan Doyle's sleuth, Sherlock Holmes, is quite adept in the three modalities of reasoning. The error that Holmes and many of his critics have made has been to confuse two of these modalities of reason and ignore the characteristics of the third: abduction. "You know my method. It is based on the observation of trivial details," asserts Sherlock in "The Boscombe Valley Mystery" (1.285). Holmes's method is the character's rational idiosyncrasy, and it is contingent on the *esprit de finesse* (Pascal's term) with which he composes his abductions. Watson certainly practices his friend's "method" of observation in the development of *The Hound of the Baskervilles*. Most of the investigation at the Baskerville manor is carried out by Watson, and yet his results fail to complete the picture of the crime. Trivial details are the basis for the master's art, but it is what Holmes makes of these details that validates his role in the case.

3. The reference is best understood in terms of Friedrich Schleiermacher's "divinatory method," a psychologistic approach to the understanding of the text: "The divinatory [method] is that in which one transforms oneself into the other person in order to grasp his individuality directly" (Palmer, *Hermeneutics* 90).

4. See Barthes's *S/Z* on the hermeneutic code. The narrative means by which a story postulates a mystery, delays its solution, and withholds or allows the formulation of an answer all serve to constitute a recognizable schema that is detectory in that it withholds information (such as a name) while producing the grounds for the process of inquiry.

The Labyrinthine Text
The Fiction That the Reader Makes

In 1932, Borges reviewed an unusual text comprised of a synopsis of events, ticket stubs, ink or paint stains, and photographs. *Murder off Miami*, the work reviewed, is composed of elements that are presented and sold together as a text, which according to Eco is "a coherent series of propositions, linked . . . by a common topic or theme" (*Sign* 204). Borges comments on the distinctive nature of this detective "text" by noting that the inclusion of the match and the blood-stained curtain, the lock of hair, and so on, along with the testimonies, reminds him of "the methods of those painters who instead of painting an ace of spades glue it to the canvas" [el procedimiento de esos pintores que en lugar de pintar un as de espadas lo pegan en la tela (*Textos* 46)]. But what concerns Borges (as his criticism of Holmes made clear) is how something that could be considered a series of propositions is to be made coherent and linked by reason. *Murder off Miami* is a bare outline, the "raw materials" of a text that anticipates a resolvent "there" to constitute its meaning (zealously guarded by the third envelope with a name) or to recontextualize its disparate elements. Without this anticipated reader (the conjectural reader "made" by detective fiction) the narrative text announced by the title is so much debris, a laundry problem, and several startling confessions.

Borges comments on the difficulties that the case reviewed poses: "The good reader must compare those testimonies, examine those photographs, question that human hair, decipher that match, exhaust that bloody rag and finally guess or induct the *modus operandi* of the criminal and his identity" [El buen lector debe cotejar esos testimonios, revisar esas fotografías, interrogar ese cabello humano, descifrar ese fósforo, fatigar el jirón ensangrentado y finalmente adivinar o inducir el *modus operandi* del criminal y su identidad (*Textos* 46)]. No sign relates to its object in a single way. The historically bound form of the detectory story—even in the unusual guise of *Murder off Miami* —offers a wide range of possibility for the exploration of the sign and its contexts. In a discussion of the work of Roman Ingarden, the critic Wolfgang Iser notes the idea that "the literary intentional object lacks total determinacy in so far as the sentences in the text function as a guideline, which leads to a schematic structure that Ingarden calls the 'represented objectivity' of the work" (*Act* 170). He goes on to quote Ingarden:

> In consequence: the represented object that is "real" according to its content is not in the strict sense a universally, quite unequivocally determined individual that constitues a primary unit; rather, it is only a schematic formation with spots of indeterminacy of various kinds and with an infinite number of determinations positively assigned to it, even though formally it is projected as a fully determinate individual and is called upon to simulate such an individual. (Ingarden in Iser, *Act* 170)[1]

Every epistemic relation involves some sense of arbitrariness because of the "slippage" that occurs in interpretation and is associated with the "spots of indeterminacy" referred to by Ingarden. This is why the characteristic appearance of results before the causes that are of paramount importance to detective fiction provides ample ground for abductive reasoning. The indeterminacy of the clues (facts) in the fictional mystery is a fascinating projection of multiple possibilities of interpretation— even failure.

Gian Paolo Caprettini suggests that, in the detective story, the choices that the reader makes to discern what is relevant or irrelevant in the discourse comprise one series of hypotheses "separating the enigmatic and discreet discourse of symptoms from that of evidence (often a deafening one)" (137). A second series is constituted by the inferences of the detective, "a clearly defined corpus," subject to accretion in the development of the narrative. The hypotheses produced in both instances are interpretants of the facts and represent the elaboration of narrative frames needed to structure the events progressively over time:

> The mechanisms of the detective story work in relation to certain hypotheses (more or less spontaneous, more or less critically evaluated), to which readers are led to refer, according to the way in which the tale is presented to them. If the detective story can be defined as a tale which consists in the *production of symptoms*, then it is obvious that the reader, invited to decipher them, can never completely escape the pressure. On the contrary, reading implies continuous decisions in order to control the pressure of the clues. (156)

Readers perform their abductions against the background of expressed precepts and conferred rules that the author has at his or her disposal. The text of *Murder off Miami* is understandable as such only in relation to the set of thought processes that the presentation of "crime material" can elicit from its reader. As the critic Roger Caillois states, and *Murder* makes evident, a mystery story can be reduced to a manner of presenting the facts ("Detective" 10).

In the detective story, it is not simply the pressure of discerning what are relevant and irrelevant "symptoms" in the growing narrative body that keeps the reader guessing. There is also the principle of misdirection at work in the detective text. The writer will set up certain indicators in one direction that the reader may or may not follow in relation to what is revealed about the facts of the case, and also in relation to what the reader knows about the conventions of the genre. It is the detective writer's craft to mislead in order to prolong the story. In the issue of prompting the reader to draw the wrong inference, the writer has an old device at his disposal that is in fact at the heart of detectory schema. The recourse is the formulation of *paralogismos*, which Aristotle defines as "the art of framing lies in the right way:"

> Homer, more than anyone else, has taught other poets to say what is false in the right way. This is by use of false reasoning. People think that if 'X' always follows 'Y', then 'Y' will always follow 'X.' But this is false. Hence, if 'X' is

> false but 'Y' is true when 'X' is true, the poet should add
> on the statement that 'Y' is true. Then our minds, knowing
> 'Y' is true, will also infer that 'X' is true as well. (*Philosophy*
> 428)

The erroneous inference is to be made (and calculated to be made) by the reader in search of the antecedent, and herein lies the interest (and amusement) afforded by detective fiction.

The photographs alluded to by Borges provide a good example for the issue of "framing lies" and its relevance to detective fiction; they are used by the author (or assembler) of the text as a consequent case from which the reader must arrive at some conclusion (or antecedent) by means of conjecture. Borges notes the complications involved: "First stage: Two photographed individuals look alike and the reader should understand that they were father and son. Second stage: Two photographed individuals look alike so that the reader suspects that they are father and son, and then it turns out that they are not. Third stage: Two photographed individuals look so much alike that the suspicious reader decides that they cannot be father and son, but then they are" [Primera etapa: dos retratados se parecen y el lector debe comprender que eran padre e hijo. Segunda etapa: dos retratados se parecen para que sospeche el lector que son padre e hijo, y luego no lo son. Tercera etapa: dos retratados se parecen tanto, que el lector suspicaz resuelve que no pueden ser padre e hijo, y despues lo son (*Textos* 46)].

Peirce has written about the iconic quality of photography in the following terms: "Photographs are produced under such circumstances that they were physically forced to correspond point by point to nature." Therefore, concludes Peirce, they "are in certain respects exactly like the objects they represent" (*Collected Papers* 2.159). The similarity between the object and its image is an issue of contention and is measured by degrees: In certain respects, the image is not like the object it represents. Hence, a letter can be hidden in plain sight because the image that the searcher has of the letter does not correspond to the reality of the object as it appears in the context of the desk that is meant to hide it in plain sight. The relationship between signs is equally slippery, especially when similarity plays a role in the identification of the sign relation. On the way to naming the individuals depicted in the photographic images, the interpreter encounters similar and dissimilar elements, value judgments, and cultural presumptions that make identification open to manipulation. In the third and final stage of Borges's conjectures, the reader's cunning is expected to bring about his or her own undoing. Having been given B, the reader is left to infer the truth of A, which he or she, anticipating a bluff, has discarded—but A is true and Aristotle's recipe for false reasoning has once again been implemented for the esthetic end that is enacted in the reception of the work.

The cycle of detection described by Todorov reverts to the scene of the crime with the regularity of ritual, reducing the anomalies present in a world made strange by crime to a norm and system. Innovative detective fiction resists this formalized reduction of possibilities by recognizing that the clue exists in a web of interpretative relations that generate multiple interpretants and allow for the creation and synthesis of new ideas from that which is known. Such disruption or novel interpretation of generic norms exploits the abductive potential of Dupin's method of inquiry and expands the stock repertory of the genre by sometimes denying the neat ending or re-formulating historically stratified relations and compositional structures.

Automatized generic norms trivialize the detective story into a formulaic and safe search for "whodunnit."[2] The Russian Formalists focused on the tiredness of the form and suggested that this automatization results in parody: "A new form appears not in order to express a new content, but in order to replace an old form which has already lost its artistic value," writes Viktor Sklovskij (Bann and Boult, 53). Detective fiction, whose artistic value has always been in question, can be and still is being written with much success today. The most instructive parody of the form concentrates on the most contrived aspect of the detectory schema, the univocal solution to the mystery, while it maintains as the central feature of the new literary interpretation the general convention of the investigation, which is the most powerful metaphor of the genre. More importantly, parody renders visible the conventions that make up the genre. One need only recall Thurber's treatment of the detective story reader

to understand how that revelation is possible. Parody makes
evident that which had remained in the background, informing
the reading (constituting a reader), marking the parameters of
interpretations (the range of presuppositions), and contex-
tualizing the creative experience.

What the detectory reader does with narrative is to
construe the narrative in terms of a labyrinth. The labyrinth is
the most direct image of the role of the reader in relation to the
text. It is made up by the paths of conjecture; hence, the use of
the term *conjectural reader* that appears in these pages to describe
this most conspicuous offspring of the genre. Every narrative
functions to some degree by the temporary suspension of an
answer. The suspension is guaranteed by the linear, sequential
nature of language. At the sentence level, if predication appears
first, the natural question is to ask, momentarily, the predication
of what. If the nominative appears, the reader asks what will we
learn about the name, and how the name will be predicated.
How a text deals with these questions very often determines the
genre to which it belongs and also reveals the compositional
strategy being used for the engagement of the reader. Any
hesitation in the answer to the natural questions of meaning in
the text will lead the reader to formulate questions about the
sentence and, in a general sense, about the narrative itself. These
delays in the composition of narrative, these suspensions of
anticipated answers, have been called the *hermeneutic code of
narration* by the critic Roland Barthes (84–8), who considers all
narrative to depend on this textual presence, regardless of genre.

The detectory schema, which represents the structuring of
the path from an enigma to its solution, is wholly dependent on
this hermeneutic code, which is foregrounded in the detective
story. It is important to reiterate that the articulation of this path
is dependent on the reader, who recognizes the elements of
textual composition in terms of a hermeneutic code or system of
rules that regulates the mystery and its resolution. The schema
represents the potential structuring of that path and cannot be a
complete realization of it without this reader. Each *hermeneuteme*
or element of the schema might suggest or assert that there is a
question to be asked or a mystery to unravel, but this assertion is
contingent upon its recognition. Roland Barthes identifies the

following hermeneutemes in *S/Z:* certain textual features signal the proposal and thematization of the enigma and the promise of an answer. The first hermeneuteme signals the existence of a mystery; the second underlines what the object of the enigma is; and the third, which can be implied by the detective's early feats of abduction, as when Holmes describes an absent person by the marks of his walking cane or when we hear Dupin's mind-reading abilities corroborated by the anonymous narrator, serves as a contractual agreement (explicit or implicit) that the narrative will yield an answer to the question posed; others, such as the snare, the equivocation, and the partial answer prolong the guessing game by evading the truth (with the false clue, for example). "Jamming" the answer is an unpopular example of closure in detective fiction since it elides the solution, though it may serve to heighten the suspense, as when a key witness is found murdered, dashing the hopes of information that would bring the reader closer to the disclosure of the answer, which is the end result anticipated by the reader of detective fiction (209–10).

The detectory reader reads and questions primarily in terms of the hermeneutic code. If the text is conceived in terms of a labyrinth that delays and misdirects the reader's quest for meaning, the reader counterposes to this textual labyrinth his or her own imaginary one, which is in fact another text made up of the conjectures formulated by the reader. The image of the labyrinth carries this significance in Borges's work as well as in the work of Eco. Eco elaborates the maze metaphor in *The Name of the Rose* by having his detective tread a labyrinthine library in order to arrive at a hidden text, which explains the reason for the deaths in the abbey. The library, like a good detective story, protects the answer and delays the detective from discovering what he seeks. In fact, the detective's progress and setbacks in the library/labyrinth can be conceived in the terms of the hermeneutic code described by Barthes, which is fundamentally the process of resolution of an enigma and the basis of all detective stories. Eco has been able to make use of this central idea of Borges's work, along with the metaphor of the library, the mirror, and the play of numbers, as a part of the plot and development of *The Name of the Rose*. Borges's short stories "Ibn

Hakkan al-Bokhari, Dead in His Labyrinth," "The Library of Babel," "Death and the Compass," and others have all been put to use by the Italian author. Eco elaborates on the ideas in these stories of Borges, using Borges's recurrent themes and obsessions in order to build a more complex and suspenseful mystery.

The authors of the works studied in the following pages— Borges, Borges and Bioy Casares (otherwise known under one name as Honorio Bustos Domecq), and Eco—use the generic conventions of the detective story as a point of departure for their fiction. They also assume the reader's knowledge of these conventions in order to develop the detectory story in its most promising feature: the search for a rational answer in the face of mystery. Reading a detectory story is reading about a search for an answer through inferences derived from clues encountered in the process, which might very well define the implicit interpretive process of any reading act. The critic Alexander Coleman has noted that Borges's esthetics of narration, made explicit in "Narrative Art and Magic" (1932), argue for "a massive expansion of the detective method, with causation apparent in all details as they are arranged in prediction, execution, and fulfillment . . . . Borges will take over the figure of Dupin for his own purposes, and extend the metaphorical possibilities of this master of ratiocination until he begins to lurk unexpectedly behind many of Borges's characters" (*TriQuarterly* 363). In his collaboration with Bioy Casares, Borges projected the abstracting consciousness of Dupin into the figure of Don Isidro Parodi, and utilized the strict structuralization of the detectory schema to restrain the dialectical play of their collaboration as well as to keep the rampant, bombastic style of their creation, Honorio Bustos Domecq, in check. Innovative detective fiction is equally prone to contextualize the reader's expectations in the realm of probability and error. In *The Name of the Rose*, the detective's ordering of the signs of the series of crimes that take place in an abbey results in contradiction and the impossibility of a logical reduction of the mystery into an a priori ordered whole or unified theory. The challenge that this fiction of conflict and fallibility poses to the act of reading consists in the degree of effort demanded of the reader to perceive connections in the process of reconstituting a text whose completeness could be imaginary or unattainable.

NOTES

1. Iser critiques Ingarden on the issue of true and false concretizations of the work by saying that "there can be no doubt that the determinacy of a work arises out of its concretization, but what is open to doubt is whether each reader's individual concretization can be subjected to criteria of adequacy or inadequacy" (*Act* 171).

2. Detective story writers, notes Raymond Chandler, compete on almost equal terms: "It is one of the qualities of this kind of writing that the thing that makes people read it never goes out of style. The hero's tie may be a little out of mode and the good grey inspector may arrive in a dogcart instead of a streamlined sedan with siren screaming, but what he does when he gets there is the same old futzing around with timetables and bits of charred paper and who trampled the jolly flowering arbutus under the library window" (3–4). Chandler emphasizes the problem-solving aspect of the detective story and its intellectual character turned to formula.

PART TWO

Borges and the Labyrinths of the Detective Story

Borges, Detective Story Reader

Borges's interest in the literature of the English language is evident in the frequent mention he makes of the work of Thomas Browne, Algernon Charles Swinburne, Thomas De Quincey, Robert Louis Stevenson, and H.G. Wells. It is evident, too, in a number of articles published by him in the 1930s on subject matter rather foreign to Latin America: the fiction of G.K. Chesterton, the works of authors such as Michael Innes, Emmuska Orczy, Ernest Bramah, R. Austin Freeman, and other masters of the detective genre.[1] Borges promoted the development of detective fiction in Argentina and the southern continent by writing these review articles, through his involvement in the translations of detective novels distributed by Emecé in the Seventh Circle series, and in the selection and translation of the fine, and often curious, detective stories which he edited with Bioy Casares in the two volumes of *Best Detective Stories* published in 1943 and 1951.[2]

The fascination that Borges felt in reading detective fiction led to his wanting to try his hand at the writing of the mystery story. His first collection of stories, *A Universal History of Infamy*, does not show compositional traces of the genre that would later underwrite so many of his stories, but it is a varied chronicle of the lives of outlaws and criminals that the novice narrator had culled from different sources and modified to suit his imagination. There is one exception extant in the volume, however, and that is "Streetcorner Man." In Borges's later fiction at least two stories stand as clear examples of the genre: "Ibn Hakkan al-Bokhari, Dead in His Labyrinth," which shares traits with Chesterton's brand of mystery story, and "Death and the

Compass," which stands as an example and critique of the genre at the same time.[3]

Many of Borges's stories show traces of the detective story. Ronald Christ makes much of this influence in his analysis of "The Approach to al-Mu'tasim" by pointing out that the mystery is central to the story, which he considers "the embodiment of Borges's own concern with that genre." (*Narrow Act* 114). Borges's concern is also evident in "The Examination of the Work of Herbert Quain," where the author explains that Quain had failed as a detective story writer because critics found his first novel too derivative of Agatha Christie, and because the novel appeared at a time when Ellery Queen's *Siamese Twin Mystery* was popular among detective story readers. Other critics have pointed out the relation, however dim, that stories like "Emma Zunz" (actually the chronicle of a crime narrated from the criminal's perspective), "The Shape of the Sword," and "Theme of the Traitor and the Hero," have with detective fiction. The key to these interpretations of the presence of detective fiction in these stories does not lie in the fictions but with the perception of the critics, who are familiar with the detectory schema and the conventions of the genre. Their interpretations have an origin, identified in this comment made by Borges in *Twenty-Four Conversations*: "We the contemporary readers of detective stories . . . are the children of Poe: we have been created by him" (Alifano, 46).

Borges's insistence a reader is created suggests the role that detective fiction played in helping him conceive of a "literature of skepticism," informed by a reader's suspicions of the veracity or relevance of the things presented in the text. In the readerly suspicion exercised by detective fiction one can sense an intensification of the normal process of reading, which is *leer* in Spanish, from the Latin *legere*, "to bring together," but also "to select"and "to choose." In this etymology one can also see the reader as an active principle of composition and as a counterpoint to writing. Detective fiction provides a principle of suspicion that is adequate for the process of reading the literary text, a text that relies on allusion, repetition, convention, and generic or extraliterary references. The textual identity that the reader acquires from reading and becoming familiar with the detectory schema is the structuring agent that Borges anticipates for his fiction. The reader, like the narrator before the finished text, is a displaced creative consciousness that participates in determining the design and significance of the story. In saying this, it is important not to lose sight of the importance that the concept of order has for the organized and premeditated text, or the principle of textual "magic" that Borges exercised in his literature.

In "Narrative Art and Magic" (1932), Borges leads one to infer that "causation," or causality, is the main problem and concern of the novel (*Rodríguez Monegal and Reid*, 37). In contrast to "the overwhelming disorder of the real world," Borges contraposes "a vigorous scheme of attentions, echoes and affinities" in fiction (38). The latter is the expression of a *magical* chain of cause and effect in which "every detail is an omen and a cause" (38). The integrity of the literary writer, for Borges, lies with this type of magic. In "Narrative Art," Borges points to G.K. Chesterton's manipulation of details as the happy encounter between plot and ineluctable logic.[4] Again, it is detective fiction which best represents the fusing of plot with surprising logic, but this should not be taken to mean that only detective fiction represents for Borges what he called a "classical," or organized, text.

Detective fiction represented for the Argentine author a consciously intellectual project that, rather than being limited to the writer side of the writer-text-reader equation, affected directly the reader's selectional bias. Borges's interest in this matter is his recognition of the permutational force of the reader's perception. His first outing into narrative fiction, in fact, was the work of a reader that gave free rein to his imagination to formulate on paper what remained between the lines in the lives of reprobates that had engaged his interest in other texts. The importance Borges gave to readers led him to postulate, in an echo of the Irish philosopher George Berkeley, that no text could exist without a reader. And although Borges did not theorize about readership in the way he did about texts in "Narrative Art" and "Postulation of Reality," for example, his comments about readers are very often associated with mystery's generic form. He saw the detective reader as an implicit premise, a

predisposition to the reading act, which paralleled and elaborated the structure of the text. Detective fiction, he believed,
was as an excellent tool to train the mind's classifying play.

"We read a detective story suspecting everything be-
forehand, but the manner of reading has been created by the
detective story," Borges said in *Twenty-Four Conversations*
(Alifano, 46). It is not merely the parodic humor that links the
"major" and "minor" works of Borges where traces of the
detective can be found, as Julian Symons suggests (*Bloody Murder*
185); the link is, rather, the assumption made by the Borges of
the existence of *a type of reader* for his fiction—a type of reader
that would not exist without Poe's invention. The genre that
developed from Poe's stories would eventually define the textual
identity of a reader precisely by its often decried compositional
regularity. Further, if an author can, by means of these very
regularities, engage a reader in a game with the mere outline of a
detective plot, literary practice will, in that move, have a raising
of the ante that promises multiple and surprising results. These
are the stakes of Borges's game.[5] In Borges, in other words, we
find a skeptical view of language, which is seen as a contingent
medium with a penchant for incoherence, but is ultimately
organized (tentatively) by the combinatorial ability of the mind.

Borges gives primacy to intellectual strategies in eliciting
order. One can intimate, from the notion that textual structure is
a relation between textual design and the conceptual schemes
that result from how the work is perceived, the making of
contiguous labyrinths, fleeting and multiple. The logical
principles of a textual scheme are not readily apparent to a
reader and hence, he or she must conjecture structures of sense.
Can one imagine now how a reader in 1841, accustomed to the
short stories of Irving, Hawthorne, Melville, or those whose
work memory fails to rescue from anonymity, would have read
"The Murders in the Rue Morgue" in the pages of *Graham's
Lady's and Gentleman's Magazine*? Here was a story that, beyond
presenting the grisly facts of a bizarre murder, surreptitiously
engaged the reader in a guessing game for the identity of the
murderer and the motives of the crime. Only in subsequent
readings would the sagacious reader be able to tell that the
orangutan was there all along in the reported foreign language

with its shrill highs and guttural lows, in the unusual force spent in the act, in the widely spaced finger marks, in the impossible but ineluctable escape route. And, more importantly, the reader would have realized that all that reported metonymical detail was an open and engaging invitation for his or her intellect to join the ranks of the armchair detectives. A worthless occupation, perhaps? Eliciting order from an incoherent domain is the mark of the intellect, Borges would argue, adding: "In some page of one of the fourteen volumes that he wrote, De Quincey thinks that having discovered a problem is no less admirable (and is more productive) than having discovered a solution" [En alguna página de alguno de sus catorce volúmenes piensa De Quincey que haber descubierto un problema no es menos admirable (y es más fecundo) que haber descubierto una solución (*Textos* 221)].

In detective fiction, the tendency of the reader, and indeed his or her most distinctive feature, is to question the value of details. By taking this position, which partially works against the "suspension of disbelief," the reader becomes aware of the elaborated nature of fiction, since the details that give the narration its verisimilitude are questioned. However, the reading process continues because of the detectory plot that is assumed to be working in the piece under scrutiny; and it is precisely this sort of scrutiny that associates it with the detective genre.

NOTES

1. The reviews appeared in the magazine *El Hogar* of Buenos Aires as part of its literary supplement; some have been collected by Rodríguez Monegal and Reid in *Borges: A Reader*. They were finally compiled by Rodríguez Monegal, in collaboration with Saceiro Garí, as *Textos cautivos* in 1986.

2. According to Donald Yates, Borges "served as a sort of patron saint to the detective story in Argentina" ("Argentine" 26). The term "patron saint" provides an uplifting contrast to the hellish role that Eco assigns to Borges. See "Jorge of Burgos: Eco's Minotaur" in these pages.

3. Borges's creative efforts in detective fiction did not at first receive universal acclaim, or threaten Agatha Christie's or Ellery Queen's positions as top writers in the field. To the contrary, though "Death and the Compass" was included in Ellery Queen's *Mystery Magazine* along with "The Garden of the Forking Paths," readers of detective fiction were vexed by Borges's handling of the formal elements of the detective story. The readers' vexation is explained by Julian Symons's, in his sweeping dismissal of Borges as a detective story writer: "Essentially Borges' connection with the crime story is parodic, and it is not surprising that the detective who sits solving crime puzzles brought to him in a prison cell is named Isidro Parodi [Symons's reference is to *Six Problems for Don Isidro Parodi*, written by Borges in collaboration with Bioy Casares and published in 1942, but translated into English in 1981]. The solutions are unconvincing. The stories are merely fanciful or jokey, but the book is, as admirers will say, minor work. . . . Major Borges tales, however, are similar to minor ones in convincing or amusing only at the level of jokes" (*Bloody Murder* 185). Critics often mention "The Garden of Forking Paths" as an example of Borges's tales of detection. The story shares, rather, some characteristics with the spy story now associated with Ken Follett, Richard Forsyth, John le Carré, and perhaps Ian Fleming. For a discussion of this genre, see John Cawelti's *The Spy Story*.

4. In "Labyrinths of the Detective Story and Chesterton" (1935), Borges abducts a number of precepts for the construction of detective stories from *The Scandal of Father Brown*. Borges notes (1) a discretionary limit of six characters, (2) the declaration of all the terms of the problem, (3) the avaricious economy of means, (4) the primacy of the "how" over the "who," (5) decorum in the treatment of death, and (6) the necessity of and amazement produced by the solution (*Rodríguez Monegal and Reid*, 72). In the formal model of the detective story, Borges found the framework for magical narrative, which is a narrative founded on causality. Ronald Christ affirms that Chesterton furnished Borges with "an esthetic disposition, a fundamental metaphor, a necessary logic, a minimal esthetic: the disposition to view subjects analytically, esthetically: the metaphor of the criminal as artist, the detective as critic; the logic of deterministic word and event ('magic' causality); the minimal esthetic of the detective story" (*Narrow Act* 129–30).

5. Marcial Tamayo and Adolfo Ruiz Díaz affirm that in Borges's writing, as in Sophocles' *Oedipus Rex*, every word counts in the general plan of the work: "Many phrases [in Borges's stories] seem equivocal, but the the reader cannot, before knowing the resolution, learn that subtle double play that motivates them. . . . Borges' equivocations are

always mysterious and exact" (27–8). The critics' pronouncement fore-shadows the Cabbalist's approach to the Holy Writ, discussed below. See also "The Reading Self" in Part 2 of this edition.

Treading the Labyrinth
Borges and the Detectory Reader

To recapitulate, the genre of detective fiction represents for Borges the creation of a type of reader, one who reads "skeptically, with a special sort of suspicion" [con incredulidad, con una suspicacia especial], and whose existence Borges conjectures by means of the following parodic characterization:

> The person could be Persian, Malaysian, a country bumpkin, a child, a person who is told that *Don Quixote* is a detective novel; let us suppose that hypothetical reader has read detective novels and begins to read *Quixote*. Then, what does he read? . . . For example if he reads: *In some place of La Mancha* . . . , of course he assumes that whatever it is did not happen in La Mancha. Then: . . . *whose name I do not want to remember* . . . , Why didn't Cervantes want to remember? Because obviously Cervantes was the murderer, the guilty party. Then . . . *not too long ago* . . . possibly what has happened will not be as terrifying as the future . . . *there lived a gentleman*: Perhaps that gentleman is alive and will be murdered or has just been murdered" [Puede ser un persa, un malayo, un rustico, un niño, una persona a quien le dicen el Quijote es una novela policial; vamos a suponer que ese hipotético lector haya leído novelas policiales y empiece a leer el Quijote. Entonces, ¿qué lee? . . . Por ejemplo, si lee: *En un lugar de la Mancha* . . . , desde luego supone que aquello no sucedió en la Mancha. Luego: . . . *de cuyo nombre no quiero acordarme* . . , ¿por qué no quiso acordarse Cervantes? Porque sin duda Cervantes era el asesino, el culpable. Luego . . . *no hace mucho tiempo* . . . posiblemente lo que suceda no será tan aterrador como el futuro . . . *que vivía*

un hidalgo : Quizá ese hidalgo está vivo y será asesinado o acaba de ser asesinado (Oral 67)].

It would be difficult to define Poe's progeny by means of sociological speculation or to categorize this reader in terms of age, gender, or a certain life style in a given country, that is, by the means available to consumer research firms. Rather, Borges suggests, this reader is constituted by his or her interpretive capacity, by the strategy he or she adopts in the act of reading. For the purposes of the detective story, the reader possesses a degree of ability developed in previous readings. This ability allows the reader to carry out the interpretive function that the text proposes or problematizes. Therefore, we can infer from Borges that the constitution of a literary genre depends on a reader capable of identifying the codes at work in the text and able to interact with them on the basis of previous reading experiences that allow for an initial act of recognition. Umberto Eco explains that "recognition occurs when a given object or event, produced by nature or human action (intentionally or unintentionally), and existing in a world of facts as a fact among facts, comes to be viewed by an addressee as the expression of a given content, either through a pre-existing and coded correlation or through the positing of a possible correlation by the addressee" (*Theory* 221).[1] Recognition and closure are intimately associated in the detectory schema.

There is a potential for error in this act of recognition, which requires an abductive form of interpretation. The recognition of the text's principle of composition can be real or imagined. *Don Quixote* is not, after all, a work of detective fiction; *Macbeth* is an Elizabethan tragedy, and *Oedipus* a Greek one. The reader is prompted by the work to accept its most compelling principles; after all, if Oedipus is not guilty, the play would not work as the tragedy it is intended to be. However, it is possible to "misread" *Oedipus*, to read the play according to principles that are incompatible with its narrative thrust and show it to be lacking, or at odds with itself. Oedipus's guilt in the death of his father is an aspect of the plot that relies on the audience to assume it as a given, though in fact it is not. The questions that Borges elicits from the opening lines of *Don Quixote* can be accepted as a suitable grid for interpretation if other passages of the work confirm the suspicion. In fact, other sections of the work challenge this line of questioning, and the reader's suspicion can in turn be directed at, for example, the issue of disputed authorship that the novel raises, since it masquerades as a translation from the Arabic. But foregrounding the reader's role in this way implies that the unity and coherence that are usually assumed to be properties of the text are actually dependent on the codes that the reader possesses or that he or she is able to infer from the reading. Borges has written, "Literary genres depend less on the texts, perhaps, than on the way these texts are read" [los géneros literarios dependen, quizás, menos de los textos que del modo en que estos son leídos" (*Oral* 66)]. This formulation of the reader recognizes the process of reading as a culturally determined activity in which the text only acquires sense or meaning according to the conventions the reader has assimilated and any others that he or she is able to postulate from the reading.

The primacy of a reading self foregrounds the processes through which we make sense of things, the systems of codes, conventions and presuppositions that allow a message to mean something to someone else. The reader of a detective story, for example, recognizes in the thematization of an enigma an invitation to actively consider mysterious events whose answer has yet to be determined. In Borges's story "Ibn Hakkan," an introduction tells us first of two characters in Cornwall, and includes a sketch of the setting, with its "bleak moor, the sea, the dunes, and an imposing, tumbledown building" [el negro páramo, el mar y un edificio majestuoso y decrépito (*The Aleph* 116; *Obras* 1. 600)]. This leads to the "emphasizing of the subject which will be the object of the enigma" (Barthes, 209): "After all these years, the facts surrounding [Ibn Hakkan al-Bokhari's] death are still unclear" [Al cabo de los años, las circunstancias de su muerte siguen oscuras" (*The Aleph* 116; *Obras* 600)]. The thematization of the enigma is followed by its proposal. Unwin, the listener of the other's retelling of the mystery, asks *why* these circumstances might still be unclear. Dunraven, the teller of the tale, goes on to formally propose the mystery. The circumstances of the death are still unclear, he says, because "in the first place, this house is a labyrinth. In the second place, it was watched over by a slave and a lion. In the third place, a hidden treasure vanished. In the fourth place, the murderer was dead when the murder happened. In the fifth place—," [En primer lugar, esa casa es un laberinto. En segundo lugar, la vigilaban un esclavo y un león. En tercer lugar, se desvaneció un tesoro secreto. En cuarto lugar, el asesino estaba muerto cuando el asesinato ocurrió. En quinto lugar. . . . (116; 600)]. Unwin stops Dunraven in the midst of this potentially unending series of baffling circumstances. Barthes writes that the proposal of an enigma "signal[s] in a thousand ways that an enigma exists" (210); one of the charms of the detective story is the principle of economy that rules both the proposal of the mystery and its resolution. This is a principle of economy closely related to that of Occam's razor in science and philosophy: keeping elements down to a minimum, a principle that is still prized today. Unwin states the principle in his objection to Dunraven's multiplying series as follows: "Don't go on multiplying the mysteries. . . . They should be kept simple. Bear in mind Poe's purloined letter, bear in mind Zangwill's locked room" [No multipliques los misterios. . . . Estos deben ser simples. Recuerda la carta robada de Poe, recuerda el cuarto cerrado de Zangwill (116; 600)]. Above all, the reader anticipates the elements that comprise a mystery as a series of clues in the text.

The total effect of the narrative depends on the reader recognizing this series as a general law comprising the text (or series of texts). After the thematization and proposal of the mystery, the bleak moor of the setting recalls the dark moor where the adventure of *The Hound of the Baskervilles* took place; the occupations of the two characters, Dunraven and Unwin, recall the two aspects of true reasoner advocated by Dupin in his description of acumen: the poet and the mathematician. The name of the town's rector, Mr. Allaby, stands revealed by his function to the fleeing Zaid, who uses the rector to dispel any suspicions that might arise about his being in the town of Pentreath. The epigram that reads " . . . like the spider, which builds itself a feeble house" [son comparables a la araña, que edifica una casa (*The Aleph* 116; *Obras* 600)] refers to the detectory reader's endeavors in conjectural space with the resulting labyrinths of sense, as well as to Ibn Hakkan's cousin Zaid's building of a labyrinth in the story. The spider web also appears to signify entanglement (in the plot? in the possibilities of the plot?), as Zaid dreams of being imprisoned by a web of serpents (by his own perfidy?), an association made by the character when his skin comes in contact with the spider web in a cave where he hides from his enemies along with Ibn Hakkan.

The initial act of recognition, dependent on how the mystery is thematized or postulated, permits the events to articulate toward the resolution of the enigma. The detective in the text is in a sense an inferential machine that produces lines of reasoning that the reader may share in anticipation of the end. It is significant that in "Ibn Hakkan" the poet and the mathematician share the story of the mystery while walking through the maze built by Zaid on the shores of Cornwall. There is a center to be reached in this classic labyrinth, whose many branching ways lead to "the very center of the network" [al centro de la red (116; 601)], if the explorers always turn to the left. In that certainty of the presence of the center and a method of arriving at it, the promise of an answer is heralded by the text. There is also an intimation that the story is a coherent whole in the red color motif evident in the description of people, places, and things. The labyrinth is red, the beard of Ibn Hakkan's impersonator is red, red is alluded to in the *Rose of Sharon*, the ship that brings the rightful bearer of Ibn Hakkan's name to the shores of Cornwall, and "Red" is the name of the sea that will be the ship's destination after it departs from the southwest of England for the port of Suakin.

Having reached the room that is at the center of the labyrinth and the end of the story (as it is known to the people of Pentreath), Dunraven reveals that his enumeration of the facts of the case is only a partial answer, and the reader is snared by a question at the end of what seemed to be the explanation of the truth of the case: "Can this story be explained?" [¿Nos es inexplicable esta historia? (121; 603)]. The reader is left with Unwin to fit the pieces of the puzzle together, since "The *facts* were true, or could have been thought as true, but the way [Dunraven] told them they were obviously lies" [Los hechos eran ciertos, o podían serlo, pero contados como tú los contaste, eran, de un modo manifiesto, mentiras (122; 604)]. What Unwin is calling into question is the necessity of the meaning of the narration as told by Dunraven. There is a more sensible way of telling the story that will account for the facts in a manner fully supported by the facts, and that at the same time organizes them in another structure of sense closer to the plausible. Why would a man impelled by an irrational fear of persecution build a huge red labyrinth by the English shore?

Unwin's task is to construct a hypothesis to account for this baffling circumstance, and another one, the bizarre defacing of the victims killed in the labyrinth. Unwin then tells his story of equivocation and mistaken identity, in which a man, Zaid, driven by greed, cowardice, and jealousy, builds a maze to lure Ibn Hakkan, kill him, and steal his treasure and his name. Dunraven considers this story, aware that "the solution of the mystery is always less impressive than the mystery itself. Mystery always has something of the supernatural about it and even of the divine; its solution, however, is always tainted by sleight of hand" [la solución del misterio es siempre inferior al misterio. El misterio participa de lo sobrenatural y aun de lo divino; la solución del juego de manos (123; 604–05)]. He accedes to Unwin's version of the solution, adding his own critical touches to the story on the proviso that "if [Unwin's] guess is correct" then his objections will tie the loose ends of the new narrative. Unwin's narrative conjecture is thus further elaborated by his critical reader, who grants Unwin's tale the correctness prescribed by the conventions of the genre that are the basis for his guess, that is, by the classic rules of the game that are demanded by the reader.

But what if the story told is one that leads to the realization that the sequential process of naming and discovery in the text was wrong? Barthes explains the process of naming thus: "Whoever reads the text amasses certain data under some generic titles for actions (stroll, murder, rendezvous), and this title embodies the sequence; the sequence exists when and because it can be given a name, it unfolds as this process of naming takes place, as a title is sought or confirmed" (19). Naming is an inferential process. A detective novel by Herbert Quain, *The God of the Labyrinth*, presents that very scenario of the incomplete or deficient naming. Borges explains:

There is an unresolved murder in the introductory pages,
a slow discussion in the middle, and a solution at the end.
After the solution of the enigma, there is a long and
retrospective paragraph that includes the phrase: *Everyone
thought that the encounter between the two chess players had
taken place by chance.* That phrase suggests that the solution
was false. The reader, restless, examines the pertinent
chapters and discovers *another* solution, which is the
correct one. [Hay un indescifrable asesinato en las páginas
iniciales, una lenta discusión en las intermedias, una
solución en las últimas. Ya aclarado el enigma, hay un
párrafo largo y retrospectivo que contiene esta frase: *Todos
creyeron que el encuentro de los dos jugadores de ajedrez había
sido casual.* Esa frase deja entender que la solución es
errónea. El lector, inquieto, revisa los capítulos pertinentes
y descubre *otra* solución, que es la verdadera.] (*Obras*
1.462).

Borges points out that "the reader of that unique book is more
perceptive than the *detective* " [el lector de ese libro singular es
más perspicaz que el *detective* (1.462)]. What the reader of Quain
had to do was disregard the solution that the detective had
presented and return to the beginning to reread the story in the
light of an intuition. The conclusion that there is "*otra* solución"
implies that there is a better, more complete formulation of the
meaning of the events, one that will replace the false opinion of
the detective. The reader's intervention is creating an entirely
new story—one that, as de Man explains, "is a story of the failure
to read" and that "narrates the unreadability of the prior
narration" (*Allegories* 205). The reader of Quain's novel provides
a less deluded (or more reliable) version of the events that
reveals what de Man calls "the negativity of fiction."[2] Quain's
reader intuits that the detective's interpretation does not account
fully for the events that it pretends to represent, and that
realization leads him or her to consider that the detective's
purportedly infallible account is not the record of what actually
took place, but a fallible interpretation of it. The end was a
beginning. Truth must be sought again by the "restless reader."

In "Elements of Rhetoric," Borges writes that "that
intricate game of changes, of successful frustrations, of en-
thusiasms, exhausts for me the esthetic act" (Rodríguez Monegal

and Reid, 39). Elsewhere he has noted that "a volume, in and of itself, is not an esthetic fact, it is a physical object among others; the esthetic fact can only take place when it is written or read" [Un volumen, en sí, no es un hecho estético, es un objeto físico entre otros; el hecho estético sólo puede ocurrir cuando lo escriben o lo leen (*Obras* 2.354)]. Note the importance he gives to the role of creative elaboration by the reader (and by the writer at the time of creation) in his conception of the "esthetic fact." This event or act requires the conjunction of the reader and the text, and it is in this conjunction that the text is defined, perhaps, or comes into existence, insofar as it is read or interpreted. With this idea Borges is vindicating, for the humanities and for the study of communication, a disputed conception from the physical sciences, one often found formulated in textbooks under the following guise: "The scale of observation is what creates the phenomenon."

Borges adapts Berkeley's *esse est percipi* ("to be is to be perceived") to explain what occurs in the act of reading: "Poetry is in the commerce between the reader and the poem, not in the series of symbols registered in the pages of a book" [la poesía está en el comercio del poema con el lector, no en la serie de símbolos que registran las páginas de un libro (*Obra poética* 15)]. Borges did not adopt wholesale Berkeley's belief in an eternal and indivisible space and consciousness but rather limited Berkeley's idealist thesis to the confines of a "seen-here-and-now" that is concrete and related to the psychology of sensation (or observation). For Borges, there does not seem to be a transcendental subject; rather, the subject is reduced to a consciousness of difference, for whom items in a series are not necessarily connected to each other (*Other Inquisitions* 185). Reading is an encounter that modifies both subject and object. The psychologistic impression upon the reader when recognizing some differences and modifying them upon perception results in a physical modification of the subject that is registered as a kind of *delectatio nervosa*: "The essential thing is the esthetic fact, the *thrill*, the physical modification prompted by each reading" [Lo esencial es el hecho estético, el *thrill*, la modificación física que suscita cada lectura (*Obra poética* 15)]. There is no abstract god of the intellect for Borges, but he plays with the idea ironically, as has been seen in his defense of Dupin, who imagines himself to be an all-encompassing intelligence. The exchange between Dupin's double nature, represented by Dunraven and Unwin, poet and mathematician, the creative and resolvent, makes evident the dialogic nature of understanding in Borges's thinking and the lack of finality in the reasoners' process of conjecture before the face of mystery.

"La modificación" in Borges seems to imply a learning process that takes place in the course of reading and modifies both the text and the "textual being" that is the reader. The "esthetic act" implies the formulations of "networks of sense" that are the reader's various attempts to get to the truth of the matter. In the case of detective fiction, the process is motivated by, for example, the burning question, "Who is the guilty party?" The modification of the network of sense that the reader of Quain's novel must make in order to account for the unaccountable is a telling example of the modification Borges has in mind. Borges has noted a relation between *esse est percipi* and the economy of Occam's formula by suggesting that the latter allows or prefigures the other (*Other Inquisitions* 123). The relation is important, because it reinforces the proposition that perception, in the transaction between reader and text, is also arrived at through interpretation, or that perception is also a semiotic operation.

In "The Silver Blaze," the inspector, who has missed the clue of a matchstick, says with an annoyed expression "I cannot think how I came to overlook it," to which Holmes answers, "It was invisible, buried in the mud. I only saw it because I was looking for it" (Doyle, 1.446). The Italian semiotician Caprettini makes two important points on the basis of this characteristic exchange. First, the exchange between Holmes and his interlocutor makes clear that hypotheses are crucial to discovery; and, second, in an extension of this first point, "an observation is a planned and prepared perception" ("Peirce" 144). Caprettini quotes Karl Popper to make this point. He could as well have quoted Borges in "The Modesty of History," who wrote, "A Chinese prose writer has observed that the unicorn, because of its own anomaly, will pass unnoticed. Our eyes see what they are accustomed to seeing" (*Other Inquisitions*, 167). Discernment is the product of the exercise implied in the "esthetic fact"—the meeting of reader and text— that allows for the improvisation of different montages to account for the particulars of the event over time. The "esthetic act" is a reiterative exercise of interpretation that should be tempered by Holmes's stern indictment: "You have not observed. And yet you have seen" (Doyle, 1.211). The model of proficiency embodied by these exemplary mentors—Dupin, Holmes—idealizes the modification of the reader's perception. To know how to read is to know the laws of the text. But knowing the laws of the text is also to expose one's reading to conjectural error.

NOTES

1. This pragmatic principle is at work in Jonathan Culler's discussion of literary competence: "The important thing is to start by isolating a set of facts and then to construct a model to account for them" (*Structuralist Poetics* 128). Culler points out that structuralists have often failed to do this in their own practice and adds, however, that the principle is implicit in the linguistic model. Culler quotes Barthes: "Linguistics can give literature the generative model which is the principle of all science since it is a matter of making use of certain rules to explain particular results" (128).

2. The "negativity of fiction," in de Man's account of it, makes the text *allegorical*; that is, the words that comprise the text stand for some idea other than what they name and are no longer the record of what actually took place but an interpretation.

The Reading Self
The Golem Meets His Maker

When Borges writes in "The Postulation of Reality" that "the very act of perceiving, of heeding, is of a selective order; every attention, every fixation of our conscience, implies a deliberate omission of that which is uninteresting" (Rodríguez Monegal and Reid, 31), he does so in the midst of a discussion that suggests that, in the act of writing, a certain kind of writer that he calls a classicist anticipates the reader as a compositional element of the text. What the "classicist" does is to produce a kind of writing that is "generalized and abstract":

> The author proposes to us a play of symbols, rigorously organized without a doubt, but whose eventual animation remains our responsibility. He is not, in fact, expressive; he limits himself to recording a reality, not representing it. The prodigious events to whose posthumous allusion he invites us imply charged experiences, perceptions, reactions: these can be inferred from the narration, but they are not in it. To state it more precisely: he does not write of initial contacts with reality, but rather of their final conceptual elaboration [El autor nos propone un juego de símbolos, organizados rigurosamente sin duda, pero cuya animación eventual queda a cargo nuestro. No es realmente expresivo: se limita a registrar una realidad, no a representarla. Los ricos hechos a cuya póstuma alusión nos convida, importaron cargadas experiencias, percepciones, reacciones; éstas pueden inferirse de su relato, pero no están en él. Dicho con mayor precisión: no escribe los primeros contactos de la realidad, sino su elaboración final en conceptos]. (*Discusión* 68; Rodríguez Monegal and Reid, 31).

The classical method, in its "notorious inefficacy," relies on three modes of composition, according to Borges. One is the imparting of important facts; another consists "of imagining a more complex reality than the one stated to the reader and recounting its derivations and effects"; the third is the use of circumstantial invention, "those laconic details with long-range consequences" (Rodríguez Monegal and Reid, 32–33). The fascination that detective fiction would hold for a writer practicing this method of composition is readily apparent, since, as the three compositional modes make clear, it is up to our perception of things to consider these imparted facts as sufficiently valid to change their status from "circumstantial" detail to sign or clue. In Borges's conception of the classical text, the reader works from effects to possible causes that will explain the state of the fictional world. Defining the task of the classicist writer—an approach to the composition of a text that Borges contrasts to the "romantic" (not in an historical sense, but as another approach to composition)—he explains that "the classicist does not distrust language; he believes in the adequate virtue of each one of its signs" (30). But by "adequate virtue" Borges is not implying the linguistic sign's power to name and "close off" its subject; rather, he is emphasizing that the sign's virtue lies in its imprecision.

The inefficacy of the classical text can be reversed by a reader who restricts the twists and turns of chance. Writing in the classical mode is an act of confidence that relies, for one thing, on the public character of language. A genre, for example, is a shared convention; an image, once forged, "constitutes public property" (32). In contrast, a "romantic text" (the term is, ironically, Borges's) attempts to express (or exhaust) a certain reality by imposition, by emphasis, by what Borges understandably calls "the partial lie" (32). Already in 1926, in *El tamaño de mi esperanza* [*The Extent of My Hope*], Borges had this intimation about language:

> Every noun is abbreviation. Instead of enumerating cold, sharp, cutting, unbreakable, shining, pointed, we say dagger; in place of the withdrawal of the sun and the encroaching of shadows we say sunset [Todo sustantivo es abreviatura. En lugar de contar frío, filoso, hiriente,

inquebrantable, brillador, puntiagudo, enunciamos puñal;
en sustitución de alejamiento de sol y progresión de
sombra decimos atardecer (45–46)].

How many adjectives are needed to arrive at the name of the
dagger? How many qualifying sensations to name a lemon? Or a
rose? Or, as Hilary Putnam reminds us, what constitutes the
"core fact" of a single word (114)? When Borges writes, "What
we name substantives are nothing but an abbreviation and its
doubtful probability" [Lo que nombramos sustantivos no es sino
una abreviatura de adjetivos y su falaz probabilidad (*Inquisiciones* 65)], he is envisioning the act of naming as taking place
in a field of relations that "deceitful probability" opens up to
choice and error and ultimately, to the examination of contexts
on the way to one of the many possible arrangements of textual
reality that occur with the utterance of a name.[1]

The text does not name. The reader invents names for the
aspects of fiction he or she encounters in reading. The "imprecision" of the classical text—and certainly, detective fiction is a
popular example of the classical text as Borges defined it—
anticipates a reader. In the case of detective fiction, Borges has
noted, the text has created one. A reader created by and from
fiction is an idea that intrigued Borges, and he came back to it
again and again in his work, where it can be found under many
guises. Perhaps the most interesting is his elaboration of the
Cabbalist conception of "the golem." In "A Vindication of the
Cabbala," Borges writes: "I do not wish to vindicate the doctrine, but rather the hermeneutical or crytographic procedures
which lead to it" [no quiero vindicar la doctrina, sino los
procedimientos hermenéuticos o criptográficos que a ella
conducen (*Obras* 1.209; Rodríguez Monegal and Reid, 22.
Borges's interest in the Cabbala goes beyond a mere predilection
for arcane tales.[2]

For the Cabbalists, there is no element of chance or
imprecision in the sacred Scriptures. Nothing is casual in the
Scriptures because even the letters of the text were the
instruments of God, used in the elaboration of His divine
message. Hence, everything in the sacred text must be
determined and rigorously significant, including the number of
letters of each versicle. The exegetic labor of the Cabbalist

scholar, his decoding labor and the many grids of sense that he imposes on the divine text in order to elucidate its transcendental meaning, had to be foreseen by God, whose intelligence is infinite. The *modus operandi* of the Cabbalists, Borges reminds us, is based on a logical premise: "A book impenetrable to contingency, a mechanism of infinite purpose, of infallible variations, of revelations lying in wait, of superimposed light . . . How could one not question it to absurdity, to numerical excess, as did the Cabbala?" [Un libro impenetrable a la contingencia, un mecanismo de infinitos propósitos, de variaciones infalibles, de revelaciones que acechan, de superposiciones de luz ¿cómo no interrogarlo hasta lo absurdo, hasta lo prolijo numérico, según hizo la cábala?" (*Obras* 1.212, Rodríguez Monegal and Reid, 24)]. The key for the Cabbalist enterprise of interpretation is to invent (or imagine) as many laws at work in the text as is humanly possible, in order to decipher the Scripture of God. The many intriguing attempts at decoding performed by the Cabbalist scholar are similar to the ways of cryptography. Borges compares the work of the Cabbalist to the process of decipherment reported by Poe in "The Gold Bug," a story in which cryptography was necessary in order to arrive at buried treasure in a barren inlet of the North Carolina coast (*Siete noches* 131).

In recounting the Cabbalist conception of the golem, Borges writes of a "man" created by combinations of letters. The golem is the imperfect product of an interpretive effort, a shapeless entity foreseen in the text of texts and engendered from "the task of counting, combining, and permutating the letters of the Scriptures" (Borges and Guerrero, *Book of Imaginary Beings* 113). The golem-maker is, essentially, a creative interpreter of textual reality. The conjunction of art and magic alluded to in Borges's essay can now be appreciated in the creation of this amorphous entity that represents the creation of a text, or a reader-as-text. The golem is the product of an act of interpretation. The golem in turn also interprets what he (or she) is told by his maker, but cannot speak. As a textual being, he performs the tasks that are demanded of him, but, as reported in Jewish lore, he can become independent and a threat to his maker. In the earliest version of the central European golem, written by Yehudah Loew, rabbi of Prague, the programming goes wrong and his maker, a Talmudic scholar, is forced to remove the letter *aleph* from the inscription that animates the creature's body. The inscription is thus transformed from *'emet* (truth) to *'met* (he is dead) and the being turns to dust (Bilsky 13). Borges gives fictional treatment to the Cabbalist notion in "The Circular Ruins," where a wizard succeeds in dreaming a pounding heart into existence only after he has uttered the correct and prescribed syllables of an "all-powerful name." In this story, Borges adds to the golem myth a dimension of the infinite. The magician bewitches his creation and is in turn bewitched by it. Only after he succeeds in creating another entity does he find out that he too had been dreamt by another and that fire cannot destroy him:

> He walked into the ragged flames. They did not bite his flesh, they caressed him and flooded him without heat or combustion. With relief, with humiliation, with terror, he understood that he was also an illusion, that someone else was dreaming him [Caminó contra los jirones de fuego. Estos no mordieron su carne, éstos lo acariciaron y lo inundaron sin calor y sin combustión. Con alivio, con humillación, con terror, comprendió que él también era una apariencia, que otro estaba soñándolo]. (*Obras* 1.455).

The wizard master of fiction, whose command of interpretation has allowed him to conceive of a mediating entity between himself and the text, is thus revealed to be dependent on his creation, to have been anticipated by another interpreter as one more interpretation in a chain of creations, built from the past and undying in subsequent interpretations.

In Borges's poem "The Golem," a rabbi, after giving himself "to permutations / of letters and complex variations," frets about the being he has brought into existence:

> Why did I decide to add to the infinite
> Series one more symbol? Why to the vain
> Skein which unwinds in eternity
> Did I add another cause, effect, and woe?
>
> At the hour of anguish and vague light
> He would rest his eyes on his Golem.

Who can tell us what God felt,
As He gazed on His rabbi in Prague?

[¿Por qué di en agregar a la infinita
Serie un símbolo más? ¿Por qué a la vana
Madeja que en lo eterno se devana,
Di otra causa, otro efecto y otra cuita?

En la hora de angustia y de luz vaga,
En su Golem los ojos detenía.
¿Quién nos dirá las cosas que sentía
Dios, al mirar a su rabino en Praga?]*
(*Obras* 2.264–65; *Personal Anthology* 79)

In reference to the poem, Borges indicated to Richard Burgin that "in the end it is suggested that as the Golem is to the magician, to the Cabbalist, so is man to God" (*Conversations* 75).[3]

Human texts are not absolute. Human truth is a fragmentary, limited, and finite kind of truth. The reading consciousness, without the resource of an omnipresent and self-correcting Text, constitutes and is constituted by the patterns and designs of language. By means of the transactional nature of the linguistic sign, the act of reading restores to the word *text* its etymological Latin sense of "weave" or "web." It is in this web of sense that the reader is doubly snared in the attempt to constitute meaning. The openness sensed in the heterogeneity of textual elements is confronted by the irreducible otherness that constitutes the textual sign. The site of confrontation is the reader, who is simultaneously drawn in by the interpretive adventure and shaken by the jumps and starts of linguistic construction from settling too comfortably with a finalizing version of what is taking place or what is at stake in the narrative at hand. Narrative discourse never makes fully clear how a reader can best and fully correspond to the various intonations that the text attempts to impose on his or her own voice.

Every reading is an imaginative act that speaks the text into existence by an approximate duplication of a text that represents the written evidence of an earlier attempt at interpreting human actions, motives, and thought. In this sense, the detectory reader is constituted, like the golem, by the laws of interpretation derived from linguistic evidence. As in the making of the golem, this conjectural reader in the act of eliciting sense is "Imprisoned in that sonorous net / Of Before, After, Yesterday, While, Now, / Left, Right, I, Them, Those, Others." [Aprisionado en esta red sonora / de Antes, Después, Ayer, Mientras, Ahora,/ Derecha, Izquierda, Yo, Tú, Aquellos, Otros (*Personal Anthology* 78; *Obras* 2.264)]. In the act of interpreting, the reader is anticipated as the semiotic protagonist of textual design.

An aspect of Borges's thoughts on the "esthetic act" and the creation of readers is echoed by the work of Georges Poulet, whose phenomenological approach to reading leads him to recognize that "a book requires a reading consciousness for its realization as a work" (56). A comparison of Poulet's elegant elaboration of the relation between readers and texts and Borges's thoughts on the same might prove valuable in defining the latter's conception. A key term in Poulet's theory is "intentionality," defined as "the structuration of an act by which the subject imagines, or conceptualizes or is conscious of an object, thereby bringing the object into being; but the intuition of the object simultaneously constitutes the subject as a vessel of consciousness. The subject is thus (in intending the object) paradoxically the origin of all meaning but is also the effect of consciousness" (55).

Notice how Poulet's "intentionality" reiterates what Borges discusses under the rubric of "Berkeley's esthetics"—that perception is an act of interpretation, that a text by itself is an empty notion, that "poetry is in the commerce of the poem with the reader" and that, therefore, both are inextricably bound by the results of that exchange. Poulet goes on to postulate a "reading self" who is not the reader's consciousness or the biographical author. The reading self is a "third" that results from reading, an "other" created from the reader's intercourse with the text. As a reader, Poulet explains, "I am a conscience astonished by an existence which is not mine, but which I experience as though it were mine" (60). In regard to the text, Poulet goes on to elaborate: "The work constituted by the animating intention of the reader becomes (at the expense of the reader whose own life it suspends) a sort of human being . . . a mind conscious of itself and constituting itself in one as the subject of its own objects" (59).

In this pronouncement, Poulet approximates the creation of a golem, a subject revealed through reading who, as Poulet clarifies, "is not the author" (59). In the context of Borges's writing, however, the golem and its creation have a sense different from Poulet's theory of passive reception of a being in the text (or "ghost in the machine"). For one thing, Borges's conception of the making of the reader, based on the literature of the detective, has an ineluctable sense of "game" or "gaming" that is assumed by the creative poles of the field of possibilities we call text. Secondly, Borges's well-developed notion of "mirroring" or infinite multiplicities denies a pivotal point in the object that Poulet conceives as being present in the written work and that permits a consistent return of "the subject of its own objects." A multiplicity, the theorists Gilles Deleuze and Félix Guattari explain, "has neither subject nor object—only determinations, sizes, and dimensions which cannot increase without changing its nature (thus the laws of combination increase as the multiplicity does)" (*On the Line* 14). The text for Borges is closer to Deleuze and Guattari's concept of multiplicity, a conglomerate of materials and intentions wearing a mask of coherence and whose sense is up to the reader to conjecture. It is at the moment of interpretation that the mask of the reader is revealed. This is a tracing of the codes by means of which he or she implements sense, and it is further colored by the compositional designs that the reader's wishes and desires have made evident in his or her own commerce with the text.

*"El Golem" from *El otro, El mismo* (1964) in *Obras Completas*. 3 vols. Ed., Carlos V. Frías. Barcelona: Emecé, 1989. Copyright Emecé Editores. Reprinted with permission.

NOTES

1. On the issue of perceptual judgment, Peirce writes: "Every judgment consists in referring a predicate to a subject. The predicate is thought, and the subject is only thought-of. The elements of the predicate are experiences or representations of experience. The subject is

never experiential but assumed. Every judgment, therefore, being a reference of the experienced or known to the assumed or unknown, is an explanation of a phenomenon by a hypothesis, and is in fact an inference" (Peirce in Fann, 12).

2. Borges acknowledges *Major Trends in Jewish Mysticism* by Gershom Scholem and Joshua Trachtenberg's *Jewish Magic and Superstition: A Study of Folk Religion* as two sources for his interest in the Cabbala (Christ, "Art" 162). In his writings, reference to the Cabbala first appears in "A History of Angels," where Borges discusses the theory of *Sefiroth* and the existence of ten heavenly worlds, each corresponding to one of the names of God (*The Extent of My Hope* [*El tamaño de mi esperanza*); "Una vindicación de la cábala" is included in *Discusión* (1932), and, of course, aspects of the Cabbala figure prominently in "The Aleph," "The Theologians," and "Death and the Compass." The idea of the golem is first found in Borges's review of Gustav Meyrink's novel of the same name for *El Hogar* in 1938 (*Textos*, 230–31). The idea of the golem receives important fictional treatment in "Las ruinas circulares," and in the poem "El Golem." The golem also makes an appearance in *El libro de seres imaginarios*, written by Borges in collaboration with Margarita Guerrero. Rabi first notes Borges's familiarity with Jewish mysticism in "Fascination de la Kabbalah" (de Roux, *L'Herne* 265–71). The theme and its relation to the author is researched by Jaime Alazraki in "Borges and the Kabbalah" (*Tri Quarterly* 240–67).

3. With respect to "The Golem" and "The Circular Ruins," Borges declares: "In Lubbock, on the edge of the desert, a tall young lady asked me if when I wrote 'The Golem' I hadn't been attempting a variation of 'The Circular Ruins;' I replied that I had had to travel the entire continent to receive that revelation, which was true. . . . Both compositions have, on the other hand, their differences: the dreamer dreamed is in one, the relation of the divinity with man and perhaps of the poet with the work in the other that I composed later" [En Lubbock, al borde del desierto, una alta muchacha me preguntó si al escribir 'El Golem', yo no había intentado una variación de 'Las ruinas circulares'; le respondí que había tenido que atravesar todo el continente para recibir esa revelación, que era verdadera. . . . Ambas composiciones, por lo demás, tienen sus diferencias; el soñador soñado está en una, la relación de la divinidad con el hombre y acaso la del poeta con la obra, en la que después redacté" (*Obra poética* 168–69)].

"Death and the Compass"
Lönnrot's Last Case?

Borges did not theorize extensively on the making of the reader beyond the idea expressed in conversation about Poe's progeny and the avowed interest in the reader and the act of reading that he made evident in his prologues. Perhaps this fact is a recognition of his own limitations: "I know now," he wrote in 1961, "that my gods grant me no more than allusion or mention" (*Personal Anthology* x). What Borges did do was narrate, leaving to the critic the task of emphasizing his gesture or tracing an allusion. This is the case with Borges's references to the legend of the golem. It could be argued that the creation of the golem bears a relationship to the One Text, as an image of unity of the text as object and of the subject resulting from the text. But then we encounter a narrative that prompts us to rethink the terms of that relation.

One such narrative is "Death and the Compass" ["La muerte y la brújula"], about which Borges declares: "No apology is needed for the repeated mention of the Kabbalah, for it provides the reader and the all-too-subtle detective with a false track, and the story is, as most of the names imply, a Jewish one. The Kabbalah also provides an additional sense of mystery" (*The Aleph* 269). Given Borges's interest in this aspect of Jewish mysticism, the statement appears to be an understatement of the role of the Cabbala in the story. Elsewhere, Borges has noted that "The Cabbala not only is not a museum piece, but is, rather, a sort of metaphor of thought" [La cábala no sólo no es una pieza de museo, sino una suerte de metáfora del pensamiento (*Siete noches* 137)]. Does "La muerte y la brújula," with its Cabbalistic theme, have something to tell about the constitution of the golem? The story foregrounds the making of the reader in terms of the "game" already discussed. One thing that the story makes clear is that when one does not know the nature of the game, one must conjecture its rules; the story also proposes that what defines the game are the rules the players play by, and that those rules intuited by the players also define the players as participants in a particular game, called, for example, chess, or backgammon, or detective fiction.

The golem, it has been noted, is constituted by the laws of interpretation used by the Cabbalists to determine the doctrine of the text. "Death and the Compass" provides a dynamic model that makes evident how the author/criminal and the reader/detective are constituted by the laws of genre. In this dialogic model, the Scharlach/golem comes into being as the Lönnrot/golem does by means of the rules of an ongoing game (this is why they can repeat themselves in the future, or past).[1] Both golems are created by the rules they recognize and follow in their game of misdirection and discovery. The single golem that results from the Cabbalist's "esthetic act" is thus superseded by the dynamic correspondence that the narrative model of Borges's detective story reveals.

If questioned about the existence of an *actual* Scharlach or Lönnrot behind the golem that represents them in the fiction they have both created, Borges would probably answer that no, behind Scharlach or Lönnrot there is another golem, the product of yet another constitutional pattern and "generic" circumstance in some further text. Golems represent arrangements in the sense of "bringing in a player" to account for the game. What grounds their existence is the action of playing *as if* the game responded to a unity expressed in general rules of play that are, again, the product of conjecture. The golem represents mediation; it establishes reading as an action that requires the hypothetical notion of a player, and in this action, the text defines the reader as a temporary arrangement: "An arrangement is precisely this growth of dimensions in a multiplicity that necessarily changes its nature as it increases its connections" (Deleuze and Guattari, *On the Line* 15). The arrangement is the principle of adequate reading that a text demands in order for sense to take place. Deleuze and Guattari emphasize this reader's changing nature, since they are interested in highlighting a certain aspect of textual instability and heterogeneity. One could imagine a reader whose composition, arising from a dense text such as José Lezama Lima's *Paradiso* or James Joyce's *Finnegans Wake,* is multiple and whose role would be to generate many lines of conjecture arising from as many different codes or grids of sense as the text demands.

Golems (or detectory readers in the case of detective fiction) are "varieties of measures" that drastically alter fixed notions of origin such as authorship. In the prologue to his first book of verse, Borges wrote:

> If the pages of this book contain some well-crafted verse, may the reader forgive my daring in having composed it before him. We are all one; our trifles are of little import, and circumstances influence our souls to such a degree that it is almost a chance occurrence that you are the reader and I the writer—the diffident and zealous writer— of my verses [Si las páginas de este libro consienten algún verso logrado, perdóneme el lector el atrevimiento de haberlo compuesto yo antes que él. Todos somos unos; poco difieren nuestras naderías, y tanto influyen en las almas las circunstancias que es casi una casualidad esto de ser tú el leyente y yo el escribidor—el desconfiado y fervoroso escribidor—de mis versos]. (*Obra poética* 19)

One can only conjecture how this statement, with its modest tone and contrite rhetoric, must have been read in 1925, but more important is the sense in which the paragraph attempts to dissolve the differences between author and reader. Both entities are part of an equation that is mediated by the work of art. The circumstances of differing personal histories, psychology, belief system, education are unavoidable, but Borges likens the author and reader, knowing full well that in the site of exchange and reciprocity that is the text, their differences will meet and blur any question of origin beyond the temporal one of who expressed artistic will first in the act of composition.

In "Death and the Compass," the investigator and the criminal play out the game of difference between the reader and the author over the text of the crime. In order to snare the detective, the criminal, aware of the line of inquiry taken by the investigator, will lay out clues from which the detective will develop the detectory schema. The criminal's motivation in this case is revenge. It is not unusual to find this kind of battle of wits in a detective story. Ever since Dupin's confrontation with Minister D—in "The Purloined Letter," criminals and detectives have shared an uneasy distinction within the genre. For example, both have inordinate pride—criminals' pride in their ability leads them to commit a crime deviously plotted and enacted, while detectives are proud of their power to conceive of the way the fiendish plot was conocted and carried out by conjectural means. Both detectives and criminals are not beyond breaking the law, which is understandable enough in the case of the criminal, but which seems peculiar in the case of the detective, who is the agent of order in the text. The detective and the criminal seem mysterious and cryptic in their deeds and pronouncements, especially to the reader, who is kept at a distance for the purposes of delay and misdirection in both the criminal's and the detective's case. Detectives, finally, have the godlike power to judge and punish, which they wield over the other characters in the fiction; criminals are similarly godlike (one might say demonic) in the way they dispose of human life and property with motives that are apparently beyond understanding.

The detective and the criminal, conjointly, are a source of wonder for the reader. Borges's story problematizes the pragmatic strategy demanded of the reader by detective narratives: A rabbi lies murdered in his room at the Hôtel du Nord where he was lodged as delegate to a Talmudic conference taking place in the (unnamed) city. Borges has acknowledged that the fictional city that appears in "Death and the Compass" follows the spatial disposition of Buenos Aires. The abandoned villa of Triste-le-Roy, for example, where the denouement takes place "stands for the now demolished Hotel Las Delicias in Adrogué . . . ten or fifteen minutes south of Buenos Aires" (*The Aleph* 263). More important than the fictional reflection of the author's private maze is the fact that Borges uses the procedure employed by Poe to mask the site of an actual crime in "The Mystery of Marie Rogêt." In Borges's hands the technique yields startling results. Poe places a crime occurring in New York, and reported by local newspapers, in Paris. Borges places a crime that has not happened (a fictional crime) in a city disguised as somewhere else. Regardless of the name the reader might choose for the fictional city—Buenos Aires, London, Montevideo, Paris, Prague—Borges's fictional city suggests another place by the shortcomings of the reader's association. The Hôtel du Nord also names what it does not happen to resemble. "Hôtel" names the structural "otherness" that can simultaneously be interpreted from its appearance:

> The first murder took place in the Hôtel du Nord—that tall prism which overlooks the estuary whose broad waters are the color of sand. To that tower (which, as everyone knows, brings together the hateful blank white walls of a hospital, the numbered chambers of a cell block, and the overall appearance of a brothel) there arrived on the third of December Rabbi Marcel Yarmolinsky [El primer crimen ocurrió en el Hôtel du Nord—ese alto prisma que domina el estuario cuyas aguas tienen el color del desierto. A esa torre (que muy notoriamente reúne la aborrecida blancura de un sanatorio, la numerada divisibilidad de una cárcel y la apariencia general de una casa mala) arribó el día 3 de diciembre el delegado de Podólsk al Tercer Congreso Talmúdico, doctor Marcelo Yarmolinsky]. (*The Aleph* 56–66; *Obras* 1.499)

Each aspect of the hotel, its whiteness, for example, remits that feature to another space and blurs the coherence of the hotel proper. The hotel's whiteness suggests a hospital, the multiple rooms suggest a jail, and any number of features, ranging from the lighting to the décor, relate the hotel to the bordello. The fact that the hotel is a tower standing by waters the color of sand is an image that, curiously, reminds the Borgesian reader of the Tower of Babel. The philosopher Jacques Derrida explains in relation to this fabled tower:

> The "Tower of Babel" does not figure merely the irreducible multiplicity of tongues; it exhibits an incompletion, the impossibility of finishing, of totalizing, of saturating, of completing something on the order of edification, architectural construction, system and architectonics. ("From 'Des Tours de Babel'" 244)

The indeterminacy foreshadowed by the open description of the hotel is not an auspicious beginning for the detectory reader. One must wonder if the solution of the mystery will be found, indeed, if it can be found. But the detectory reader knows that crimes, no matter how devious and fiendish, are encoded by the criminal in order to be just as fiendishly and cleverly decoded by the detective. There is a symbiosis between both the creative and resolvent poles of the text that is a form of complicity in the production of meaning. The detectory reader anticipates an almost perverse collaboration between criminal and detective that one assumes will guarantee the cohesion of the work. Clues of this cohesion are not slow in coming. What is known about the hotel is that it is situated in the north of whichever city. The reference falls in neatly with the title of the story, as does the event that has taken place in the peculiar building. And then, there is the repeated reference to the number three in the quoted section: there are three descriptions of the building, and the ordinal number "third" is featured in the date and the name of the congress held in the city.

At the scene of the crime, the investigator Erik Lönnrot encounters a sheet of paper with single sentence, written on a typewriter: "The first letter of the Name has been uttered" [La primera letra del Nombre ha sido articulada (*Obras* 1.500)]. In the conventions of the genre, the detective begins by noting trivial and seemingly insignificant details, which the typewritten page obviously is. It is the detective's stock role to give significance to these trivial details, which no one else notices at the scene, as a coded signal of the mystery's resolution. From the detail that he has noted, the detective begins to construct a pattern that the police have certainly not conceived. By his punctilious observation of details, the detective suggests that the reader is being misled by the obvious lack of acumen that these ubiquitous agents of the law represent. In order to sustain the fiction, various hypothetical predicates must be formulated by the reader upon recognizing a clue. Like the reader, the detective, inscribed as he is in the tradition that defines him, must gamble on the meaning of the details encountered as if they held the promise of resolution to the case: "Each word," writes Borges, "though it may be laden with centuries, begins a blank page and compromises the future" [Cada palabra aunque esté cargada de siglos, inicia una página en blanco y compromete el porvenir" (*Obra poética* 463)]. The seductive snare of each sentence found, its rich promise of hidden meaning and eventual discovery, is the challenge of detective fiction, which is a narrative based on the reader's discernment of the relevant and the irrelevant. The reader of detective fiction, recognizing the bizarre circumstances of the crime and the detective's role in the scene, expects the logical explanation to occur, and expects, perhaps humbly, a certain flair in the detective's announcement of his line of thought. For the reader, to be confronted with the unthinkable constitutes a large measure of the mystery story's delight.

"The first letter of the Name has been uttered," reads the note found in the array of circumstantial detail that comprises the scene of the murder of the rabbi. From this site of incoherence, Lönnrot infers the note to be part of the design of the crime. When he proceeds to articulate a series of logical presuppositions (the first letter of how many, whose name has been articulated, and so on) he establishes the relevance of the typewritten note, for the relevance of the sentence to the context in which it was found must be judged in the general pragmatic sense espoused by William James; that is, the truth of an assumption must be judged by its practical effects, by the set of actions that it determines and to some extent controls. In his elaboration of the meaning of the sentence, Lönnrot induces a ritual that is based on a secret name. In anticipation of this explanatory end, he builds a "data base" by reading treatises on Jewish mysticism. He learns that the name he seeks is the *Tetragrammaton*, the four letters that together spell the name of God. In his research, Lönnrot might have read the following:

> It is said in the Cabbala that the name of God comprises the whole Pentateuch, except that the letters are shuffled and thus, if someone possessed the name of God, or if someone reached the *Tetragrammaton*—the four letters that form the name of God—and knew how to pronounce it, that someone could create a world and could also create a golem as well, that is, a man" [En la cábala se dice que el nombre de Dios es todo el Pentateuco, salvo que están barajadas las letras así, si alguien poseyere el nombre de

Dios o si alguien llegara al *Tetragrámaton*—el nombre de
cuatro letras de Dios—y supiera pronunciarlo, podría
crear un mundo y podría crear un golem también, un
hombre]. (Borges, *Siete noches* 138)

It is a tribute to Borges's wry humor that one of the books found
at the scene of the crime, and forming part of the rabbi's personal
collection, is Borges's own essay, "Vindication of the Cabbala."
After a second and third murder that complete the sides of
"a mystical equilateral triangle," Lönnrot postulates, against the
evidence, the site of a fourth murder that is yet to take place. He
anticipates the place and the time by the symmetries he has
recognized in the preceding murders, by "the secret morphology" he has intuited in the series of crimes: The labyrinth
has the shape of a rhombus, a figure whose equidistant vertices
are points corresponding to specific sites in the city, and whose
geometrical disposition represents the four letters of the name.
At the fourth and final point of this construction, the criminal
Scharlach, like an avenging Daedalus, awaits his victim and
verifies his complicity in the entire pattern of events to an
astonished Lönnrot—"I realized that you conjectured that the
Hasidim had sacrificed the rabbi; I set myself the task of
justifying that conjecture" [Comprendí que usted conjeturaba
que los Hasidim habían sacrificado al rabino; me dediqué a
justificar esa conjetura" (*Obras* 1.506)]. Red Scharlach reveals this
and something else about Lönnrot's interpretive endeavors,
which shed light on the indeterminacy of the reading process.
"Reading is an 'argument,'" writes Paul de Man, "precisely
insofar as it has to go against the grain of what one would expect
to happen in the name of what has to happen" (*Writings* 222).
The irony in Lönnrot's situation works at the level of the reading
act, the one activated by the reader, who recognizes with the
detective the way in which language undoes claims of its
existence as a realm of autonomous meaning in the potentially
fallible act of communication.

In the story, irony has been prefigured in a reader who has
been "tricked" into assigning value to a clue because of an
illusion, the illusion proposed by detective fiction that unique
and adequate sense can be made out of contiguous details. Sense
can be made out of textual elements by means of an educated

guess, the consequent application of rules of combination and a close reading strategy guided by attention to detail, but as the denouement of detective stories often impress upon the reader, there is no guarantee that the meaning produced in this way is true to the letter of the text. Lönnrot seeks an interpretation suited to the letter of the criminal case, and yet his Cabbalistic system of representation will not be true to the facts of the case:

> You will argue that reality does not have the least obligation to be interesting. I will reply that reality can do without that obligation, but that is not the case with hypotheses . . . . Here we have a dead rabbi; I would prefer a purely rabbinical explanation, not the imaginary mishaps of an imaginary thief [Usted replicará que la realidad no tiene la menor obligación de ser interesante. Yo le replicaré que la realidad puede prescindir de esa obligación, pero no las hipótesis . . . . He aquí un rabino muerto; yo preferiría una explicación puramente rabínica, no los imaginarios percances de un imaginario ladrón].
> (*Obras* 1.500)

Lönnrot fails precisely because he is a reader of detective fiction. Advantage is derived by Lönnrot's adversary from this fact, which determines certain assumptions about the way in which the detectory schema will develop towards the resolution: "The conventions of detective fiction make possible the adventure of discovering and producing a form, of finding the pattern amid a mass of details, and they do so by stipulating what kind of pattern one is reading toward" (Culler, *Structuralist Poetics* 148). Scharlach stipulates that Lönnrot will identify key elements of the mystery in Cabbalistic terms and thus "feeds" to the detective the clues (as Borges "feeds" to his reader the numerical ones) needed for the development toward the fateful moment of discovery.

Lönnrot has sought the elegant solution, the one the reader of detective fiction has come to expect. In contrast, Police Inspector Franz Treviranus is not interested in rabbinical explanations: "I am interested," he informs Lönnrot at site of the crime, "in capturing the man who stabbed this person" [Me interesa la captura del hombre que apuñaló a este desconocido] (*Obras* 1.500). Treviranus's idea is that the initial victim was killed by accident and that the criminal had confused him with a dealer in precious stones who was lodged across the hall of the hotel. Treviranus turns out to be right. But he does not so much propose a plot as a sprawl of equivocations and disorder. "Chaos is dull," writes G.K. Chesterton, explaining what amounts to the poetry of the detective story, "because in chaos [a] train might indeed go anywhere, to Baker Street or to Bagdad. But man is a magician, and his whole magic is in this, that he does say Victoria, and lo! it is Victoria" (*Man Who Was Thursday* 7). Treviranus's suggestion that the murdered rabbi happened to be at the wrong place at the wrong time and that the real target of the murderer was the gem dealer lodged across the hall belongs in an all-too-familiar world. Lönnrot (and the reader) are readily willing to discard Treviranus's scenario in order to elaborate a reasoned labyrinth that is as much invented as discovered by the intellect confronted with the enticing clues of the case. Treviranus is quickly relegated to the background of the story and identified in the reader's repertory of detective lore with Inspector Seagrave from Collins's *The Moonstone*, the prefect of police in "The Purloined Letter," or the often-mistaken Inspector Lestrade in Doyle's masterpieces of detection.

In regard to the battle of wits that is the centerpiece of the story, Borges writes: "The killer and the slain, whose minds work in the same way, may be the same man" (*The Aleph* 230). This is a pragmatic note that can be understood within the context of our discussion of the golem(s), but it might prove worthwhile to trace the idea. In 1927, Chesterton wrote in *The Uses of Diversity* that "the detective is always outside the event, while the criminal is inside the event. . . . Some would explain it by saying that the policeman is always outside the house when the burglar is inside the house" (35). In his fiction, however, specifically in *The Man Who Was Thursday*, Chesterton proposes a different scenario. In that novel, all the anarchists are policemen, and the chief criminal is also the head of police. Chesterton's is a conception that Borges fully developed by having his detective and chief criminal meet in a house of double symmetry:

> Seen from a short distance, the house of the villa of Triste-le-Roy abounded in pointless symmetries and maniacal repetitions: to one glacial Diana in a murky niche

corresponded a second Diana in another niche; one balcony was reflected in another balcony; double stairwells opened into double balustrades. A two-faced Hermes projected a monstrous shadow [Vista de cerca, la casa de la quinta de Triste-le-Roy abundaba en inútiles simetrías y en repeticiones maniáticas: a una Diana glacial en un nicho lóbrego correspondía en un segundo nicho otra Diana; un balcón se reflejaba en otro balcón; dobles escalinatas se abrían en doble balaustrada. Un Hermes de dos caras proyectaba una sombra monstruosa]. (*Obras* 1.504–505)

The dual arrangement makes evident the fundamental fact that language comes into virtual existence the moment that two entities become aware of a "you" and an "I."[2] By suggesting the criminal and the detective are the same man, Borges reminds us that within the codified exchange the "I" is interchangeable; the subject pronoun merely names a site in language measurable by its effects. Borges notes that "Lönnrot is not an unbelievable fool walking into his own death trap but, in a symbolic way, a man committing suicide" (*The Aleph* 230).

The disposition of Triste-le-Roy is also an allusion to the fact that mirrors will create a labyrinth: "two opposing mirrors are enough to create a labyrinth" ["bastan dos espejos opuestos para crear un laberinto" (Borges, *Siete noches* 44)]. The rhombus by which Lönnrot is able to anticipate the resolution of the case and with which he replaces the false clue of the triangle that Scharlach sent him *is* the triangle, doubled and seen in two halves, each reflecting the other. Lönnrot, the interpreter of Scharlach's geometric figure, becomes a witness to his own dissolution. By means of a configuration of sense whose truth value is assumed by the detective to be operative, Scharlach carries out his intention to "rub out," literally to, erase, the otherness of the detective and so prompt his assimilation into a fiction that will prove to be his undoing.

The focus of Scharlach's fiction makes its reader conceive a narrative in terms of a universal—in this case, a geometric— figure. To achieve this effect, Scharlach counts on the detective to eliminate all the nonreinforcing elements from the scheme that would deny "triangularity." For this, the criminal relies on the inference derived from the fact that the secret name has four letters, and that the crimes have occurred at three of the cardinal points of the compass: the north, the east and the west. The eastern crime is a mock representation of a murder, though the detective does not know this, and neither does the reader. At this point, Scharlach sends a letter to the police informing that the series of murders is complete, and that the mystical triangle is complete. The letter is signed with the name of Baruch Spinoza, the seventeenth-century Jewish philosopher whose Cartesian-based *Ethics* are conceived and developed in rigorous geometric terms. The letter is calculated to have the effect stipulated by Aristotle in his discussion of framing lies in the right way. Lönnrot (and the reader) disregards the letter as an attempt at misdirection, and calculates that a fourth murder will take place south of the three previous points.

In his story, Borges extends a clear (and numerical) invitation to the reader to play along with the detective. The coherence of the story is clearly determined, as has been noted, by the consistent reference to the number three, which is calculated to be taken into consideration by the detectory reader. The numerical clues call attention to the story's composition as another source of a mysterious pattern. The number four makes a marginal appearance both as part of the exposition of the initial crime in the name of the Tetrarch of Galilee, a trader in gems who is lodged in the room across from the one occupied by the murdered rabbi, and as the date in which the victim is found murdered. After the third murder, there is a veritable profusion of the number four in the text: There are four descriptions of the heterogeneous establishments that serve as backdrop to the scene of the fourth murder, and four (and the rhombus) is hinted at by the harlequin suits worn by the alleged criminals, who leave at four o'clock with their intended victim. Four is also the number of versions reported in the local newspapers dealing with the series of deaths. The deceiver's scheme (Scharlach's and Borges's) relies on the reader's intellect to provide the sensical figure's economy by the recognition of particular features, which in this case are the number of angles, the dimensions of the figure's sides. Equally important is the necessary reference (performed by the reader) to a model conceived and composed by previous perceptions of the form (a geometric one, in Borges's exposition). Scharlach provides three equidistant points and hints at a fourth by means of a temporal clue. Lönnrot is more than willing to pursue that resolution. The primacy of signification in the detective's universe is reason enough for Lönnrot, who is consumed by the signification system he postulates for his solution.[3]

The fate of Lönnrot and Scharlach is sealed in the self-regarding doubling evident in the final scene. Borges could have left the story at this point of frightful, self-cancelling duality, but he adds a further twist: Lönnrot turns critical of the plot that is about to cancel him out of existence. Ever the detective, he appeals to the economy of means dictated by the genre: "In your labyrinth there are three lines too many, " he tells Scharlach, "I know of one Greek labyrinth which is a single straight line." [En su laberinto sobran tres líneas. Yo sé de un laberinto griego que es una línea única, recta." (*Obras* 1.507)] In doing so, he proposes the paradoxical straight-line labyrinth resorted to by Zeno the Eleatic to refute movement: "Movement is impossible (argues Zeno) since the moving object must cross a middle point to reach the final one, and before that, the middle of the middle, and before that the middle of the middle of the middle, and before that . . ." [El movimiento es imposible (arguye Zenón) pues el móvil debe atravesar el medio para llegar al fin, y antes el medio del medio, y antes el medio del medio, del medio y antes . . .]. (Rodríguez Monegal and Reid, 106; *Discusión* 130)

Lönnrot also appeals to infinite regression as an argument against his end. He recognizes his (and Scharlach's) written nature: "Scharlach," he says,

> when in another incarnation you stalk me, feign to commit (or do commit) a crime at A, then a second crime at B, eight kilometers from A, then a third crime at C, four kilometers from A and B, halfway between the two. Wait for me later at D, two kilometers from A and C, halfway, once again, between both. Kill me at D, as you are now going to kill me at Triste-le-Roy" [cuando en otro avatar usted me dé caza, finja (o cometa) un crimen en A, luego un segundo crimen en B, a ocho kilómetros de A, luego un tercer crimen en C, a cuatro kilómetros de A y B, a mitad de camino entre los dos. Aguárdeme después en D, a dos kilómetros de A y de C, de nuevo a mitad de camino.

Máteme en D, como ahora va a matarme en Triste-le-Roy].
(*Obras* 1.507)

Like a modern Abel, Lönnrot formulates his situation as an encounter with a new Cain. Cain and Abel, Scharlach and Lönnrot are "sites" playing out their assigned roles, their periodic "deaths."[4] Their game is a repetition of past games, the moves of which they are reenacting in a tradition of set moves. Lönnrot's scheme recalls Agatha Christie's *The ABC Murders*, only without the coincidence of the victims' names and toponyms that characterizes that series of murders. And in "Chess" ["Ajedrez"], Borges writes of the players sitting in their respective corners moving the well-worn game pieces. As described by Borges, the pieces seem alive in their conventional, formulaic antagonism. In fact, after the players' deaths the game will go on: "Eventually, when the players have withdrawn, / when time itself has finally consumed them, / the ritual certainly will not be done" [Cuando los jugadores se hayan ido, / cuando el tiempo los haya consumido, / ciertamente no habrá cesado el rito (Rodríguez Monegal and Reid, 280; *Obras* 2.191)]. The best way to understand this allusion to the infinite is to relate it to the detectory reader who plays the game of the fiction by way of the rules that define him or her and the game—unendingly.

Scharlach's devious designs find resonance in Borges's prefiguration of the reader in his text. Borges's anticipation of his reader in "Death and the Compass" is an object lesson of fictional deception. The lead paragraph sets up a number of contingencies for the reader's consideration: The peculiar nature of the story is clearly stated—the case to be displayed is "rigorously strange" ["rigurosamente extraño" (*Obras* 1.499)] and without parallel in the detective's experience; the detective will not, we are told, prevent the last murder or name the culprit. But all these unsettling declarations are referred by the reader to the set conventions of the genre, which has the effect of dissipating their strangeness. The announced failure of Lönnrot's investigation is disquieting and sheds a degree of suspicion on his method, but this early revelation of the end could be part of the game, and, after all, the inversion of detective story conventions is not an unprecedented event.

As early as 1912, R. Austin Freeman gave the solution of the mystery at the beginning of *The Singing Bone*. In 1932, Anthony Berkeley Cox revealed the name of the murderer in the second sentence of *Before the Fact*. The rest of the book tells how the murder is planned with the victim's knowledge (la Cour and Mogensen, 94). All these maneuvers can be interpreted as the writer's way of imposing difficulties in the composition of the mystery. Compare the following opening paragraph by Robert Barr with Borges's opening gambit: "Some years ago I enjoyed the unique experience of pursuing a man for one crime, and getting evidence against him of another. He was innocent of the misdemeanor, the proof of which I sought, but was guilty of another most serious offense, yet he and his confederates escaped scot free in circumstances which I now purpose to relate" (Sayers, *Omnibus* 304). The encyclopedia of facts that comprises the detectory reader thus conspires to erase the uniqueness of the fictive truth that will be encountered at every turn of the reading.

Lönnrot's failures are presented apologetically, while the merits of his investigation are set out plainly: The detective could not name the murderer but was able to foresee his name in "la morfología secreta" of the sequence of murders. The "secret morphology" that is so announced finds immediate resonance in the name of the criminal, Red Scharlach. Does the reader read "red" in relation to Erik Lönnrot's name before finding an indexical value related to Scharlach's own? *Red* is found in the detective's and in the criminal's name but it is upon finding *red* in the latter's name that the color acquires any significance in the reading (and what might that significance be?). Upon recognizing the relation, the reader has to implement some code to account for the similarity. This enactment requires the transfer of terms among linguistic codes; for example, the reader must arrive at the realization that the morpheme "rot" is the German equivalent of "red" and accept that "Erik" does support the contiguous relation with that index (as in Erik "the Red" and, as Scharlach conjures up, "scarlet"), though that postulated relation might be later discarded in the new contexts of the story. Borges's game of allusion progressively draws his reader, now alerted to the power of naming, into the level of fiction. The choice of assigning value to color is revealed as a deviously arbitrary decision by the resulting irony. The criminal's name in Borges's story also echoes the name of Doyle's master sleuth, Sherlock Holmes. The reader finds that in coding the name of Scharlach as a color index of pragmatic significance to the meaning of the text, the phonetic value of "Scharlach" is relegated to a background that the generic associations of the text refuse to sustain. The associative tensions created by the act of naming result in an irony that signals the irreducible allusive links that bind the criminal with the detectives in fiction.

The denotative resonance of color between the names suggests a hidden configuration at work in the text, or better yet, "hovering" between the reader and the text. A relation so intriguing is a convincing argument for its significance. Notice that the resonance between the names is not a clue that works at the diegetic level of the narration. It does not figure in the detective's calculations that unfold the narrative. It prefigures, rather, another reader who is able to make the association and give meaning to a reality that "stands" behind the sign, a reality meant only for him or her who makes the discerning choice. "A thread of red," writes Borges, "also runs through the story's pages. There is a sunset on the rose-colored wall and, in the same scene, the blood splashed on the dead man's face" (*The Aleph* 230). The search for a hidden morphology in the codification of names has constituted a reader with a certain sensibility who is implied in the interpretive act, an act that is intertextual: "There's the scarlet thread of murder running the colourless skein of life, and our duty is to unravel it, and isolate it, and expose every inch of it," pronounced Sherlock Holmes in *A Study in Scarlet* (Doyle, 1.33). But the necessity of a meaning in the text is contingent on the context assigned to each fragment encountered in comprising the narrative, and in the assumption made by the reader that the part is in some way genuinely like the whole.

In the closing moments of the story, the detective is finally a critic of the plot he has helped to create and suggests a simplification of its development. We have seen Lönnrot seeking in the paradoxical nature of Zeno's scheme the plot configuration that might possibly allow for the irresolution of an irreversible end: "In your labyrinth there are three lines too many," says Lonnrot, following Occam; "I know of one Greek labyrinth which is a single straight line. Along that line so many philosophers have lost themselves that a mere detective might well do so, too." Scharlach agrees to oblige him with that figure; he aims, perhaps imagining the linear trajectory of the bullet, at two points, the entrance wound and the bullet's exit from the body: "Then, very carefully, he fired" [Después, muy cuidadosamente, hizo fuego] (*Obras* 1.507). Borges has brought his story to conclusion with a rhetorical figure, a metaphor of fire that evokes death as the name of the action without insuring it. With that figure of speech, Borges has merely said what the action is not like. Does he say "shot," "killed," or "put an end to Lönnrot's life"? No, these are the reader's conjectures. Hillis Miller points out that Scharlach does not literally "make fire" and identifies the locution as a *catachresis* (60), a figure (or trope) that, de Man notes, "coins a name for a still unnamed entity, which gives face to the faceless" (*Resistance* 44). Confronted with indeterminacy, the reader might just as well imagine the escape of the detective or observe the reference to another of Borges's artifices, where fire is revealed as the vehicle of dreams, recurrence, and configurative repetitions.

Borges leaves unresolved the opposition of presence and absence in the text and forces the reader to recreate the act that originated the interpretation. A new labyrinth has to be created from this opposition, one that invokes the Spanish language, the ordinary conventions of the detective genre, and logical presuppositions in order to arrive once again at a signifier, presumably hidden, at Tzinacán's vision in "The God's Script:" "the faceless god that is concealed behind all the gods" [el dios sin cara que hay detrás de todos los dioses (*Obras* 1.599)]. It is this transfer of terms from realms outside the text that constitutes the pragmatic projection of the reader as a strategy of textual interpretation. The effort to name what has no proper name, the desire to join in a prefigured game, is the conventional enticement of detective fiction. Each sign encountered along the way demands an attempt to go straight to the truth of a matter constituted by style, rhetoric, and form and restricted by the economy of the detective plot, which Borges elaborates as an argument of unforeseen complexity designed to reveal to the reader his or her own name.

NOTES

1. One could stipulate that, hypothetically, the Lönnrot-Scharlach game could reflect into the past only as far back as 1841, the year that marked the formalization of the detectory schema into the conventions of detective story with Poe's creation of "The Murders in the Rue Morgue."

2. This idea is found in *Ensayo sobre el origen de las lenguas* (*Essai sur l'origine des langues*) by Jean-Jacques Rousseau: "As soon as a man was recognized by another as a sensible being, thinking and similar to him, the desire or necessity of communicating his feelings compelled him to search for the means appropiate for the task. Those means can only be derived from the senses, the only instruments by means of which a man can act on another. From that, then, we have the institution of sensible signs for the ends of expressing thought. The inventors of language did not reason this process, but instinct suggested to them the consequences" [Tan pronto como un hombre fue reconocido por otro como un ser sensible, pensante y similar a él, el deseo o la necesidad de comunicarle sus sentimientos y sus pensamientos lo llevó a buscar los medios apropiados para ello. Tales medios sólo pueden sacarse de los sentidos, únicos instrumentos por los que puede un hombre actuar sobre otro. De allí, pues, la institución de los signos sensibles para expresar el pensamiento. Los inventores del lenguaje no se hicieron este razonamiento, pero el instinto les sugirió su consecuencia" (11)].

3. In the representation of Lönnrot's journey to meet his maker, Borges uses "tricks" deployed in *Historia universal*, such as "the paring down of a man's whole life to two or three scenes" (*Universal History* 13). Here he pares down the work of his intellect to the two or three lines that are his *oeuvre*. In attempting to illustrate "infinite intelligence," Borges offers the following example: "The steps a man takes, from the day of his birth to the day of his death, trace an inconceivable figure in time. The Divine Intelligence perceives the figure at once, as man's intelligence perceives a triangle. That figure (perhaps) has its determined function in the economy of the universe" [Los pasos que da un hombre desde el día de su nacimiento hasta el de su muerte, dibujan

en el tiempo una inconcebible figura. La Inteligencia Divina intuye esa figura inmediatamente, como la de los hombres un triángulo. Esa figura (acaso) tiene su determinada función en la economía del universo"]. (*Other Inquisitions* 128; *Otras inquisiciones* 123)

4. In "Del culto de los libros," Borges points out that "the Scot [Thomas] Carlyle, in various of his works and particularly in the essay on Cagliostro . . . said that universal history was a Sacred Scripture: one that we decipher and write uncertainly, and in which we are also written" [el escocés Carlyle, en diversos lugares de su labor y particularmente en el ensayo sobre Cagliostro . . . estampó que la historia universal es una Escritura sagrada que desciframos inciertamente, y en la que también nos escriben"]. (*Other Inquisitions* 120; *Otras inquisiciones* 114).

PART THREE

The Readers Write: Bustos Domecq and
Six Problems for Don Isidro Parodi

Bioy Casares and Borges
The Making of "Biorges"

In the collection of detective stories titled *Seis problemas para Don Isidro Parodi* [*Six Problems for Don Isidro Parodi*], Borges shared authorship with Adolfo Bioy Casares, and became the better-known half of a new author named Honorio Bustos Domecq. The subsuming of their names under the name of Bustos Domecq, and the placing of their writing under the rule of Bustos Domecq's, would eventually earn Borges and Bioy Casares the additional sobriquet of "Biorges." Initially, "Biorges's" production was received skeptically by those around them, and this created problems in the publication of their work. Ultimately, "Biorges" opted for private means of publication in order to circumvent popular or literary standards (and objections) that lay in the way of a project they felt deserved a fair chance at a readership. The following pages recount the development of the literary collaboration undertaken by Bioy Casares and Borges.

As individuals, outside of the writing contract represented by Bustos Domecq, the Bioy Casares-Borges collaboration proved to be a productive and important one. In "An Autobiographical Essay," which appeared in 1970 as part of *The Aleph and Other Stories*, Borges recalls the joint compilation of anthologies of Argentine poetry, fantastic fiction, detective stories; together, he and Bioy Casares wrote articles and prologues, prepared annotated volumes of Sir Thomas Browne and Baltasar Gracián, collaborated on translations, and founded a magazine, *Destiempo* (246). A high point of the collaboration between Bioy Casares and Borges came in 1943 with the compilation of the first of two collections of detective fiction which would prove crucial to the development of the genre in Argentina and Latin America. The editions have undergone substantial changes: The edition of 1943 that Rodríguez Monegal mentions *Jorge Luis Borges*: in *A Literary Biography* (378) now describes *Los mejores cuentos policiales 2*, published by Alianza/Emecé, which includes not sixteen but fifteen stories, such as "The Purloined Letter" by Edgar Allan Poe, "The Red Haired League" by Arthur Conan Doyle, "The Honor of Israel Gow" by G.K. Chesterton, and Ellery Queen's "Philately," among others. Gone are the stories by Guillaume Apollinaire and Georges Simenon reported by Rodríguez Monegal. The collection retains the originally selected stories by Argentine authors Adolfo Luis Pérez, Manuel Peyrou, and the uncharacteristically immodest contribution, given the title of the collection, by Jorge Luis Borges. The editors' selection for the volume was "La muerte y la brújula" ["Death and the Compass"].

In time, critical acclaim for the story would make it difficult to argue with the choice. The critic Donald Yates has affirmed that if Argentina had produced that story and only that story, mention of the country would still be assured in any history of the detective genre (*El cuento* 11). "Death and the Compass" might not be the most characteristic story of the detective genre, but some of the other choices that appear in the volume are not what many aficionados would consider "mainstream" either. Present in the pages of the current edition are Nathaniel Hawthorne's "The Repeated Death" from *Twice-Told Tales*, and a story from Jack London, another author not usually associated with the detective genre. The independence of the editors' choices can be best understood in terms of Borges's own argument: "Literary genres depend less, perhaps, on the texts than on the way these texts are read" [los géneros literarios dependen, quizás, menos de los textos que del modo en que éstos son leídos" (*Oral* 66)]. Borges's pronouncement goes a long way to explain why, for example, Robert Louis Stevenson is represented in the first edition of the volume with a fragment of *The Master of Ballantrae* that lacks both a detective and the story of an investigation.

In his review of a collection of Borges's stories, published in 1942 under the title of *The Garden of Forking Paths*, Bioy Casares casts some light on this issue, which is closely related to the recognition of the value of the detectory schema, and the reader created by Poe:

> Perhaps the detective genre has not produced a book. But it has produced an ideal: an ideal of invention, of rigor, or elegance (in the sense that this word receives in mathematics) for the plots. To highlight the importance of construction: that is perhaps, the significance of the genre in the history of literature [Tal vez el genéro policial no haya producido un libro. Pero ha producido un ideal: un ideal de invención, de rigor, de elegancia (en el sentido que se le da a la palabra en las matemáticas) para los argumentos. Destacar la importancia de la construcción: éste es, quizá, el significado del género en la historia de la literatura]. (Bioy Casares in Camurati, 73)

In relation to the story that gives its name to Borges's collection, Bioy Casares goes on to write: "It is a detective story, without detectives, or Watson, or the other inconveniences of the genre, but it has the enigma, the surprise, the right solution, that may particularly be demanded of, but not delivered by some detective stories" [Se trata de una historia policial, sin detectives, ni Watson, ni otros inconvenientes del género, pero con el enigma, la sorpresa, la solución justa, que en particular puede exigirse, y no obtenerse, de los cuentos policiales (Bioy Casares in Camurati, 74)]. Bioy Casares and Borges are clearly advocating with these "irregular" choices a reading tradition over a textual one. The first anthology verifies the editors' implied criteria by including, among the other interesting choices, an outstanding story by Ryonosuke Akutagawa, "In a Grove," which consists of a series of testimonies to the high police commissioner by several characters who are the possible suspects of a murder. In 1951, Bioy Casares and Borges produced another anthology for Emecé which included "Smoke," by William Faulkner, along with "The Twelve Figures of the World" by Honorio Bustos Domecq.

The anthologies were a great success and Emecé Editores, faced with a growing readership for the mystery story, saw their way clear to begin a mystery novel series which would be edited by Bioy Casares and Borges (Rodríguez Monegal, *Borges* 379). Pressed for a title for the series, Borges settled with Bioy Casares to name the series after the circle occupied by violent men in Dante's *Inferno*. Borges recalls the occasion: "If it had been the sixth, eighth or fourth it wouldn't have worked, but 'The Seventh Circle' was perfect; we were lucky and we used that title for the series" (Alifano, 44). The first volume published was *The Beast Must Die* by Nicholas Blake, and Wilkie Collins's *The Moonstone* soon followed, a novel that has been described by T.S. Eliot as "the first, the longest, and the best of modern English detective novels" (Collins, 7).

Bioy Casares and Borges's greatest invention would be, however, Honorio Bustos Domecq. Borges recalls the third man they had created: "In the long run, he ruled us with a rod of iron and to our amusement, and later to our dismay, he became utterly unlike ourselves, with his own whims, his own puns, and his own very elaborate style of writing" [A la larga, nos manejó con vara de hierro, y para nuestra diversión, y después para nuestra consternación, llegó a ser muy diferente a nosotros, con sus propios caprichos, sus propios chistes, su propia y muy elaborada forma de escribir (*The Aleph* 246)]. Bustos Domecq's first book was *Six Problems*. The collection of detective stories was also the first of its kind in Argentina (Yates, *El cuento* 10). It was published in 1942 by the magazine *Sur*, but Domecq's debut was not a success. Readers found the stories dense, too comic or not comic enough. Undeterred, Bustos Domecq published *Dos fantasías memorables [Two Memorable Fantasies]* in 1946 and inspired a "disciple," B. Suárez Lynch (another permutation of the originating pair), to publish a truly digressive detective novel, *Un modelo para la muerte [A Model for Death]*, that same year. The novel was given a generous prologue by Bustos Domecq himself.

If Bustos Domecq's first excursion into fiction was not a success, his disciple's was even less so. Borges explains that "the stories became so impossible to unravel and so baroque that it was very difficult to understand them" (Murat in Rodríguez Monegal, *Borges* 370). But Suárez Lynch's novel was not published for commercial distribution. For the promotion of

Bustos Domecq's second and last volume—two other Domecq-inspired creations would be published under Borges Casares and Bioy's names—and for his disciple's first (and last), Bioy and Borges resorted to a fictitious publishing firm, "Oportet & Haereses," a small, private venture that would dictate the limited circulation of Domecq's second outing and of Lynch's novel in 1946.[1]

The critic Emir Rodríguez Monegal reveals the joke half-hidden in the name of the apocryphal firm by noting the allusion "al oporto y al jerez," that is, to port and sherry (*Borges* 370). In an obvious manner, the name of the firm does allude to those characteristically peninsular spirits as Bustos's other surname refers to Pedro Domecq's *solera* founded in 1730 in Jerez de la Frontera. Borges has also explained that Domecq "was the name of a great-grandfather of Bioy's and Bustos of a great-grandfather of mine from Córdoba" (*The Aleph* 246) but, given the free play that the name and history of the character allows, one might interject that Domecq is also the surname of Philip Trent's love interest in E.C. Bentley's celebrated parody of the detective genre dating from 1913. A distant relation, perhaps? Monegal's proposition, however, does generate the metaphor of Bacchic play and laughter in relation to the work of Bustos Domecq, and to the work of Suárez Lynch in particular. Borges recalls the writing of *A Model for Death*, Suárez Lynch's detective novel: "At the beginning, we made jokes, and then, jokes on jokes, it was like in algebra: jokes squared, jokes cubed . . . " (Murat in Rodríguez Monegal, *Borges* 370). Rodríguez Monegal (reader/detective) has grasped on to the phonetic similarity to port evident in the first term of the coupling "Oportet & Haereses," and that has allowed him to recognize in both names a clear reference to viniculture. The coupling of the two nouns, their phonetic similarity to the names of the spirits mentioned, and the obvious reference to the Andalusian company in Domecq's name tend to close off the field of possible associations. The reader has eased himself onto the joke. But why exclusively port and sherry?

The name of the publishing company invented by "Biorges" is a perfect example of the kind of clue often found in the puzzle type of detective story. The ambiguity of the name hints at the charm of the game proposed by this mode of mystery, which engages the reader while aiming to misdirect the process of interpretation that it sets in motion. The key to interpreting the clue lies in forestalling rash interpretations while questioning the motivation of the narrator. The powers of reason are thus called into play, along with a measured consideration of the context of the problem. Often, the resolution of the enigma demands that the interpreter look at the clue from an unusual angle, one that lines up the narration and the particular clue in an unconventional way and reveals the true thinking of the devious criminal. This approach is championed by Poe in "The Purloined Letter" and accounts for the dazzling solution reached by Dupin. The revelation of the solution that was in plain view all along is, in the final account, why these stories of reasoning detectives are read and marveled at by detective story readers. A solution arrived at from plain fact is very much in the spirit of the Parodi stories. It also embodies the playfulness of the ratiocinative mode of interpretation, which compels the reader to consider the angle that would best allow one to understand the mystery. As in "The Purloined Letter," the resolution of the mystery of the publishing house's name requires the same type of acumen that one needs to solve the popular riddle, "What is black and white and red all over?" The series (the first two terms of which are colors and in which "red" is the first and final term) leads the hearer away from preterite verb forms, which are what he or she needs to arrive at the proper solution. It is not until the hearer disengages the third term from the color series that the riddle stands revealed and the answer appears to have been there all along: a newspaper. The shift in the hearer's understanding is a response to the puzzle, and it is only this shift, or modification, that permits true understanding to take place.

Rodríguez Monegal, when he was commenting on the publishing house's name, probably did not think of Latin as an angle for resolving the case. But let us hypothesize that the authors were conscious of the fact that the English word *heresies* is derived from the Latin "haereses" (*herejías* in Spanish), and see what comes of it. We have before us "an opinion or practice at odds with an orthodox principle." The linking of "Haereses" to "Oportet" seems unjustified now. However, "Haereses" fits the spirit of Bioy Casares and Borges's enterprise, when we consider the nature of Bustos Domecq's stories against the background of what constitutes a detective story and its mode of presentation and development. By parodying the form, Bustos Domecq is deviating from a generic norm and thus becomes a heresiarch at odds with the detective canon. Moreover, the *Oxford Latin Dictionary* defines "oportet" in the following way: "It is demanded by some principle or standard; it is right, proper, requisite."

Even more interesting, "oportet" links to the mode of distribution chosen by Bioy Casares and Borges for Bustos Domecq's heresies after the initial "failure" of his parodic doctrine. By choosing to print Bustos Domecq privately, Bioy Casares and Borges were circumventing the "official" routes of publication, which would hesitate to provide open access to a readership, given the genre and nature of Bustos Domecq's writing. Here was a need to reach a readership in spite of the prevailing intellectual climate or the predisposition of the existing channels of distribution and publication. Recall that in 1947 the "apócrifa empresa editorial" of Oportet & Haereses published "New Refutation of Time" by Jorge Luis Borges, a thirty-five page essay that is key for understanding the author's conception of time and self (Rodríguez Monegal, *Biografía* 364). In it, Borges writes: "Are the enthusiasts who devote a lifetime to a line by Shakespeare not literally Shakespeare? [¿Los fervorosos que se entregan a una línea de Shakespeare no son, literalmente, Shakespeare? (*Otras inquisiciones* 177)].[2] Rodríguez Monegal explains that at the time, "Borges represented not only an emergent culture. . . . It was a specifically literary quest, but in the context of the Argentina of those years it also had the dimensions of a moral quest" (*Borges* 403). Borges's question represents one of the boldest and earliest statements of the radical deconstruction of historicism that would characterize the Argentine author's thought and literary practice. Borges, in other words, was writing against the intellectual climate and practice of the time.

In their discussion of publishing during the years 1500–1550, the historians Lucien Febvre and Henri-Jean Martin write: "Booksellers were primarily concerned to make a profit and to sell their products, and consequently they sought out first and foremost those works which were of interest to the largest number of their contemporaries . . . " (260). Febvre and Martin's appraisal of what motivated the booksellers in the sixteenth century still holds true today. Notice, then, the importance of private publication for marginalia, or heresies, outside the mainstream interest of established publishing houses or of an existing readership.

Private printing serves a strategic role in the dissemination of ideas and constitutes the creation of "reading enclaves" allied with the decentralizing forces of society and the free currency of ideas. Consider also this statement on the history of printing: "Printed materials encouraged silent adherence to causes whose advocates could not be located in any one parish and who addressed an invisible public from afar" (Eisenstein, 42). The Bioy Casares-Borges duo, in November of 1947, the same year that "New Refutation" was published, circulated the manuscript of "The Monster's Celebration," a satirical piece on Perón's partisans and their leader's demagoguery. The central episode was the lynching of a young Jewish intellectual by a fascist Peronist mob, told in the argot that would characterize much of *Six Problems* and *A Model for Death*. In 1955, the story was "officially" published in the Uruguayan weekly *Marcha*, after Perón was deposed from power (Rodríguez Monegal, *Borges* 406). Evident in this anecdote is the importance of access to the means of printing and distribution for the dissemination of ideas, be they the introduction of a genre considered irrelevant to the circumstances of the country, or a tract in confrontation with the prevailing political climate of the times.

The audience for Borges's essay, "Biorges's" story, Bustos Domecq's fantasies, and Suárez Lynch's baroque punning was limited to a fortunate few, but the mere fact that the works existed in print and could spread suggested that new readers and readerships could be created if there were multiple ownership of presses. Freedom of the press might be the right of those who own the presses, but not necessarily, and this private sector might have been seen by Bioy Casares and Borges, in turn, as the best insurance for the preservation of civil liberties in the days of the Peronist regime. Necessity, indeed, prompted the private printing of "The Monster's Celebration," and of Bustos Domecq and Suárez Lynch experimental writing.

The validity of this reading of the meaning of "Oportet" and "Haereses" lies in the credibility of the new code by which I have interpreted the two terms. What happened to the port and sherry? By emphasizing the terms "haereses" and "oportet" in relation to the linguistic code of Latin (a move suggested by the word ending and composition, and the presence of Eco's novel in this discussion), it has been possible in one sense to liberate, and in another to detoxify, the association made by Rodríguez Monegal and to open up the possibility for the interpretation just proposed. The relation of similarity between the terms "oportet" "haereses" and "port" "sherry [jerez]" short-circuited other associations for Rodríguez Monegal that might (or, admittedly, might not) have been intended by its authors.

Is Rodríguez Monegal wrong, then? Not necessarily. A Latin reading is only one of many that are possible. Borges had, of course, avowed an interest in the subject of heresies (two essays come to mind: "A Vindication of Basilides the False" ["Una vindicación del falso Basílides"], published in *Discusión*, and "The Biathanatos," included in *Other Inquisitions*). And why would the "haereses" appear in connection with the publication of Bustos Domecq's stories? Seen against the canon of detective stories, *Seis problemas* is a comical compilation of heresies: The detective is in jail, the characters whose troubles Don Isidro resolves receive popular acclaim for their ingenuity, the plots are often preposterous, and the language of the stories is often mystifying for the average reader. A Latin interpretation only allows for a fuller and more relevant discussion of "Biorges's" travails in creating Bustos Domecq and disseminating a body of work that flew in the face of readers' expectations and tastes at the time of publication; it gives precedence to Latin over the multifarious other linguistic codes that are inherent in the symbol and supports a coherent set of propositions. "Oportet & Haereses" can *also* be port and sherry. The mystery encoded in the words naming the firm lingers and depends on which code is chosen to decipher the inscription; both interpretations, Rodríguez Monegal's and the one I present in these pages, are in fact independent of each other and always subject to elaboration by yet another reader.

NOTES

1. "Oportet & Haereses" published *Dos fantasías memorables* (1946), *Un modelo para la muerte* (1946), and "Nueva refutación del tiempo" (1947). Bioy Casares and Borges published under their own names two other contributions by Bustos Domecq to the marketplace of ideas: *Crónicas de Bustos Domecq* (1967), and *Nuevos cuentos de Bustos Domecq* (1977).

2. Ruth Simms's translation of this key question from "New Refutation" misinterprets Borges. The identification with Shakespeare would not be the product of a lifetime of devotion, but rather, of the intensity of the reading instance that identifies the reader with the line (or work) by Shakespeare. "The reader is in some way the poet"— Borges would explain years later—" . . . when we read Shakespeare we are, however momentarily, Shakespeare" (Borges and Ferrari, *Libro* 206). In the context of the essay, Borges is using Hume as a point of departure in that "time must be composed of indivisible moments" (183); Borges concludes: "I do not know what right we have to the continuity that is time" (175). This assumption can frequently be seen at work in Borges's stories where the character's identity (and death) are determined in a single instant. Interestingly, in the later interview, Borges does not deny history, but conceives it as repeated instances: "perhaps in some cases we can prolong Shakespeare even more, since the text by Shakespeare has been enriched . . . not only by the commentators, but by history, by those repeated experiences that are called history" (Borges and Ferrari, *Libro* 206).

A Compendium of Heresies
Six Problems for Don Isidro Parodi

Ellery Queen's list of the one hundred most important collections of detective fiction in the world includes Honorio Bustos Domecq's parodic *Seis problemas* (1942), hereafter referred to in this chapter as *Six Problems*, as well as the Mexican writer Antonio Helus's *La obligación de asesinar* (1946) [*The Murder Imperative*] (la Cour, 146).[1] In *Six Problems*, essentially a product of dialogue and discussions over detective plots, Borges and Bioy Casares introduce to the English type of detective story the oral quality that Borges had attempted to recreate in "Street-corner Man," his first story. They also made the turn of phrases that hide and reveal, the slang known as *lunfardo,* and street-corner humor into the idiosyncratic features of narratives which are, in spite of it all, detective stories—rigorously structured tales of hidden truth, guilt, and discovery. Chesterton wrote that detective fiction is a drama of false identities, more concerned with masks than with faces (*Generally Speaking* 6). In Don Isidro's "problems," language is the mask of the culprit. By fore-grounding this aspect of the mystery story, "Biorges" empha-sizes the importance of the "esthetics of suspicion" in discourse. The drive toward resolution characteristic of the form is not forsaken, however; Don Isidro himself is as central and respon-sible as God in seeing through the multiple deviations of symbols and references, as well as through the deceit and forgetfulness of his witnesses, in order to arrive at a revelation of the hidden scheme in the final account of the events that he pronounces in his prison cell.

What is commonly known as the classic or English de-tective story has certain features that lend themselves to caricature, or it has, rather, an inherent element of caricature. One has only to think of the detective's slightly dull foil, or the eccentricity of the brilliant detective who, by the limits of characterization imposed by the genre, cultivates habits such as smoking a meerschaum pipe in the dark, or playing the violin for mental concentration. Detectives may consume opiates or stimulants, or cultivate roses or orchids. Then there are the conventions of composition, such as the detectives' cryptic remarks, or their pronouncements that wrap up the solutions to the mysteries. The element of caricature of this line of detective fiction is amplified in the *Six Problems*, with the result that Bustos Domecq's stories achieve a greater comic effect than is the norm in the genre (whether this effect was intended in the model or not), not just from characterization, but from dialogue and situation as well. Parody is the ground condition on which the Parodi stories develop.

With the character of Don Isidro Parodi, Borges and Bioy Casares attempt to surpass the characteristic eccentricities of the classic reasoners. *Six Problems* appeared in 1942 with a verbose introduction by a character with the name of Gervasio Montenegro, who praises the work of Bustos Domecq with malapropisms and dizzying rhetoric. Montenegro's introduction is followed by a biographical sketch of Bustos Domecq written by a fictional school teacher, Miss Adelma Badiglio. Bustos Domecq's detective is in jail, unjustly accused and convicted of a crime he did not commit; his stimulant is Paraguayan tea, or *mate*, which he drinks from a small powder blue mug, and his entertainment is cards, with which he is sometimes able to work out the solution of the crime. It is important to note that the situations that Parodi solves are often preposterous, but never are they so fantastic that they invalidate the process of resolution, or allow the case to be dismissed as a joke, at least not by a reader of G.K. Chesterton, Ernest Bramah, or Emmuska Orczy—that is, not by a reader familiar with the armchair detective tradition of preposterous crimes and dazzling solutions.

The stories are parodic; as the writer Severo Sarduy explains, "the substratum and basis for this genre . . . is the carnival, a symbolic and syncretic spectacle where the 'abnormal' reigns, where misunderstandings and transgressions multiply along with eccentricities and ambivalence, and whose central action is a parodic crowning, that is to say, an apotheosis that is at the same time an act of mockery" (556–57). The parodic crowning that takes place at the end of the Parodi stories is, of course, the crowning of truth, but the stories do not make mockery of truth in the sense that the word is understood today of laughing at or discrediting the object of mockery; rather, the Parodi stories preserve the multidirectional quality of parodic laughter that Bakhtin observes in relation to earlier parody, "which was free of nihilistic denial." Thus, truth is made richer and more contradictorily complex by Bustos Domecq's parody, which represents "a critique on the one-sided seriousness of the lofty direct word" (*Dialogic* 55). The stories also make evident that parody, as Linda Hutcheon points out, can have ideological or even social implications (98). The stories do not escape, however, the paradoxical legitimacy of parodic discourse. On the one hand, as Roland Barthes indicates, parody suggests a "complicity with high culture . . . which is merely a deceptively off-hand way of showing a profound respect for classical-national values" (Barthes in Hutcheon, "Modern Parody" 101); on the other, Domecq's stories represent an anarchic force, "one that puts into question the legitimacy of other texts" (100).[2]

Borges's comments on the detective story cast a light on the nature of Bustos Domecq's experiments with the genre:

> A detective story actually begins with the last chapter, and the entire book has been written for the purpose of getting to the last chapter; this agrees with Poe's aesthetics (and he invented the detective genre), Poe, who said a short story ought to be written for the last line. That is, of course, a way to turn out admirable stories but at the same time, it's a kind of trap in the long run. I think it's possible to write short stories which aren't written for the last line. In any event, I don't know whether anyone had attempted that type of story before Poe, or perhaps before Hawthorne. But I believe stories can be written which are continuously pleasing, continuously exciting, and which do not lead us to that last line out of mere astonishment or mere bafflement. (Borges in Sorrentino, 62)

The density of the characters' speech in Bustos Domecq's stories, the convolutions of the mystery, and the amusement produced by the misunderstandings and contradictions of character and plot work their spell to undo the linearity of detective story construction. However, one could say in relation to Bustos Domecq's stories that the reader encounters astonishment and bafflement from the *first* line of the stories; in either case, the interpretation does not invalidate the description of stories not written for the last line as being pertinent to Bustos Domecq's narrative.

Several of Bustos Domecq's stories have highly inventive plots, and at least one has been included in a wide-ranging detective story anthology, the one edited by Bioy Casares and Borges in 1951. The frame of these stories is the monologue of a visitor whom Parodi has obliged with an audience. Several other monologues are usually added to the initial one, all pronounced before an attentive Parodi. The ending, appearing as a "Part Two," is Parodi's wrap-up solution, addressed to one of the visitors, though not necessarily the first one, who might turn out to be the guilty party. In this respect, *Six Problems* follows the classic detective story evoked by Ronald Christ, with its "causal patterns of prophetic propositions and echoing, complementary solution" (*Narrow Act* 120). Specifically, inventiveness in the plots of the Parodi stories can be measured by the imaginary distance between the consequence and the antecedent that Parodi is able to bridge by sheer abductive prowess. The illuminating conjecture by Parodi is presented in the final sections of these stories, with the revelation of the underlying principle of the mystery.

In their compositional rigor, these stories share in the logical formula of the sonnet: "A sonnet has two parts, . . . the first part or proposition . . . and the second or resolution . . . where the initial movement is completed, either badly or well" (Vázquez, 15). Whether one considers these stories to have been completed badly or well has to do with how much the reader is willing to accept or has accepted "the general effect of a detective story," which, as enunciated by John Sturrock, "is to inflate whatever it contains with potential meaning, and to show how a plot can seize on anything it likes, however mean or ordinary, and integrate it within a single meaningful, literary structure" (127). This general effect is often compressed in *Six Problems* to a single, meaningful paragraph, which makes many of these stories not for the intellectually squeamish, nor for friends of the easy solution. Sturrock's exposition of the general effect of detective stories is at the heart of Bustos Domecq's project, with each story being a virtual exemplum of that effect.

A second principle that should be noted in Bustos Domecq's writing agenda is that the same set of facts can often be explained in several different ways. This principle arises from the nature of these stories, in which each character proposes a version of baffling circumstances, and very often adds several baffling conclusions of her or his own.

Unique as these stories are, they are not without precedent in the genre. First and foremost, there is "The Mystery of Marie Rogêt," Poe's sequel to "The Murders in the Rue Morgue," of which the editors say: "The Mystery of Marie Rogêt" was composed at a distance from the scene of the atrocity, and with no other means of investigation than the newspapers afforded" (Poe, *Complete* 27). This story in particular spawned many an entertaining offspring in the likes of "The Thinking Machine," conceived by Jacques Futrelle in the character of Professor Augustus S.F.X. van Dusen, and Baroness Emmuska Orczy's "old man," whose involvement with detection is summed up by the character with this line: "Crime only interests one when it is a complex game of chess full of crafty moves" (*Old Man* 43); there are still others, such as Rex Stout's sedentary Nero Wolfe, and Ernest Bramah's detective Max Carrados, who makes up with insight for the fact that he is blind.

The enterprising spirit of the "armchair detectives' " such as those mentioned above, is evident in the following excerpt from one of the notable Max Carrados's cases: "They discussed the cases according to their interests, and there the matter generally ended so far as Max Carrados was concerned, until he casually heard the result subsequently from [Louis] Carlyle's lips or learned the sequel from the newspaper" (Sayers, *Omnibus* 191). These characters delivered solutions to the most baffling cases by what they were wont to call "a quaint piece of deduction." Most, like Orczy's old man, did not bother to verify their hypotheses by visiting the scene, nor were they known to use any aid other than newspaper reports and photographs. Borges comments on this development of the genre:

> In the earliest example of the genre ("The Mystery of Marie Rogêt," 1842) and in one of the most recent ("Unravelled Knots," by the Baroness Orczy [1926]), the story is limited to the discussion and abstract resolution of a crime, perhaps quite distant from the event or after many years. The everyday methods of police investigation—fingerprints . . . interrogation, and confession—would seem like solecisms therein. One might object to the conventionality of this veto, but such a convention, in this instance, is irreproachable: it does not aim to avoid difficulties, but rather to impose them. (Rodríguez Monegal and Reid, *Borges* 71–72)

The ten years before World War I produced the most important collections of cases from these curious types. These are the years of the Edwardian mystery, which would culminate, for many, with *Trent's Last Case* in 1913. By making the investigator's "obviously correct" solution turn out to be completely wrong, Edmund C. Bentley is reputed to have revolutionized the crime novel (Bentley, x–xi). But collectively, the armchair detectives could be considered to be a further elaboration of the character Dupin, the pure reasoner. The distance that exists between these detectives and the site of the crime, and their relation to the narration of the crime—that is, the interpretation of the events—highlights the role of the detective (and of the reader) as the abstracting consciousness that is at the narrative center of the work of fiction. The armchair detective is the closest analogy to the reader, whose reasoned interpretation is the basis for the reality of the text.

Naturally, this is the model Bustos Domecq emulated. The second thrust of Bustos Domecq's project was the creation of a narrative language, which might have proved to be the driving force of the entire Bioy Casares-Borges enterprise because it is evidently the source of a boisterous humor that these men uncharacteristically expressed through Bustos Domecq's writing. The language of Bustos Domecq's characters also created a stilted but recognizable portrait of Buenos Aires society. This

notable linguistic innovation by Bustos Domecq received
attention from one of the few contemporaries to sympathize with
his project. In one of the earliest commentaries *Six Problems*,
published in 1943, the eminent Mexican essayist Alfonso Reyes
noted that in the volume

> we are transported to strange and baroque places, we visit
> the most secret corners of Buenos Aires life and in front of
> our eyes passes a gallery of types of all categories and
> races in a cauldron of imagination [sic], each one speaking
> the language that best suits him. To the point that, if one
> puts aside the interest of the plot, the book has the value of
> a social testimony, strongly illuminated by poetical lights"
> [nos vemos transportados a los escenarios más abigarra-
> dos y curiosos, recorremos los más ocultos rincones de la
> vida porteña y desfila a nuestros ojos una galería de tipos
> de todas las escalas y todas las razas mezcladas en aquel
> hervidero de inmigraciones, hablando cada uno su
> lenguaje apropiado]. (Rodríguez Monegal, *Borges* 369;
> *Biografía* 333)

In the opinion of some critics, the nature of Bustos
Domecq's existence and creative life derives from the desire of
two well-to-do cronies to satirize the "Italian immigrants" or the
"lower classes" of Argentine society (Avellaneda, 361–62;
Simpson, 186, respectively). The cast of characters or "voices" in
Six Problems is, however, much more comprehensive than that
but, more important in the context of this discussion, most of the
"deplorable" fun does spring from the "cauldron of im-
migrations" [hervidero de inmigraciones] that characterizes the
River Plate region and that Bustos Domecq represented in the
language of his stories.

The contrasting accents and suggested intonations, the
variants in word usage and the apparent incomprehensibility of
some of the characters' testimony all lead to the realization that
nationality, at least for the people of that "Argentina" imagined
by Bustos Domecq, is the product of a conjecture derived from
circumstances. It is the association of contiguities—these cattle,
these railroads, this port, these newspapers, these deaths—that
make a community living in the crossroads of the world conceive
itself as specifically "Argentine," for example, rather than

"Uruguayan." Flora, fauna (this tree, this bird), terrain, and, often, the native inhabitants can postulate, by the metaphorical and metonymical means used by readers of literary texts, a "nation."[3] In his book *The Invention of Argentina* Nicholas Shumway writes: "The guiding fictions of nations cannot be proven and indeed are often fabrications as artificial as literary fictions. Yet they are necessary to give individuals a sense of nation, peoplehood, collective identity, and national purpose" (xi). In this context, it is possible to conceive the citizens of a nation as readers and interpreters of a national text that they claim as their own, and in which they themselves are written.

Borges and Casares Bioy, rather than conceive themselves as above this national text, are well aware of being in the collective sauce of Bustos Domecq's humorous concoction: "Each word is a shared symbol" [Cada palabra es un símbolo compartido], Borges wrote in *Dr. Brodie's Report* (10), noting also in the prologue to his collection of verse, *Obra poética*, "a language is a tradition, a way to feel reality, not an arbitrary repertory of symbols" [un idioma es una tradición, un modo de sentir la realidad, no un arbitrario repertorio de símbolos (*Obra poética* 3–9)]. *Six Problems* is evidence that Bustos Domecq recognized the flux of social conflict and sought this conflict of diversity in language, in its heteroglossia, to produce the "testimonio social" that Alfonso Reyes rightly recognizes in his quality of writing.[4] The condition first identified and named by the Russian theorist Mikhail Bakhtin as heteroglossia is an added difficulty that Bustos Domecq imposed on the sedentary sleuth Isidro Parodi, who depends on the language of his visitors for the success of his investigations, since he arrives at the solution of his cases without "the resources of methodical investigation: the drill, the compass, and the microscope" [los recursos de la investigación metódica: del taladro, el compás y del microscopio (Borges, *Textos* 77)]. Parodi's problems (and their resolution) foreground discourse, which becomes the shifty subject under scrutiny by a reader intent on foreshadowing the right answer, the correct scenario of the original crime.

NOTES

1. *Six Problems* is the first collection of detective stories published by "a writer" of the Spanish language. Domecq's inclusion in Queen's honor roll of the detective story is remarkable if one considers that the first English translation of the volume was not published until 1981. The only other translation of this work, besides this belated though welcome effort, is a 1967 Paris edition of *Six Problèmes*, translated by F.M. Rosset for Denoël.

2. The critic M.E. Cossío enumerates the various models for parody that he sees at work in Bustos Domecq's stories: the norms of the detective genre, various literary and popular discourses, the world of the detective story (where each problem finds its smoothly fitting key), history, the role of the reader, and the role of the critic (151–53).

3. For a full discussion of this idea, see Benedict Anderson, *Imagined Communities*. In *The Invention of Argentina*, Shumway quotes Edmund S. Morgan's *Inventing the People* as to the U.S.'s guiding fictions, e.g. the American way of life, manifest destiny, the melting pot (x).

4. "Heteroglossia" is a term that Mikhail Bakhtin introduces as "the base condition governing the operation of meaning in any utterance. . . . At any given time, in any given place, there will be a set of conditions—social, historical, meteorological, physiological—that will insure that a word uttered in that place and at that time will have a meaning different than it would have under any other conditions . . . " (*Dialogic* 428). The instability of language that is assumed by this condition sets the stage for Isidro Parodi.

The Mystified Reader
"The Twelve Figures of the World"

The first of Parodi's problems presents the reader with the character's *curriculum vitae* and the reason for his present and future accommodations: cell number 273 of the Penitenciaria Nacional. Parodi is serving a twenty-one year sentence (1919–1940) for the death of one Agustín Bonorino. Parodi was framed for this crime by a tenant in arrears who seized an opportunity to furnish the police with the name of his landlord, and thus to avoid his responsibility with the payment. Time has taken its toll: "A sedentary life had worked a change in the homicide of 1919; he was now in his forties, sententious and fat, and had a shaved head and unusually wise eyes" [La vida sedentaria había influido en el homicida de 1919: hoy era un hombre cuarentón, sentencioso, obeso, con la cabeza afeitada y ojos singularmente sabios (*Six* 18–19; *Seis* 16)]. Like Max Carrados, who carries with him the prison of his blindness, Parodi is forced, because of judicial corruption, to solve his cases at a physical distance from the scenes of the crimes. Parodi thus serves the cause of justice in a carnivalesque society where one of its criminals is also its most renowned sleuth.

"Homicide" and even "sleuth" name Parodi equivocally; he had been (in 1919) a barber, a hairdresser who evidently owned and rented rooms in the city of Buenos Aires.[1] In 1933, a man suspected of murder and arson visits Parodi. Bustos Domecq records this, the first of Parodi's celebrated cases, in 1941. Domecq describes the actions of the suspect on the morning in which he realizes he is being followed and decides to visit Don Isidro:

Ambling down the corridor, [Achilles Molinari] returned
with his razor, a brush, a sliver of yellow soap, and a cup
of steaming water. He flung the window open wide,
stared down at the unknown man with exaggerated calm,
and slowly, whistling the tango "Marked Card," began to
shave [(Aquiles Molinari) se fue a los fondos; volvió con la
maquina de afeitar, la brocha, los restos del jabón amarillo
y una taza de agua hirviendo. Abrió de par en par la
ventana, con enfática serenidad miró al desconocido y
lentamente se afeitó, silbando el tango *Naipe marcado*]. (*Six*
17; *Seis* 15)

Parodi is already aware of some of the events recounted by
Molinari from his study of the evening newspapers, with which
Parodi exercises his "spiritual agility" (*Six* 17). After fourteen
years, Parodi has made himself at home in cell 273. He
complains to his visitor about foreigners of questionable back-
grounds and especially Italians (though his own surname
suggests a similar origin), who are to found in all the best places
in the country, including the Penitenciaria Nacional.

Bustos Domecq records Parodi's nationalist outburst and
provides information about Molinari's character. Molinari is a
sportswriter associated with a newspaper in Cordone. The rest is
Molinari's narration of the mysterious events that culminated in
murder. Molinari expresses his personal debt to the Eucharistic
Congress, which he says has left an indelible mark on his
spiritual life (Bustos Domecq is the author of *The Eucharistic
Congress, an Argentine Organ for the Propagation of the Faith*); he
has been interested, however, in joining a brotherhood that is "a
forward-looking community . . . closer to the mystery than many
who go to Mass every Sunday" [más cerca del misterio que
muchos que van a misa todos los domingos (*Six* 20; *Seis* 17)].
Molinari defends the practices of a Drusic sect with the following
equivocal pronouncement: "People accuse the Druses of
believing in idols, but in their assembly room there's a metal
statue of a bull that must be worth a king's ransom. Every Friday the Akils—they're the initiates—gather around the bull"
[Algunos dicen que creen en ídolos, pero en la sala de actos hay
un toro de metal que vale más que un *tramway*. Todos los viernes
se reúnen alrededor del toro los akils, que son, como quien dice,
los iniciados (*Six* 21; *Seis* 18)]. The rebuttal that Molinari intends

is undone by the assertion that follows the preposition. The evaluation of what "algunos dicen" about idolatry is counter-posed to the monetary value of the object of veneration. He is blind to the fact that the accusation of idolatry is not laid to rest by the worth of the idol.

The visiting suspect's tale is itself suspect of discrepancy with the reality it attempts to depict. Equivocating further, Molinari reports that his initiation was set on a Sunday, not on the accustomed Friday of the Druses' regular meetings. Molinari notes this irregularity but reports that he was informed by his host that "for an examination as important as this one the Lord's day was more appropriate" [un examen tan importante convenía más el día del Señor (*Six* 22; *Seis* 18)]. The suspicion is raised (in Parodi, the careful reader) by the peculiarity of using a day of Christian significance for an initiation into a Drusic cult, but this unorthodox practice does not alarm Molinari, who proceeds with the telling of the events.[2] It soon becomes apparent that Molinari does not polemicize with the information that he obtains and that he tends to merge his understanding of things with the explanations given him by his host, the Druse Ibn Khaldun. Alerted to this fact, the detectory reader has to "make up" for the witness's shortcomings and rearticulate the message that he conveys. This is Parodi's task in the text. Molinari's speech is mannered with Argentinisms, but not extremely so. Some inconvenience for the fact-gathering detectory reader is caused by the similarity of the names mentioned by Molinari: He owes money to the Sastrería Rabuffi, takes a train from Retiro Station, telephones from a store on Rosetti Street and notices that his host looks like Repetto, "but beardless" (there is no allusion to Repetto before this time or, for that matter, at any time later). The devious similarity of Retiro, Rabuffi, Repetto, Rosetti, exemplifies a game with mirrors: a hoax, no doubt, but also an illusion. Which of these echoed repetitions is significant to the plot? Does the beard hide the fact that Ibn Khaldun and Repetto are the same man?

Molinari's initiation into the brotherhood is resisted by some of the Druses, but finally his task is set for him by Ibn Khaldun. From among one hundred and fifty prostrated, veiled Druses who form a rudimentary labyrinth, the sportswriter is to find "the four masters that make up the veiled tetragon of the Godhead" [los cuatro maestros que forman el velado tetrágono de la Divinidad (*Six* 24; *Seis* 20)]:[3]

> I command you to bring Yusuf. You will descend to the auditorium, remembering in their exact order the twelve figures of the heavens. When you reach the last figure, the sign of Pisces, you shall return to the first, which is Aries, and so on in rotation. Thrice you will weave a circle round the Akils and your steps will lead you to Yusuf—so long as you have not changed the order of the figures. You will tell him, "Ibn Khaldun summons," and you will bring him here. Then I shall command you to bring the second master, then the third, then the fourth [Yo te ordenaré que traigas a Yusuf; tú bajarás a la sala de actos, imaginando en su orden preciso las figuras del cielo; cuando llegues a la última figura, la de los Peces, volverás a la primera, que es Aries, y así, continuamente; darás tres vueltas alrededor de los alkils y tus pasos te llevarán a Yusef, si no has alterado el orden de las figuras. Le dirás: "Abenjaldun te llama" y lo traerás aquí. Después te ordenaré que traigas el segundo maestro; luego el tercero, luego el cuarto]. (*Six* 24–5; *Seis* 20)

The hidden figure is characteristic of Borges's writing. As is the case in "Death and the Compass," the correct ordering of the mysterious pattern might either determine the success of Molinari's enterprise, or prove a snare, designed to bring about his mental or physical undoing.

The fate of the world rests on Molinari's shoulders that Sunday night. One error on his part, he is told, could plunge the world into chaos. The configuration of four is to be derived from the strict application of the order of the zodiac to the uniform conglomeration of worshipping Druses: "those white backs, those bowed heads, those smooth masks" [esas espaldas blancas, esas cabezas agachadas, esas máscaras lisas]. (*Six* 25; *Seis* 21) Molinari labors in the maze that his steps construct in answer to the requests of Ibn Khaldun. He treads a figure that is organized by his recollection of the zodiac and motivated by his need to identify the four checkpoints named by Ibn Khaldun from the disorder of the assembled worshippers with the bull in their midst.

The sign of these four is hidden from Molinari by the uniformity of the elements that compose it. The fact that Molinari, caught in the maze, cannot see this formidable symbol while he is composing it, leads him to attribute an esoteric, transcendental quality to his endeavors. The disorienting, mystifying nature of his undertaking is what he conveys to Parodi in his narration, which preserves the fantastic nature of his actions while at the same time dimming the profile of the murder that is committed in his blindfolded (both figuratively and literally) presence. Parodi and the detectory reader share the task of demystifying the story, of locating in Molinari's representation of the events the "facts" of the case that will explain the death of a man and the destruction by fire of a man's dwelling. Molinari, mystified, blames himself for getting the order of the figures wrong and causing the death and the fire. He recalls Ibn Khaldun's warning:

> These signs rule the world. While the examination lasts, we shall entrust you with the order of the figures. The entire cosmos will be in your power. If you do not change the order of the Zodiac, our fate and the fate of the world will continue in its predetermined course. If you make a mistake—if, for instance, after Libra you come up with Leo or Scorpio—the master you seek shall perish and the whole wide world will fall victim to the menace of wind and water and fire [Esas figuras rigen el mundo, mientras dure el examen, te confiamos el curso de las figuras: el cosmos estará en tu poder. Si no alteras el orden del zodíaco, nuestros destinos y el destino del mundo seguirán el curso prefijado; si tu imaginación se equivoca, si después de la Balanza imaginas el León y no el Escorpión, el maestro a quien buscas perecerá y el mundo conocera la amenaza del aire, del agua y del fuego]. (*Six* 27; *Seis* 22)

The detectory reader recognizes in the supernatural version of the events narrated a misdirected perception of the facts of the case. By means of a reference to the conventions of the detective genre, there must be a rational explanation for the events that have resulted in murder and arson. "Twelve Figures" also presents an interesting development of the conventions of detective fiction. The murder or crime in the puzzle type of the mystery story takes place traditionally in a closed world that restricts the number of suspects, for example, and whose laws can be known. Into the closed world enters the detective, usually an outsider, who with his power of observation is able to conjecture clearly on the nature of the deception that is taking place in this closed world thrown into chaos by the destabilizing forces of crime. In Bustos Domecq's story, it is an innocent who enters the closed society, and his presence is thus utilized by a criminal consciousness within that world to carry out a crime. The outsider's presence in the society at the time of the murder makes him the most likely suspect of the crime and, given the facts of Molinari's initiation, the criminal has an added advantage in the fact that the outsider, mystified, believes that by some fault of his the world has become chaotic.

In relation to the nationalistic theme that is evident in the Parodi stories, "Twelve Figures" also provides a model for both the contiguous existence of enclaves in River Plate society, each with its traditions and rules of exclusion and inclusion, and the "translation" of individuals across cultural boundaries. Bustos's is a parodic rendering of this process, but there is evidence of the cross-cultural theme in the "Twelve Figures" story. Given the encyclopedic nature of Bustos Domecq, who is a detectory reader product of detective fiction, but who is not exclusively limited to being this type of reader, one could conjecture a meaning from the history of culture that can be associated to Ibn Khaldun's name. The character's name might be an allusion to the North African scholar Ab-ar-Rahman Ibn Khaldun, who wrote the first historical analysis on tribalism. Ibn Khaldun regarded *asabiyah*, loosely translated as group solidarity or community, as the primary principle underlying tribal society. His study focused on the relation between tribal societies and urban life, and pointed out the interdependence of the two. Tribal people reinvigorate the life of the city, but at the same time are weakened by urban life. With "Twelve Figures," Bustos Domecq parodies the process described by Ibn Khaldun by having an urban dweller attempt to join a tribal society with dire consequences for both the character and the order of *asabiyah*, already weakened by greed and the novelties of urban life.

The mystification of Molinari's understanding mediates his recounting of the events that mix his initiation with the facts of the murder. His perception of the events has been affected both by the unfamiliar circumstances of the group initiation, and also by others more familiar. Preparation for the ritual included a rigorous fast and relentless study of the Bristol Almanac, illustrated with the signs of the zodiac: "three days on plain tea, not to mention the strain of concentration" [tres días a puro té solo y el gran desgaste mental que yo me exigía] accounts for part of Molinari's disorientation (*Six* 28; *Seis* 23). But in relating the fantastic series of events that he has experienced, Molinari anticipates the incredulity of his listener, and he defensively engages the projected doubt of his addressee: "I felt that all the eyes in the oil paintings were staring at me. You'll probably laugh—my younger sister always said that I have something of the mad poet in me" [Me pareció que me miraban todos los ojos de los cuadros al óleo—usted se reirá, tal vez; mi hermanita siempre dice que tengo algo de loco y poeta" (28; 23)]. Molinari's personal character also comes into play in the distortion of the events that he is unable to order in a rational manner.

Molinari relates his growing realization of the events' fantastic character by incorporating into his narrative a stock image from gothic mystery: the animated, scrutinizing eyes in the paintings, heightening the effect that he felt of being in a fictional construction, a movie set, or in a scene from a popular genre. If the situation itself is "fictional," as he felt at that moment it was, the narrator anticipates himself as a dupe in the eyes of his interlocutor. But this realization is momentary. In his own eyes, Molinari is not a distorter of factual reality. The grounds of his narration and proof of the validity of his experience is the successful assembly of the four Druses that sustain the world.

The figure composed of the four Druses that he has sequentially delivered to his mentor Ibn Khaldun reveals the logic of the mystery to Molinari. By means of the mental map of the zodiac, he has constituted a figure whose existence Ibn Khaldun has proclaimed as an article of faith. The figure thus constituted represents for Molinari the verification of the cosmic order indicated by the "twelve figures of the world": "A hundred and fifty identical Druses, and here were the four masters!" [¡Ciento cincuenta drusos iguales y allí estaban los cuatro maestros! (*Six* 26; *Seis* 22)]. It stands to reason that he would find himself guilty of the crimes committed when he fails (or believes he has failed) in the second, more difficult trial he must undergo to join the sect. This knowledge mediates his entire account. Parodi's task is to exculpate the sportswriter from his fetishized belief in the syntactical correctness of the zodiacal figures.

A figure, like a text, is an ordering; its being denies the structureless infinity of space and the formlessness of chaos that extends beyond the individual's ability to name and measure. Confronted by the immediate success of his trial, Molinari attributes his triumph to the secret, underlying structure of the figures of the zodiac. Molinari has been able to match the requested name to the person in a multitude of like entities by the internalization of this celestial map, a feat that attests to its relevance and apocalyptic power. The zodiacal map has become the frame of reference for Molinari's reading of the events, and, since the events have resulted in death, the map frames his guilt as well. Molinari recalls the circumstances: "When I heard the laugh and the cry, I must have become momentarily confused and changed the order of the figures. That cost a man his life— maybe even the lives of the four masters" [Sin duda cuando oí la risa y el grito, me confundí un momento y cambié el orden de las figuras: esa confusión había costado la vida de un hombre. Tal vez la de cuatro maestros (*Six* 29; *Seis* 24)]. Molinari is trapped by his belief in a prescribed order that also prescribes his responsibility in the affair. He comes to Parodi, first and foremost, to confess his guilt. Parodi, himself the victim of a different sort of "frameup," seeks a different reading of the facts, but must first release Molinari from his position, which, fixed by the stars, weighs on his understanding and sanity with alarming consequences: Molinari is desperate.

Parodi sets himself to the task. He asks Molinari to recite the celestial figures in the accustomed order, then backwards. Molinari's fixation has amusing consequences. Without altering their sequential order, he proceeds to disassemble the words in their syllabic composition to produce reversed renditions of each—but in their proper syntagmatic order: "Riesa, Rustau . . . " [El Ronecar, el Roto . . . (*Six* 32; *Seis* 26)]. Parodi notes his foolish persistence. Molinari then produces a random ordering of the names, fearing the worst. Parodi sends him back to work "speechless, redeemed, dumbfounded," (*Six* 33) but seemingly relieved of his position as keeper of the sacred, mystical order of the world.

The second part of the story consists of Parodi's reading of the events narrated by Molinari. Parodi narrates the other's discourse on the basis of the detective model, focusing on human motivation and subterfuge. For example, a character that Molinari identifies as the treasurer of the Drusic Association is presented as a writer by trade in Molinari's account. Molinari makes reference to his books, "sus libritos" (*Seis* 18), as the product of this character's trivial occupation. On the night of Molinari's initiation, this character is nervous, since Ibn Khaldun has promised to read his books; later, the treasurer behaves in an unusual manner and, by shaking everybody's hand, makes clear to all that he is leaving the house, "a thing he never does" [cosa que nunca hace (*Six* 27; *Seis* 22)], according to Molinari.

Parodi makes the obvious connection between the treasurer's books and his occupation. These "libritos" are, in Parodi's retelling of the story, account books. Some discrepancy in the figures and the risk of discovery have made the treasurer nervous. His unusual behavior suggests to Parodi the possibility that he is indeed *not* leaving and that he is taking advantage of the rather uncommon circumstances to put an end to his employer—"Dr. Ibn Khaldun . . . a pioneer in the importation of linoleum substitutes" [Abenjaldún, uno de los grandes *pioneers* de la importación de substitutos del linoleum (*Six* 31; *Seis* 25)]—and to destroy the record of his business transactions. Parodi accentuates the other's discourse in such a way as to make the criminal results conform to the human motivations that he intuits from the narrated facts. Parodi provides Molinari's fantastic tale with a detective plot. That is Parodi's angle. It is the angle of the particular type of reader created by Poe.

Molinari recalls his mentor's benevolent confidence in the success of his trial and how Ibn Khaldun even helped complete the set by offering to find the fourth master of the universe: "Ibn

Khaldun himself had so much faith in me by now that I found him playing a game of solitaire instead of praying. He herded Izz-al-Din into the alcove and, speaking like a father, said to me, 'This exercise has worn you out. I shall seek the fourth initiate—Kahlil'" [El mismo Abenjaldún, que ya me tenía tanta fe que en lugar de rezar se había puesto a jugar el solitario, se lo llevo a Izedín al archivo, y me dijo, hablándome como un padre: "Este ejercicio te ha rendido. Yo buscaré al cuarto iniciado, que es Jalil" (*Six* 26; *Seis* 21)]. Parodi proposes a sleight-of-hand to an intrigued Molinari, who is to pick out the cards that Parodi calls out from the deck he keeps in his cell. Molinari is successful in performing this exercise three times; Parodi offers to pick out the last card, claiming concern for his visitor: the four named cards lie before an amazed Molinari. "Don't be so amazed," says Parodi.

> Among these cards there is one that is marked—the first I asked for, but not the first you gave me. I asked for the four of hearts, you gave me the jack of spades. I asked for the jack of spades; you gave me the seven of clubs. I asked for the seven of clubs; you gave me the king of hearts. Then I said you were tired and that I would pick the fourth card myself—the king of hearts. I picked the four of hearts, the marked card [No abrás tanto los ojos. Entre todos esos naipes iguales hay uno marcado: el primero que te pedí pero no el primero que me diste. Te pedí el cuatro de copas, me diste la sota de espadas; te pedí la sota de espadas, me diste el siete de bastos; te pedí el siete de bastos y me diste el rey de copas; dije que estabas cansado y que yo mismo iba a sacar el cuarto naipe, el rey de copas. Saqué el cuatro de copas, que tiene estas pintitas negras]. (*Six* 34; *Seis* 28).

Parodi's card trick presents a model for the Druse's hoax and Molinari's preternatural success. The affinity of Abenjaldun for cards had already been suggested by his playing solitaire during Molinari's ordeal. The tango that young Molinari whistled the morning he visited Parodi provided the key to the trick. The allusion to the tango "Naipe marcado" ["Marked Card"], however, appears in Bustos Domecq's narration of the morning in question. It is not addressed to Parodi, but to a reader who would valorize it as a clue and use it in anticipation of the resolution of the mystery.[4]

Parodi's card trick models the Druse's ruse. The Argentine detective shows that Ibn Khaldun had used the "universal" pattern of a card trick for the purposes of mystifying Molinari. Parodi is able to duplicate the pattern, though he equivocates about the identity of the human "marked card" in the naming sequence performed by Ibn Khaldun. Yusuf and the four of hearts are the marked categories in the respective sets of Druses and cards. Each one is the member of the set that is recognizable to the person performing the trick. But Parodi asserts that "Number one was Ibrahim, his closest friend. Ibn Khaldun had no trouble recognizing him even among a crowd" [El 1 era Ibrahim, su amigo íntimo. Abenjaldún podía reconocerlo entre muchos (*Six* 35; *Seis* 28)]. In effect, Ibn Khaldun asked for Yusuf first, who *must* have been his marked "card," but one week after the telling of Molinari's story Parodi equivocates. The verification of Parodi's scheme is left up to the reader.

Parodi's performance generalizes the underlying principles of the events related in "Twelve Figures" and does in fact provide a new figure for the understanding of those events. What he proposes is a system of rules that accounts for the events but allows for various combinations to be produced. In the words of Eco, "The inferred cause, proposed by means of abduction, is pure content" (*Theory* 221). Parodi *theorizes* about the event. The adequacy of the comparison undoes the fixation that Molinari experienced and replaces it with the metaphor of the card trick, revealing that the sportswriter's initial experience does not mean any one particular thing in and of itself. The set of relations that Molinari had assumed to be a fixed path leading to murder is thus put back into referential play. Parodi's explanation allows new extrapolations of meaning to take place from the text.

Notes

1. "Who knows the secrets of human nature better than a hairdresser?" writes the narrator of *The Murder of Roger Ackroyd* after mistaking Hercule Poirot's occupation (27). Dr. James Sheppard, the narrator, is engaged by Poirot as "Watson to his Sherlock" (143) partly because his usual chronicler, Col. Hastings, has departed for "the Argentine."

2. The Druses are an independent sect living chiefly in the mountainous regions of Syria and Lebanon; founded in the eleventh century, they have a faith that contains elements of Christianity, Judaism, and Islam, and share a belief in the transmigration of souls and the ultimate perfectibility of man (*Random House Dictionary*).

3. This configuration echoes a similar fable that Borges attributes to the Irish that speaks of a group of just men (the *Lamed Wufniks*) who, though ignorant of each other's existence and of their role, maintain the order of the universe (*Otras inquisiciones* 42). "The veiled tetragon of the Godhead" also figures in "Death and the Compass," which appeared in 1942, the same year that *Six Problems* was published.

4. "Recognition occurs when a given object or event, produced by nature or human action (intentionally or unintentionally), and existing in a world of facts as a fact among facts," Eco explains, "comes to be viewed by an addressee as the expression of a given content, either through a pre-existing and coded correlation or through the positing of a possible correlation by its addressee" (*Theory* 221).

"Honorio Bustos Domecq, What Is an Author?"

If Bustos Domecq had toured North America as extensively as Borges did and we, the readers of Bustos Domecq, had chanced to meet him in one of the many conference rooms that he visited, I would have addressed one question to him: "Honorio Bustos Domecq, what is an author?" I can not predict his answer, but my question would be received in two distinct—this is Roland Barthes's designation—"sites of listening," and for him to formulate an answer would necessitate dialogue between two subjects, two distinct experiences of culture and language, under the name of Honorio Bustos Domecq. The dialogue between two subjects for the purpose of answering an expressed question represents the relation between the author and the detectory reader, in which an answer is arrived at by means of the collaboration of the two entities. Bustos Domecq might have ruled his two halves with "a rod of iron" (as Borges recalls), in order to ensure his own distinct individuality; equally important and evident is the way in which the compelling power of Bustos Domecq is brought about by rules of composition. Bustos Domecq represents particular rules of composition, which in the case of *Six Problems* are clearly the rules derived from the puzzle type of detective fiction exercised by the likes of Ernest Bramah, Rex Stout, and Emmuska Orczy, among others.

At the same time, the collaboration represented by Domecq, which can be extended to include the relationship between reader and author mediated by the text, weakens the univocal role of the author in relation to the work. The reader is equally involved in the creation of meaning and is thereby a creative focus, as empowered as the author is in the elliptical figure of textual meaning. By referring his existence to previously established rules of composition, and by appearing as an interpretation of those rules, Bustos Domecq also blurs the autonomous existence usually associated with the figure of the author. Domecq also problematizes the independence of his creators. In becoming Bustos Domecq, Borges himself did not know where his input began and his collaborator's ended:

> I have often been asked how collaboration is possible. I think it requires a joint abandoning of the ego, of vanity, and maybe of common politeness. The collaborators should forget themselves and think only in terms of the work. In fact, when somebody wants to know whether such-and-such a joke or epithet came from my side of the table or Bioy's, I honestly cannot tell him. (*The Aleph* 247)

When Borges explains Bustos Domecq, he speaks of a third party whose writing differs from Bioy Casares's and his in no uncertain terms: "We have engendered a third man who is different from ourselves" (Christ, "Art" 159).

In his first book of essays, published in 1925, Borges set out to prove that "personality is a crossover dream, borne of conceit and habit, but lacking a metaphysical foothold or an intrinsic reality" [la personalidad es una *trasoñación*, consentida en el engreimiento y el hábito, mas sin estribaciones metafísicas ni realidad entrañal" (*Inquisiciones* 84)]. Bustos Domecq, the third man created by Bioy Casares and Borges, is a culmination of that project. Following Deleuze and Guattari, one could conceive the personality of Bustos Domecq as an "arrangement," one that aims to connect the multiplicities of the world by tracing other texts, other detective stories (*On the Line* 52). As an author, Bustos Domecq represents a reconciliation of the multiplicities occurring in the field of objects that is the world, in the field of representation that is the text, and in the field of subjectivity that is harbored in his monstrous double heart.

One of Borges's favorite notions was to suggest that a writer's foremost and perhaps most ephemeral invention is himself. This thought finds expression, for example, in "For Bernard Shaw," where Borges writes:

Bernard Shaw educed almost innumerable persons, or
dramatis personae: the most ephemeral, I suspect, is G.B.S.,
who represented him to the public and who supplied such
a wealth of easy witticisms for newspaper columns
[Bernard Shaw dedujo casi innumerables personas, o
dramatis personae: la más efímera será, lo sospecho, aquel
G.B.S. que lo representó ante la gente y que prodigó en las
columnas de las periódicos tantas fáciles agudezas]. (*Other
Inquisitions* 165–66; *Otras inquisiciones* 160)

The invention of "Borges" is recorded in "Borges y yo" ["Borges
and Myself" (*The Aleph* 151–2)]. The text begins with the line,
"It's to the other man, to Borges, that things happen" [Al otro, a
Borges, es a quien le ocurren las cosas](*The Aleph* 151; *Obras*
2.186), and the narrator goes on to state that in the bargain that
he has struck with this other, "I live, I let myself live, so that
Borges can weave his tales and poems and those tales and poems
are my justification" [Yo vivo, yo me dejo vivir para que Borges
pueda tramar su literatura y esa literatura me justifica (*The Aleph*
151; *Obras* 2.186)]. This symbiotic arrangement brings to Borges a
bittersweet realization, that the self interprets and is interpreted
in an interpersonal system of language: "These pages cannot
save me, perhaps because what is good no longer belongs to
anyone—not even to the other man—but rather to speech or
tradition" [Lo bueno ya no es de nadie, ni siquiera del otro, sino
del lenguaje o de la tradición (*The Aleph* 151; *Obras* 2.186)]. With
the invention of "Borges," Borges was proposing a self that is a
text, like the world.

For the philosopher Charles S. Peirce, the self is derived
from the errors that become evident in interpretation, that is,
"error . . . can be explained only by supposing a *self* that is
fallible" (*Essential* 76). Thus, in Peircian terms, the existence of a
self is derived from inference and hypothesis, which is to say
that it is derived from interpretation. In the case of Bustos
Domecq, the object of interpretation that brought this textual self
into being was detective fiction. Bustos Domecq represents the
principle of authorship that has been argued in these pages in
relation to the detectory reader, and like the golem, Bustos
Domecq represents mediation between reader and text. The
irony involved in the existence in print of Bustos Domecq is that
the mediator of Borges and Bioy Casares's detective story

readings is now producing texts as if it were an independent self. But Peirce has conjectured that interpretation gives "self" the same status as the signs of the world. Peirce proposes that man is a sign that can only be known as sign and who, like all signs, "must address itself to some other, must determine some other, since that is the essence of a sign" (*Essential* 81). Bustos Domecq is an extension of this drive to decenter the subject as a source of meaning rather than as a site where interpretation takes place through inference.

It is interesting to speculate about the source of the idea that led to the creation of that heresiarch of the detective story, Honorio Bustos Domecq. In "The Modesty of History," and perhaps anticipating his own decentering of the author function in the collaboration with Bioy Casares, Borges records his interest in a phrase found in a history of Greek literature: *He brought in a second actor.* Borges discovered that the subject of that "mysterious action" had been Aeschylus, who, as reported in the fourth chapter of Aristotle's *Poetics*, "raised from one to two the number of actors" (*Other Inquisitions* 168). Borges speculates on the Athenian public's reaction to the unannounced second actor—"Perhaps neither amazement nor shock; perhaps only a beginning of surprise"—and marvels at the significance of the transition from one to two, "from unity to plurality and thus to infinity. With the second actor came the dialogue and the indefinite possibilities of the reaction of some characters on others" (168). It remains to be seen what the reaction of the Argentine reading public was to the dialogue devised by Borges and Bioy Casares behind the mask of Bustos Domecq.

It should not be surprising to find the issue of authorship raised in relation to detective fiction. One might recall Dorothy Sayers stating that very often the average reader of mysteries "instead of detecting the murderer, . . . is engaged in detecting the writer" (*Omnibus* 43). The question that will be addressed in the following pages—what does Bustos Domecq tell us about being an author?—is an extension of this concern that characterizes the detectory reader. Bioy Casares and Borges go from being individual authors to creating the representation of another author, Bustos Domecq, and in turn, creating a further representation of a fictional author in the case of B. Suárez

Lynch, Bustos Domecq's disciple. This iteration leads us to consider the writing subject as "a variable and complex function of discourse" (Foucault, "What Is" 158). The critic Suzanne Levine asserts, correctly, that "Borges and Bioy are practical proponents of the inevitability of the anonymous text, not only by writing in first person under the disguise of other identities, but by fusing their identities in H. Bustos Domecq, B. Suárez Lynch, and other similar characters" (232). Before setting out to explore the ramifications of that idea, it might prove helpful to interject this commonsensical statement written by I.A. Richards in 1924: The work of the artist "is the ordering of what in most minds is disordered" (*Principles* 61). Richards's conception suggests, appropriately enough, that the "mind" of the artist experiences the chaotic flux of the world, and the artist reduces this chaos to relative order in the work of art.

The problem arises in the communication of this ordering. If what Richards proposes in the reception of the work of art were an extrapolation from the text by the reader of the artist's original experience, one would have little problem accepting the statement, since by sheer force of interpretation (a growing web, if the reader considers such things as biographical data, social and historical facts) the reader will obtain a clear intimation of the originating chaos. But this thought runs counter to Richards's argument, since what Richards is advocating in the reader-text exchange is the clear transmission of the author's ordering to the reader.

For the ideal transmission of the elements ordered by the mind of the writer to take place, or for someone to conceive that ideal transmission as potentially taking place by means of a stable composition of the elements of language, language would have to be a medium of exemplary stability. The concept of a stable message to be decoded by the reader is difficult to sustain. Borges wrote in 1930:

> The perfect page, the page of which not a single word can be altered without damage, is the most precarious of all. The changes of language erase lateral meanings and shadings; the "perfect" page is constituted by those delicate values and it is also the page most prone to wear [La página de perfección, la página de la que ninguna

palabra puede ser alterada sin daño, es la más precaria de
todas. Los cambios del lenguaje borran los sentidos
laterales y los matices; la página "perfecta" es la que
consta de esos delicados valores y la que con facilidad
mayor se desgasta]. (*Discusión* 48)

It is to Richards's credit that he recognized the uncertainties in
the transaction of reading in reflections that would lead his
disciple William Empson to investigate the instabilities of
literary language in *Seven Types of Ambiguity*. Richards should
also receive plaudits for the following line: "Words wander in
many directions in the figurative space of meaning" (*Speculative
Instruments* 77). With this statement, Richards acknowledges the
unstable and challenging nature of the literary text.

One way of stabilizing the transmission of messages in this
unstable medium is to postulate an author, as Michel Foucault
reminds us:

> The author is ... the principle of a certain unity of
> writing. ... The author also serves to neutralize the con-
> tradictions that may emerge in a series of texts: there must
> be—at a certain level of his thought or desire, of his
> consciousness or unconscious—a point where
> contradictions are resolved, where incompatible elements
> are at last tied together or organized around a
> fundamental or originating contradiction. ("What Is" 151)

Foucault's statement goes a long way to explain the role of a
function of discourse denominated as "author" in the creation of
stability for a text. From it, one can further establish Poe, along
with Marx and Freud, as a "founder of discursivity" insofar as he
has, beyond his stories, produced "the possibilities and the rules
for the formation of other texts" and an "endless possibility of
discourse" ("What Is" 154) in relation to detective fiction. Hence
his progeny, so denominated by Borges, and the existence of
Bustos Domecq.

Foucault's position requires elaborating: How is a text
communicated? Foucault notes that the unity of writing, "far from
being given immediately," is the result of an operation of an
interpretive nature insofar as "it deciphers, in the text, the
transcription of something that it both conceals and manifests"
(*Archaeology* 24):

> These aspects of an individual which we designate as making him an author are only a projection, in more or less psychologizing terms, of the operations that we force texts to undergo, the connections that we make, the traits that we establish as pertinent, the continuities that we recognize, or the exclusions that we practice. ("What Is" 150)

In recognizing an operation of an interpretative nature in reading, he opens the way to considering this operation not to be exclusive to the "writer." The issue becomes one of *direction*. Roland Barthes writes: "Indeed, it is the *direction* of meaning which determines the two management functions of the [classical] text: the *author* is always supposed to go from signified to signifier, from content to form, from idea to text, from passion to expression; and, in contrast, the *critic* goes in the other direction, works back from signifiers to signifieds" (174). Providing the systematic, theoretical foundations for the dissolution of this alternating directionality in interpretation has been Peirce's most important contribution to the study of fiction in our time. Peirce proposes that every sign is external, that signifiers and signifieds are interchangeable. The referent of a sign is another sign: "The interpretation of a sign is not, for Peirce, a meaning but another sign; it is a reading, not a decodage, and this reading has, in its turn, to be interpreted into another sign, and so on *ad infinitum*" (de Man, *Allegories* 3).

Lest the reader be misled by Barthes's reference to "the critic" and conclude that this discussion pertains to a professional, academic critic, it might be well to recall Borges's consideration that "every day there are fewer readers left, in the naive sense of the word, and we are left, rather, with potential critics" [ya no van quedando lectores, en el sentido ingenuo de la palabra, sino que todos son críticos potenciales (*Discusión* 46)]. If reading narrativizes or translates, in the sense of imposing an order on an existing text (a sign), reading becomes a species of writing, which is an act of interpretation. In his "Examen de la obra de Herbert Quain," Borges notes that "Quain would argue that readers were an extinct species. *There isn't a European* (he reasoned) *who isn't a writer, potentially or factually*" [Quain solía argumentar que los lectores eran una especie extinta. *No hay*

europeo (razonaba) *que no sea un escritor, en potencia o en acto
(Obras* 1.464)]. The critic is the intellectual reader, aware of the
laws of fiction, who judges by the laws of composition that he or
she abducts to be at work in the text, and whose reading is,
conversely, judged by this implicit understanding.

To consider the stories collected in *Six Problems* to be faux
Borges or faux Bioy Casares denotes how much an author's
name is like currency, dependent on the faith of the public. If the
faith in it is shaken, the currency is worthless. Borges recalls the
reception of Honorio Bustos Domecq:

> When the readers discovered that Bustos Domecq did not
> exist, they believed all the stories to be jokes and that it
> was not necessary to read them, that we were poking fun
> at the reader, which was not the case. I don't know why
> the idea of a pseudonym made them furious. They said:
> "Those writers do not exist; there is a name but there isn't
> a writer." Then a general contempt took over, but it was a
> false reasoning [Cuando los lectores descubrieron que
> Bustos Domecq no existía, creyeron que todos los cuentos
> eran chistes y que no sería necesario leerlos: creyeron que
> nos burlábamos del lector, lo cual no era cierto. No sé por
> qué la idea de un pseudónimo les ponía furiosos. Decían:
> "Esos escritores no existen; hay un nombre pero no hay un
> escritor." Se produjo así una protesta general, pero ése era
> un falso razonamiento]. (Murat in Rodríguez Monegal,
> *Borges* 369)

The test of money is whether it is accepted or not. By denying
Bustos Domecq acceptance, his readers were indirectly vetoing
Bioy Casares and Borges's proposition of the author as a
relationship among texts and as a mode of dialogue. One, after
Borges, can intuit in those readers the unsettling realization that
since two men had dreamt another (an author) who in turn
addressed them as readers, this process might imply that they
themselves had been fictionalized in some way, had been the
"devalued" victims of some confidence trick. Here lies the
mystery of readerships. The solution lies in accounting for "the
general protest" of Honorio Bustos Domecq's readers in contrast
to the general acceptance of the currency established by two
other men, Frederic Dannay and Manfred B. Lee, who wrote
under the name of Ellery Queen.

Pseudonyms are endemic to the detective genre. Eden Phillpotts, author of the celebrated Dartmoor regional novels, wrote books such as *Who Killed Cock Robin?* under the nom de plume of Harrington Hext; S.S. Van Dine also comes to mind as an obvious example. Dannay and Lee's pseudonym was the name of the main character of their fiction, Ellery Queen; between 1932 and 1933, this same Queen also "wrote," under the name of Barnaby Ross, four novels featuring a retired Shakespearian actor named Drury Lane. In this case, the readers were not even stirred by the fact that a character was writing under yet another name about yet another detective. What is at stake here is not to account for the popularity that Queen's *The Roman Hat Mystery* (1929) or *The Chinese Orange Mystery* (1934) enjoyed vis à vis *Six Problems*, but rather why the very existence of the Argentine authors would be questioned, for that is what happened. One reader, as Borges reports, said: "Those writers do not exist; there is a name but there isn't a writer."

It is a fact that a reader accustomed to Borges's or Bioy Casares's literary style would not have recognized either writer under the guise of Bustos Domecq, who truly was a *third man*. Borges recalls that this fantastic author had "his likes, his dislikes, and a personal style that is meant to be ridiculous; but still, it is a style of his own, quite different from the style I write when I try to create a ridiculous character" (Christ in Rodríguez Monegal, *Borges* 366). Years later, Borges added "people thought that, as Bustos was a joke, his writing could hardly be taken seriously" (*The Aleph* 246); remembering the publication in 1942 of Bustos Domecq's first book, Bioy Casares states: "Our friends, the critics, *are not amused*" (Levine, 172). Perhaps Borges aficionados would have been more interested had they realized, as Rodríguez Monegal points out, for example, that the parodic work by Bustos Domecq provided the author with the plot of "The Dead Man," published in 1949 in *The Aleph*, and that with *Six Problems*, "for the first time in Argentina a deliberate attempt to create narrative through the parody of narrative form and speech was successful" (*Borges* 368). But in these recognitions, it is the work of the now famous author that is set up as the point of interest, and the work of Bustos Domecq is marginal to the literary biographies of Borges and Bioy Casares. Bustos Domecq is thus not a literary entity in his own right, against the evidence of his writing.

True names and pseudonyms; perhaps it was Victor Hugo's pronouncement that inspired Borges to engage in that game: "Dieu seul sais mon vrai nom" [Only God knows my true name] (Borges and Ferrari, *Libro* 206). This was an idea that Borges also found expressed in Thomas Browne's hope that one may yet find out his or her true name in God's register. The fictitious name might yet have been a passing consideration for Borges, product of his contact with Plato's *Cratylus*, which suggests that essences are in the name and that the name is secret. But our search for the source of Borges's pseudonymous game merits a parody in Bioy Casares and Borges's collection. For an explanation of the reception to Bustos Domecq's work one might return to the metaphor of money.

In his discussion of Balzac's "Sarrazine," Barthes comments on the social myth of Parisian gold. Barthes cites Balzac: "So long as high society knows the amount of your fortune, you are classed among those having an equal amount, and no one asks to see your family tree, because everyone knows how much it costs." Barthes explains: "In the past . . . , money 'revealed;' it was an index, it furnished a fact, a cause, it had a nature, today it 'represents' (everything): it is an equivalent, an exchange, a representation: a sign" (39). The relationship between the name "Ellery Queen" and the cousins Dannay and Lee is, like old money, indexical. Ellery Queen indicates an independent and irreducible otherness that is Dannay and Lee's writing subject. The stability of this writing subject is guaranteed by the fact that the component parts are not known individually, but only by the joint inscription of their writing. Ellery Queen is a mingling accepted as oneness: a product of generic convention, the stabilizing principle of detective fiction and its norms of composition, and a singularity in the mode of creative activity. There is no Dannay and Lee outside of "Queen." The pseudonym "Barnaby Ross," with which Dannay and Lee produced the Drury Lane mysteries, is not a subversion of this order; it is an extension of the indexical function.

On the other hand, Honorio Bustos Domecq, who comes into his own by means of his difference from both Bioy Casares's and Borges's literary styles, and embodies his own style, his own jokes, his own preferences distinct from his progenitors, represents "a metonymic confusion" in the sign relation. Like Ellery Queen, Bustos Domecq has an identity derived from the reading tradition of a codified genre. But Bustos Domecq is a multiple reader, not exclusively a detectory one. He is a parodist, and though in *Six Problems* he performs to detective story standards, one senses in Bustos Domecq the unruliness of his intellect. He is like today's money, to use Barthes's figure, a sign of multiple exchanges. The concept of sign that Barthes uses in discussing Parisian gold should be clarified: "Bustos Domecq" is a symbol, arbitrarily linked to its object, which in *Six Problems* is detective fiction. The arbitrariness of the linking might have been suspected by the readers, and made them wary of a hoax; that is, the readers might have intuited the symbolical nonorigin of the author, a lack in heredity that destabilized the order of representation. One can think of this principle of heredity in terms of paternity, or as the kind of convention that gives paper money its legal value and impedes its unrestrained replication. As a symbol of the author, Bustos Domecq represents an act of transgression, and an unsettling one, because the invention of Bustos Domecq opens the concept of authorship to being a game of equivalences and representations, which denies a principle of authority in relation to the text. The interpretation of texts, without the source of meaning that the postulation of an author represents, fully enters the unending process of conjecture, error, and approximation that has marked literary history since the first reader approached the first inscribed stone.

Bioy Casares and Borges, two readers of detective fiction, became writers under a pseudonym. In fact, they became one under a name to produce detective fiction. When the reader turns into a writer, it reveals under the rubric of *writer* an ongoing dialogue, a collaboration of texts, experiences, and desires. Bioy Casares and Borges's association illustrates Paul de Man's assertion that "the distinction between author and reader is one of the false distinctions that reading makes evident" (*Allegories* 17). In other words, behind the name of Honorio Bustos Domecq there is a multiplicity, resonant with various voices and intentions, not personal or strictly bound generically, but obsessively intertextual, a shifting sign open to interpretation and imprecision.

PART FOUR

The Text as Web: A Case for Conjecture in **The Name of the Rose**

The Narrative Mask
Preface on Eco's Preface

At the onset of *The Name of the Rose*, the narrator fits himself with a mask from behind which to tell his tale. The preface claims that the novel has been translated into Italian from a nineteenth-century French book that was itself the reproduction of a seventeenth-century Latin manuscript. This seventeenth-century manuscript was in turn a version of a fourteenth-century manuscript written by a Benedictine monk, Adso of Melk, who witnessed and participated in the events related. The reader is presented with this copy-of-a-copy chain as the explanation for the textual object that he or she now holds in his or her hands. The option exercised by the author is in keeping with the timidity often associated with the composition of a first novel and could be seen as a move intended to forestall possible objections of the reader to the adequacy of his fiction.

For the author, the self-proclaimed translator or editor of the text in question, the fictional preface represents his entrance into the mirror of fiction, into that illusory country of figurations and colors where, Borges writes, the author himself is a simulacrum "obliterated by recurring night and dimly seen by the gaze of others" [que obliteran las noches y que las vislumbres permiten (*Inquisiciones* 29)]. The author is thus presenting himself as a transcriber of fiction and hence a refractory source of language. One should recall a similar instance in Borges's first book of fiction, *Universal History*, in which he set down "free versions" of narratives written by others before him.

A second interpretation of the preface is to call it the mask that the author dons in relation to the fiction. The preface begins with the inscription, "Naturally, a manuscript." This "natural" proposition of a manuscript has nothing to to do with the naturalness of writing, about which there is nothing natural. Writing is a cultural act, coded by the society in which it happens. What the author is proposing as natural has to do with writing conventions that allow the reader to recognize the appearance (and proposal) of a manuscript as a narrative trick, designed, as it has been designed many times before, to blur the line between fiction and reality, history and fabulation. The irony that must be understood in such a presentation of the manuscript is also part of the invitation extended the reader to join in the game of fiction. This appeal to codes, such as the history of Western literature, is a calculated move, which relates the culture's codes to the reader in an important way. Barthes explains: "Although they may be entirely of bookish origin, these codes, by a reversal proper to bourgeois ideology, which turns culture into nature, serve as the foundation of the real, of 'Life' " (211). The fictionality of the preface is not as important in itself as the importance that the preface represents for both the author and his desired reader in the attempt at shared fabulation that is the narrative text.

The *Name of the Rose* is, appropriately enough, a mystery. There is a detective, his amanuensis, the scribe assistant, a series of murders, the misleading pattern for resolution, and the surprising, paradoxical, revelation at the end. As a detective novel, the text harks back to a tradition that began in 1868 with *The Moonstone* by Wilkie Collins (the first and the best, according to T.S. Eliot), whose detective, Sergeant Richard Cuff, is fond of roses and something of an expert in their cultivation; in fact, Cuff is "a mine of learning on the trumpery subject of rose gardens," according to Gabriel Betteredge, one of the characters of Collins's novel (134). But none of this is announced in the preface to *The Name of the Rose*, an act of omission that confuses (or delays) the creation of the detectory reader demanded by the mystery just described. The author deceptively sets out "to tell, for sheer narrative pleasure, the story of Adso of Melk, . . . comforted and consoled in finding it immeasurably remote in time (now that the waking of reason has dispelled all the monsters that its sleep had generated). Gloriously lacking in any relevance for our day, atemporally alien to our hopes and our certainties" (5). The alert reader will do well to recall that remoteness can still house a distant mirror where the reader can see him or herself reflected or distorted by his or her own wishes and needs.

The conventional patterns that the reader encounters in the novel work to contradict the stated purpose of the preface; the detectory schema suggests a different intention from the one stated at the onset. The nature of the enigma is not made clear by the preface: Is it perhaps the very game of intertextuality recorded by the author? Is the mystery of this novel a search for origins? Or is it the search for a book that is the source of truth for the message of the novel? By his very explanation, the author has suggested to the suspicious reader a hidden code at work in the novel. Defining the enigma will become the initial driving force for the reader intent on making sense of the work. The reader is thus anticipated by the text as a detectory reader who will define the terms of the enigma and will then seek the implications of the solution. The reader's explanation of the novel will be an interpretation whose composition will depend on the elements in the text that are isolated by the reader's suspicion. By questioning the signs of the text in this fashion, the reader is postulating each proposition encountered as an *argument* in the Peircian sense. Paul de Man explains "that no reading is conceivable in which the question of its truth or falsehood is not primarily involved" (*Writings* 220). To postulate a proposition as an argument does not mean that the reader necessarily polemicizes the text, and neither does it mean that there will be a true reading. The importance of the argument lies in the process of decoding by which textual truth will be sought by the active reader.

In the worldwide search that "Eco" undertakes in order to compose the manuscript of *The Name of the Rose*, he describes a special visit to the city of Buenos Aires: "As I was browsing among the shelves of a little antiquarian book seller on Corrientes, not far from the more illustrious Patio del Tango of that great street, I came upon the Castilian version of a little work by Milo Temesvar, *On the Use of Mirrors in the Game of Chess*"(3). The visit fills the Borgesian reader with anticipated curiosity. The significance of the book that the author of the prologue finds in Buenos Aires draws on a Borgesian axiom. At a low ebb of his search, the author discovers in Temesvar's book "copious quotations from Adso's manuscript" (3). In an echo of Borges's theme of intertextuality in "The Library of Babel," the character Adso realizes in the fourteenth century what Eco demonstrates with his discovery in the twentieth: "I had thought each book spoke of the things human or divine, that lie outside books," says Adso. "Now I realized that not infrequently books speak of books: it is as if they spoke among themselves" (286). The idea expressed by Adso will prove important for the conception of Eco's novel as a labyrinth with many centers and pathways, as well as for the solution to the abbey's mystery.

The search undertaken by "Eco" in finding the story of the events in an abbey in 1324, and the discoveries that he makes at different points in the world, give an indirect answer to the perplexity of Adso, who asks, "What is the use of hiding books, if from the books not hidden you can arrive at the concealed ones?" (*Name* 286). In "The Theologians" ["Los teólogos"], Borges posited another partial answer to Adso's question by conjecturing about the survival of certain heretical doctrines in the books of their detractors. Foucault states the intertextual idea in the following manner: "The frontiers of a book are never clearcut: beyond the title, the first line and the last full stop, beyond its internal configuration, it is caught up in a system of references to other books, other texts, other sentences: it is a node within a network" (*Archaeology* 23). The notion that "books speak of other books" plays a crucial role in the resolution of *The Name of the Rose* because the detective is able to abduct the subject matter of a forbidden and singular manuscript from references, allusions, and partialities.

The plot of *The Name of the Rose* deals with a manuscript sought after by certain monks in an Italian abbey. That manuscript is the second part of Aristotle's *Poetics*. The first part deals with tragedy, and uses Sophocles' *Oedipus Rex* as a model for the discussion. No copies of the second part exist; its contents are the product of conjecture and presumably deal with the means of representation and the uses of comedy. In this aspect, the novel shares some characteristics with Borges's fiction. For example, Borges has remarked of his story "Tlön, Uqbar, Orbius Tertius" that it is a sort of detective story where the detectives are amateurs, the adventure bibliographical, the quest centered on rare or imaginary books (Rodríguez Monegal, *Borges* 327). The reader who reads Eco's fiction in the terms of Borges is not reading the novel using principles foreign to *The Name of the Rose*. The allusion to mirrors that is made in Milo Temesvar's book, "found" by the author in Buenos Aires, can be understood as a reference to the motif of the mirror that is often found in Borges's stories. The allusion to chess, it has been noted in the discussion about "Death and the Compass," has been used by Borges to conceptualize the players' role in relation to the rules of a codified game. Further, it is not a contradiction to postulate a Borgesian and a detectory reader for the interpretation of the novel, for the Borgesian reader is a detectory reader, as we have seen.

We might even use Borges's criteria for the writing of mystery novels (and while he wrote detective stories, he never wrote such a novel) to judge Eco's efforts. On the subject of detective novels, Borges wrote:

> All detective novels consist of a very simple problem which can be exposed orally to perfection in five minutes, and which the novelist—perversely—draws out for three hundred pages. The reasons for this are commercial; they obey no other necessity than to fill out the volume. In such cases, the detective novels end by being an extended short story. (*TriQuarterly* 365)

Umberto Eco draws out the plot of *The Name of the Rose* to five hundred pages, and what results from the extension is a mystery novel masquerading as multiple labyrinths that leads to other genres: the historical novel, the *bildungsroman*, and the treatise, among other possibilities. In fact, the critic Rocco Capozzi refers to Eco's novel as a "literary pastiche. . . . Obviously assembled in a writer's laboratory," that contains "intertextual traces of many authors" ("Palimpsests" 415). The reason for Eco's choice of foundational fiction (the detective genre) might have been commercial, but the filling out of the volume raises many interesting relations between the plot and the numerous themes in the novel. In other words, it is possible to read the novel by means of the kinds of readers that the other genres demand. *The*

Name of the Rose exploits the varied readership potential of a work open to several valid interpretations.

The possibilities for reading *The Name of the Rose* are as varied as the many individuals who appropriate the text by their readings. But none of the realized possibilities holds center stage as the one stable meaning of the text. Each is at best part of a chorus. To read *The Name of the Rose* by the rules of composition of a reader other than the detectory reader means, of course, to produce another reading of the novel. Hence, in the terms discussed in the introduction of this study, another reader will reach an interpretation of the novel that is complementary to the detectory reading. This complementarity of readings (and readers), and the possibility of positing different reading strategies on the basis of various aspects of the work, has been referred to by Eco as the openness of the narrative text.

The reticence of the novel's preface makes it evident that Eco is not advocating one possible reading over the other. In the preface, the author masks his real intentions, perhaps unaware of what these intentions will be revealed to be by his novel's many smart readers. Masked as well by the preface is who the adequate reader of the novel will be—is it a medievalist who has command of Latin? Is it a novel for critics interested in semiotics and intertextuality? Is it the detective story reader? The preface and the title of the novel are coyly restrained in proposing a reader for the novel. The preface thus works as the anteroom to a theater stage. Along the wall of this anteroom hang several masks, each waiting for the actor who will don it in preparation for a reading performance in which the author will appear, Proteus-like, in the very terms defined by the reader's choice of mask.

Detectory Method and the Mystery of the Rose

In the prologue to "A Scandal in Bohemia" (1891), Watson, witness to another of his companion's feats of deduction, exclaims that in the Middle Ages Holmes would have been taken for a wizard and burned. Except for the unhappy end, the words of Dr. Watson are prophetic of a book then unwritten, a prophecy that is fulfilled by *The Name of the Rose*. The name of Eco's detective, William of Baskerville, evokes in turn the renowned sleuth of Baker Street and Holmes's best known case, *The Hound of the Baskervilles*. The fictions of Doyle also crop up in relation to the work of cryptography that Eco's detective undertakes in his investigation, specifically the stories "The Red Haired League" and "The Dancing Men," both notable examples of this type of decipherment, which in turn harks back to Poe's classic "The Gold Bug." Equally significant in this context is Doyle's "The Naval Treaty," in which Sherlock Holmes, while contemplating a rose exclaims:

> Our highest assurance of the goodness of Providence seems to me to rest in the flowers. All other things, our powers, our desires, our food, are really necessary for our existence in this first instance. But this rose is an extra. Its smell and its colour are an embellishment of life, not a condition of it. It is only goodness which gives extras, and so I say again that we have much to hope from the flowers. (Doyle, 1.624)

This pronouncement by the master detective is Doyle's tribute to Wilkie Collins's Sergeant Cuff, the first detective to appear in a novel with a clearly defined detectory schema, and one with whom Holmes shares an obvious affinity. These affinities are in the order of their appearance, cryptic remarks, intellectual pride, and unerring acumen. There is also something of Wilkie Collins's great detective Cuff in William of Baskerville who, like Cuff, seems unable to laugh and who appears in a novel that alludes to Cuff's predilection for the subject of roses; but more importantly, Eco's allusion to the rose in the title of the novel and to Doyle's detective creates a chain that extends from his novel back, through Doyle, to *The Moonstone* (published in 1868) and from there, of course, to Poe's stories, published in the early 1840s. Holmes's pronouncement, incidentally, is reproduced in the collection of essays on detectory method edited by Eco and Thomas Sebeok in 1983 (79).

The Name of the Rose links to detectory schemata in other novels, too: to Dorothy Sayers's books and those written by Eden Phillpotts under the name of Harrington Hext, among others. The plot of *The Name of the Rose* is itself of classic construction. The model can be found in Agatha Christie's *The ABC Murders,* in which the murders follow an alphabetical pattern, which in turn spawned "Death and the Compass," in which the killings follow a geometrical one.

In *The Name of the Rose*, in November of the year 1327, a learned Franciscan, Brother William of Baskerville, and a Benedictine novice from Melk travel to an abbey in northern Italy where the first of a series of deaths has taken place some days prior to their arrival. The abbey, "a place where all the evils of the century had chosen to assemble" (382), provides the context for the act of detection or coherent reading of the mysterious sign that is brought into being by the complementary, antagonistic forces at work in the text.

William has been an inquisitor in the past, a role that he has abandoned, since in the proliferation of heresies that mark the century, that tangled mass of possible causes and interpretations, he no longer feels comfortable performing a task that requires the separation of the good from the evil. The distinction, William notes, is becoming more and more an occasion for roasting, and the investigator opts for applying his intellect to more discrete ends:

> I work on things of nature. And in the investigation we are carrying out, I don't want to know who is good and who is wicked, but who was in the scriptorium last night, who took the eyeglasses, who left traces of a body dragging another body in the snow, and where Berengar is. These are facts. Afterward I'll try to connect them—if it's possible, for it's difficult to say what effect is produced by what cause. An angel's intervention would suffice to change everything, so it isn't surprising that one thing cannot be proved to be the cause of another thing. Even if one must always try, as I am doing. (*Name* 207–8)

Like Holmes, who in *The Hound of the Baskervilles* makes evident his skepticism of the presence of the Evil One in the events at Dartmoor, and prefers to ignore a cause that would invalidate his scientific rational approach, William restricts his investigation to "things of nature."[1] A pronouncement from the great Holmes that carried William's apologetic and contrite tone would have caused Watson consternation, but William is a friend of William of Occam, who has sowed doubt in his mind. During the time in which the novel is set, the Franciscan expounded the philosophy of nominalism, based on direct (intuitive) knowledge of nature, an action that earned him the ban of excommunication. As Baskerville explains, his arguments with Occam have led him to doubt the possibility of discovering the "universal mind that orders all things": "The relations are the ways in which my mind perceives the connections between single entities, but what is the guarantee that this is universal and stable?" (207). The nominalist theory, affirming that only individuals (and individual *instances*) exist in nature, found its two great exponents in Roger Bacon and William of Occam. Universals exist neither in things themselves nor in the mind of God; they are abstractions. In contrast to Aquinas's proposition that knowledge is the adjustment between the mind and the thing to be known, Occam and Bacon's nominalism proposed that only the names by which men conceived things were available to the reasoner's mind, and thus the relation between the mind and ideal forms that shaped the universe was a matter for conjecture.

One result of his discussions with Occam is that William cultivates the science of the particular and the hypothetical, much to the chagrin of his young assistant: "I had the impression that William was not at all interested in the truth, which is nothing but the adjustment between the thing and the intellect. On the contrary, he amused himself by imagining how many possibilities were possible" (*Name* 306). Adso's momentary repudiation of his master's method is understandable, given the status of logic and theology in his world, as proclaimed in Paris, the seat of scholasticism of the time: "We must try to understand," Borges writes, "that for the people of the Middle Ages reality was not men but humanity, not the species but the genus, not the genera but God" [Tratemos de entender que para los hombres de la Edad Media lo sustantivo no eran los hombres sino la humanidad, no los individuos sino la especie, no las especies sino el género, no los géneros sino Dios (*Other Inquisitions* 157; *Otras inquisiciones* 156)]. Borges's philosophical disquisition represents one part of the thinking of the time; the other, already mentioned, is represented by Occam and Roger Bacon, Brother William's intellectual mentors.

As a Franciscan, Brother William would readily support Saint Francis's view that the two great evils of the Christian world of his time were the arrogance of the rich and the arrogance of the erudite doctors of the Church who had undertaken to answer all questions of faith by reason and logic, and whom one finds described in Petrarch's *Correspondence* as "hoary-headed children." The poet completes his appraisal of the scholastics of his time by advising his reader to take flight whenever these doctors of the Church begin to "spew forth syllogisms" (Tuchman, 479–80). William's advocacy of nominalism might be the result of "an ethical scruple, not a speculative incapacity" [un escrúpulo ético, no una incapacidad especulativa]. Borges explains his opinion: "Men, said Coleridge, are born Aristotelian or Platonist; one can state of the English mind that it was born Aristotelian. For that mind, not abstract concepts but individual ones are real. . . . The Englishman rejects the generic because he feels that the individual is irreducible, unassimilable, and unique" [Los hombres, dice Coleridge, nacen aristotélicos o platónicos; a la mente inglesa cabe afirmar que nació aristotélica. Lo real para esa mente, no son los conceptos abstractos, sino los individuos. . . . El inglés rechaza lo genérico porque siente que lo individual es irreductible, inasimilable e impar" (*Other Inquisitions* 123–4; *Otras inquisiciones* 119)]. As an Aristotelian, William's procedures make clear that the order of the universe might be an error "or a fiction of partial knowledge" [o una ficción de nuestro conocimiento parcial (*Other Inquisitions* 123; *Otras inquisiciones* 118)].

Borges's assertion carries at least two important consequences for the current discussion. One is that Brother William's method of detection is optimally suited and indeed, derived from the epistemological model postulated by Occam, in which the context is related to what is most familiar (or instinctive) to the observer. Brother William explains the implications: "The order that our mind imagines is like a net, or like a ladder, built to attain something. But afterward you must throw the ladder away, because you discover that, even if it was useful, it was meaningless" (*Name* 492).[2] Thus, a simpler hypothesis does not result in a universal truth in every case. A second consequence of William's assertion is that the restrictive atmosphere that pervades the monastery, expressed in the controlled access to the holdings of the library and represented in the figure of Jorge of Burgos, becomes the understandable act of preservation of a hierarchical society where communication is based on the assumed presence of a stable symbolic signifying system that is the mind of God. Correct interpretation must be established only by the authority of the fathers, by their power of *auctoritas*.

The abbey stands as a bastion of Medieval order, now decentralized by the rise of the secular state and the vernaculars in the world at large.[3] The library, containing as it does works from the East and the pagans arranged by the country of their origin, is "the sign of the labyrinth of the world" (*Name* 158). This is a labyrinth one enters at one's own risk, not knowing where (or if) one will leave it. If the library once was made to house the books it contains, "now it lives to bury them" (396). To hide books is a futile act, given the context of interactive meanings and partial messages, since from the books not hidden one can arrive by abduction at the ones concealed. The act of hiding, however, represents an effort to prevent the end of the monologue of knowledge that the Church claimed in this time, with its theocentric world view and monopoly of language.

In this mystery, official force takes the form of the character Bernard Gui, Guidoni, or Guido, the author of *Practica Inquisitionis*; the detectory reader has met Gui before, and knows his methods from the prefect in Poe's stories, or perhaps from Lestrade in Doyle's, though the character of Gui is most clearly evident in Superintendent Seegrave, who appears in Collins's novel and whose first investigative act is to terrorize the servants of the household. Bernard Gui is the true investigative foil of William. While Jorge of Burgos is an antagonist in the "metaphysical" sense that Moriarty was to Holmes, an unmoved mover, Gui is a methodological opponent, a character still defined by his role as an inquisitor, concerned with "the pestiferous stink of the Devil" that he perceives permeates the halls of the abbey (*Name* 301). In his battle against the Evil One (*his* unmoved mover), Gui does not hesitate to use that inquisitive tool (or weapon): the fear of others. Coupled with his conventional detectory knowledge that everyone has something to hide, Gui knows that the *prima causa* of every mystery is the battle between good and evil that is being played out in human action. Gui must be understood as the arm of Burgos's thinking and as the agent of repressive action needed by the official powers to forestall the spread of heresy and error in the world. In Gui's version of the events (which can be read as a parody of William's investigation), the murders are mixed with heresy, and the manuscript sought by the murdered monks must be the letters from a leader of a heretical sect that have been entrusted to the librarian for safekeeping, and which Gui produces as irrefutable proof of his conjectures. Folly, like reason, is also at work in this novel.

The historian Barbara Tuchman notes that "medieval justice was scrupulous about holding proper trials and careful not to sentence without proof of guilt, but it achieved proof by confession rather than evidence, and confession was routinely obtained by torture" (43). One fine point in the medieval system of justice is that the inquisitor never tortured. The custody of the defendants was always entrusted to the secular arm, and it was the secular arm of the Church that proceeded with the chores of intimidation. Gui explains: "One of the benefits this procedure grants the criminal is precisely that death be savored and expected, but it must not come before confession is full, and voluntary, and purifying" (*Name* 385–86). A drawback of this reasoned method (there are others too numerous to mention) which works against the inquisitor's interest is the reactive proliferation of the number of heresies that he is trying to restrict because, as Adso correctly points out, "every person, when questioned, usually tells the inquisitor, out of fear of being suspected of something, whatever may serve to make somebody else suspect" (302). Such is the case in the novel. Having obtained a confession of heresy from some unfortunates, Gui presses for a further confession to explain the murders perpetrated in the abbey, arguing that the practices of heresy of which the men were guilty have corrupted their spirit and that "can only lead to criminal acts" (381).

Under the threat of further torture, the accused confess to the crimes of the abbey and Bernard Gui closes the case. When another murder happens soon after, he is no longer concerned because with his investigation he did not attempt or pretend to round up all the heretics that might have been lurking in the monastery. His procrustean strategy has been the opposite of William's:

> Bernard is interested, not in discovering the guilty, but in burning the accused. And I, on the contrary, find the most joyful delight in unravelling a nice, complicated knot. And it must also be because, at a time when as philosopher I doubt the world has an order, I am consoled to discover, if not an order, at least a series of connections in small areas of the world's affairs. (*Name* 394)

William's summation of his art, spoken like a detective of the classic style, echoes Orczy's old man. But unlike the old man and his armchair brethren, William does not shrink from the task of direct questioning of the evidence, because his goal is an empirical truth, not just the flash and flourish of a reasoned abduction, and empirical truths need immediate proofs for validation. What is at stake in William's statement is the further making of a "meta-abduction" after the initial hypothesis. The meta-abduction represents the verification of the initial guess against the world of experience (Eco, "Horns" 207).

The meta-abduction is an extensional game of interest only to policemen and scientists, Orczy's old man would argue, while sipping tea and incessantly playing with a piece of string. The creation of possible scenarios (or worlds) is all that reading affords, and that is in itself no small task. Without an author to validate one's meta-abductions, "visiting" the site of the crime to sniff bicycle tracks, while collecting ash for further examination in the lab, is just a redundant pantomime. And why postulate another Doyle in relation to the detectory schema? Or hypostatize, for that matter, *scientific discovery* as the reader's measure of certainty? The act of reading, the old man in the corner would remind his reader, is an activity more resigned to imprecision than the actions of checking the physical evidence would lead one to believe.

One example of the imprecision of textual analysis is provided by the title of Eco's novel. Eco opted for the title over *The Abbey of Crime*, which would have proposed the detectory reader in no uncertain terms. In *Postscript to* The Name of the Rose, Eco writes that "one of the chief obstacles . . . is the fact that a novel must have a title" (2), and proceeds to explain his choice of title: "I liked [the title] because the rose is a symbolic figure so rich in meaning that by now it hardly has any meaning left: Dante's mystic rose, and go lovely rose, the War of the Roses, rose thou art sick, too many rings around Rosie, a rose by any other name, a rose is a rose is a rose, the Rosicrucians" (3). Eco considers a restricting title an obstacle to the "virtuous principle" by means of which a novel is "a machine for generating interpretations" (2). Eco's decision to title his novel the way he did indicates that he did not intend his novel to have a single meaning, and that it is the reader's task to formulate ideas about what the work is about as he or she advances in his or her reading, and not at the onset of the narrative. At the same time, Eco intends to keep his own interpretation of the novel at bay, and allow his reader to generate sense without the author's guiding regimentation of the interpretive game.

For the detectory reader, Eco's novel could be a classic detective story set in the Middle Ages that chronicles seven murders and their investigation. But it is not beyond this detectory reader to conjecture the meaning of the rose in relation to the text. The most important event in the detective assistant's life, one reported in the novel, is the sexual experience that he has with an unnamed girl. At the end of his years, when Adso sets down the chronicle of his adventures in the abbey, he admits that the memory of the girl has always been with him. The rose has long been a symbol of love and desire, but there is another connection to the girl in Adso's memory. When the girl is accused of being a witch, and burned at the stake by Bernard Gui, Adso suffers a great emotional pain that is compounded by the fact that he "could not, then or ever after, call that love by name" (*Name* 407). Adso feels the need to attach his feelings and confusion to a *name* and, in that action, to conjure all the things that are associated with that name. The name of the girl is an absence in the text, which could be conceived as a figure for Adso's desolation in his attempt to name what his love could not.

The form of the rose, the arrangement and shape of the petals, may symbolize the labyrinthine shape of the abbey's library. The rooms of the library, which make up the labyrinth, are constructed around a cylindrical chamber, and at the four corners of the central shaft are towers, one of which provides access to the library. The circular arrangement of the rooms around the center resembles the winding pattern of the petals around the center of a rose. A further comparison could be made between the library and the rose through the image of a poisoned rose whose thorns have been treated to produce the death of the person whose finger is pricked. The poisoned thorn is, of course, the book by Aristotle, which has been poisoned by the evil Jorge.

Eco's novel ends with a Latin hexameter, culled from the work of Bernardi Morlanensis: Stat rosa pristina nomine, nomina nuda tenemus (*Name* 502). In English, roughly, the verse reads: "The name of the pristine rose remains; we only have the name." An explanation of that verse could be developed in many ways: one relates it to the "where are they now?" theme that colors Adso's reminiscences at the end of the novel. The quotation also evokes the relation between things and the names that de-nominate things. William of Baskerville dismisses Aquinas's "adjustment between thought and the thing" as the ground for knowledge in favor of conjecture that accounts for the relativity of truth value. Borges expresses a similar thought: "If (as the Greek asserts in the *Cratylus*) The name is archetype to the thing, / The rose in the letters of "rose" / And the length of the Nile in "Nile" [Si (como el griego afirma en el *Cratilo*) el nombre es arquetipo de la cosa, / en las letras de *rosa* está la rosa / y todo el Nilo en la palabra *Nilo* (*Obra poética* 200)]. Eco himself informs his reader of the "possible nominalist readings of the concluding verse," which in turn reflect the nominalist theme that runs through the pages of the novel (*Postscript* 3). The evocation of the rose emphasizes Adso's growing realization that knowledge and events are passing and that only the names remain.

Finally, the rose does establish the connection previously noted among texts of detective fiction, including Cuff, his interest in roses, and his habit of whistling "The Last Rose of Summer" when he is deep in thought; and the reference to Doyle's tribute to roses (and to Cuff) in "The Naval Treaty." Holmes's and Cuff's interest in roses conveys the detectives' ability to appreciate the esthetic qualities of nature as well as the intellectual features of the mind, and suggests behind the stock characterization a complexity in character and motivation that is part of the detective. Rex Stout has similarly used this convention in his characterization of Nero Wolfe, whose passion is not the rose, but the exotic orchid.

The presence of the rose in Eco's title suggests mainly the intertextual nature of the book, and intertextuality is the means by which Eco attempts to make multiple connections with his novel to the literary world and the writing tradition that has preceded and contains *The Name of the Rose*.

NOTES

1. In *The Hound of the Baskervilles*, Holmes says in relation to the transcendental battle between good and evil: "In a modest way I have combated evil, but to take the Father of Evil himself would, perhaps, be too ambitious a task" (Doyle, 2.21).

2. The image of order, knowledge, and the ladder has been attributed to the philosopher Wittgenstein: "Er muss gleichsam die Leiter abwerfen so er an ihr aufgestigen ist" (Capozzi in Giovannoli, 200). The image of ladder as text can be found suggestively discussed in a footnote to Borges's "The Library of Babel:" "I repeat: it suffices that a book be possible for it to exist. Only the impossible is excluded. For example: no book can be a ladder, although no doubt there are books that discuss and deny and demonstrate this possibility, and others whose structure corresponds to that of a ladder "[Lo repito: basta que un libro sea posible para que exista. Sólo está excluido lo imposible. Por ejemplo: ningún libro es también una escalera, aunque sin duda hay libros que discuten y niegan y demuestran esa posibilidad y otros cuya estructura corresponda a la de una escalera (*Labyrinths* 57; *Obras* 1.469)].

3. Dante writes, in commenting on his search through "the heights and pastures of Italy" in search of the "panther" that motivates his quest (here Dante uses the imagery of the hunt, and his quarry is a language fitted for the whole of Italy, not found in local dialects): "There must be one thing by which all things of that kind may be compared and weighed. . . . everything considered as belonging to a kind becomes measurable by that which is simplest in that kind . . . we declare the illustrious, cardinal, courtly, and curial vernacular language in Italy to be that which belongs to all the towns of Italy but does not appear to belong to any of them, and by which all the municipal dialects of the Italians are measured, weighed, and compared" (635–36).

Jorge of Burgos
Eco's Minotaur

The Borges-like character who appears in Eco's novel reveals how the process of characterization might take place in an instance of fiction—in this case, *The Name of the Rose*. The casting of "Borges" in a novel that belongs ostensibly to the genre of detective fiction is a clear recognition of Borges's work in and on a genre that he considered a challenge to the inventiveness of the author. In Eco's novel, the figure of Jorge of Burgos, blind custodian of a labyrinthine library, holds the key to the solution to the mystery. Jorge's confession makes evident to the startled detective that he has arrived at a solution by connecting often irrelevant clues and events that had not, as he had inferred, been strictly produced by the will of a criminal mind. Through this confession, Eco dissolves the strict criminal/detective opposition that is expected by the reader of detective fiction. But perhaps paradoxically, it is the detective genre (defended by Borges as the best means to impose order on fabulation and as the most Aristotelic of genres) that saves *The Name of the Rose* from being a rambling disquisition on power, semiotics, and history, and, to put it plainly, from being a pastiche of quotations and unattributed borrowings. While still clearly a work of detective fiction, *The Name of the Rose* confronts the reader with a plot that, like Borges's detective fiction, disrupts the conventions of the genre and challenges the reader to produce a new interpretation about detective fiction and the toils of discovery.

The parodic reference to the blind master builder of erudite labyrinths who was at one point the custodian of books at Argentina's Biblioteca Nacional is impossible to miss. In a key article published in 1983, the same year that Eco published his

revealing *Postille a ll nome della rosa* [*Postscript to* The Name of
the Rose (1984)], the critic Walter Stephens wrote, "From a
literary point of view, it is now evident that the book owes much
to Borges's narrative and essays, and it explains how a large part
of Eco's semiotics is derived precisely from Borges" (64). The
second part of Stephens's statement is perfectly valid and
indeed, one could go further and assert that the work of Borges
is at the heart of the critical work of Roland Barthes, Jean
Baudrillard, and Gérard Genette, and that it has served as well
as the foundation of philosophical works such as Foucault's *The
Order of Things*. But the main interest in the current disquisition
is the "translational" effort on the part of the Italian author that
remits Borges, the South American writer, to the character of
Jorge of Burgos.

   From a literary point of view—to borrow Stephens's
phrase—there are few motifs as intimately related to the Argentine author as the labyrinth and the library, which appear
together as one and the same in Eco's novel; in Borges's fiction,
both serve as metaphors of impenetrable repetition and as symbols of a universe whose sense man, the map maker, must
conjecture. In *The Name of the Rose*, the centrality of the character
Jorge of Burgos to the life of the abbey is clearly stated when
he is described as "the library's memory and the soul of the
scriptorium" (130). Eco's villain is an avowed enemy of laughter
on the grounds that Christ never laughed, and he riles against
the humorous images used by the monks in the illustration of
manuscripts because they turn the masterpiece of creation on its
head on the pretext of teaching divine precepts. He says, "Little
by little the man who depicts monsters and portents of nature to
reveal the things of God *per speculum in aenigmata*, comes to enjoy
the very nature of the monstrosities he creates and to delight in
them, and as a result he no longer sees except through them"
(30). The detective, William of Baskerville, counters that Aristotle, and the Fathers of the Church, considered that laughter is
proper to man. Not everything proper to man is good, retorts the
austere Jorge, adding that "laughter foments doubt" (132). And
when in doubt, concludes the stern monk, "you must turn to
authority, to the words of a father or of a doctor; then all reason
for doubt ceases." (*Name* 132).

This encounter between the English protodetective (whose name alludes to one of Holmes's most celebrated cases) and the apocalyptic Spanish monk sets the stage for the events that follow. By postulating laughter as a transcendental event, and two clearly defined positions in the argument between the detective and the severe monk, the author isolates two poles of opposition and conflict in the monastery. The fictional world of the novel hangs in the balance: How will the development of the plot resolve this ideological stalemate? Is this learned argument related to the series of deaths that is taking place in the abbey? How many more monks will die before the hidden forces of chaos are revealed by the detective? Burgos is the clear representative of the stifling official order, a surprising role for "Borges," if one recalls his affinity for parody as a creative and analytical tool. No one would have expected the role of forerunner of Tomás de Torquemada, the Spanish inquisitor, for Borges, the skeptic, though the irony is already there in the title of Borges's collection of essays titled *Other Inquisitions*. The explanation for Eco's parodic investiture of such a character lies in the premises of the novel's plot. Like the illuminators, enjoying the monsters they create, one can imagine its author, a creature with pen in hand, a malicious smile drawn on his face, dreaming up the proper villain to play the part of the intellectual foil to his sagacious sleuth. There are debts to be paid, explains Eco, but *why* "Borges" is chosen for the role is perhaps less interesting than *how* "Borges" comes to this character.

Peirce has written that "A sign . . . is something which stands to somebody for something in some respect or capacity (*Collected Papers* 2.228)," and in this sense, "Burgos" is representamen of "Borges" that relies on Doyle's fiction for its coordinates of sense. For Burgos is a *tracing* of Doyle's Professor Moriarty, Holmes's archenemy—as William of Baskerville is a tracing of Holmes—as well as a refraction of "Borges" through the figure of Doyle's fiendish character. In other words, Burgos is "Borges" seen as "The Napoleon of Crime," who is described as follows by Holmes in "The Final Problem":

> He is the organizer of half that is evil and of nearly all that is undetected in this great city and in the annals of contemporary crime. He is a genius, a philosopher, an

> abstract thinker—he sits motionless, like a spider in the
> center of its web, but that web has a thousand radiations,
> and he knows well every quiver of each of them. His
> agents may be caught, they may be apprehended and their
> crimes forestalled—but he—*he* is never touched, never so
> much as suspected. (Doyle, 150)

The homologous relation that we might assume of Moriarty and
Burgos in their respective texts is, however, complicated by
textual difference. At the level of plot, the threads of the web do
escape Burgos, by his own admission; he has watched as the
events developed and has tried, *in retrospect*, to impose a pattern
on them based on the Book of the Apocalypse. Burgos, ironically,
ends up consuming the text that he has tried to hide, bringing
about his own death, and completing the series of deaths
announced in the sacred text. The difference between Burgos and
Moriarty is best accounted for in terms of the translation
performed by Eco, who, while creating the intertextual reference,
has also modified its context. In his novel, Eco has modified
what one should call the "playing field," keeping in mind the
conventions of the genre.

The stability implied by the image of the web in Doyle's
story brings to mind the order of the Newtonian universe in
which the scientific method reigns supreme: Things can be
known because they are connected by knowable laws operating
in the book of nature. "I never guess," Holmes has said, and he
never seems to guess, thanks to his talent for observation and
inference. There is a curious tension that one feels in relation to
Holmes's discoveries, which are always presented as bound by
a necessity that often escapes the reader. The tension is one
product of two world views in contention in the Holmes stories.
On the one hand, there is the Newtonian certainty that science
and method represent, and on the other, Hume's skepticism of
universals and his emphasis on the experience of observed fact.
Holmes's investigations carry this ambivalence. Doyle's detective is infallible in the theories that he develops by observing
details which call for an inference of something that has not
happened before. But curiously, Holmes reasons preponderately
by means of deduction; that is, he reasons *from* relatively stable
general principles *to* particulars.

The world of Holmes is one in which "all life is a great chain, the nature of which is known whenever we are shown a single link of it" (Doyle, 14). In this scheme, Moriarty is a knowable entity, but in mimetic correspondence to Holmes, who has the author-granted ability to make his deductions come true, he has the protean ability to vacate his place at the end of the one line of reasoning that would entrap him at one point in time, and then to occupy another. Moriarty's new position could be accounted for in the grid of spatial possibilities, but determining the location of the master criminal would force the process to begin anew. A computer-like mind like Holmes's and time would be needed, but in the course of events Moriarty could be feasibly found in the orderly web. The denouement played out at Reichenbach Falls between Holmes and Moriarty was inevitable: It was just a matter of time and patience.

The context that Eco has provided his detective is similarly a web, but it is a web touched by chaos. In the novel, the "lines of reason" of the textual system on which the detective and the criminal attempt to play their creative and resolvent game have a remarkable tendency to diverge from their expected paths, until their trajectory, borne in over five hundred pages, bears no resemblance to the one imagined by the detective. There are *strange attractors* at work in the plot—"attractors," because the trajectory of the mystery will converge on heterogeneous coordinates represented by the monks, and "strange," because they are unexpected by either the criminal or the detective. The strange attractors in the novel take the form of monks who share the bond of heresy, and others who are engaged in homosexual intrigue, and still others involved in a power struggle to become the librarian of the abbey; these sets of oppositional (and sometimes complementary) forces take their toll on the linearity of the events, independently of each other.

The randomness of the process makes the detective exclaim—"Where is all my wisdom, then? I behaved stubbornly, pursuing a semblance of order, when I should have known well that there is no order in the universe" (*Name* 492), but as his assistant points out, a culprit is unmasked, an explanation found, and an end reached. Perhaps the term "deterministic chaos" is a better description for the developments in the novel, as it is for Edward Lorenz's discovery of the general phenomenon of chaos in nature in the early 1960s.[1] Unpredictability is represented in Eco's novel, but the novel retains the form of a mystery to a predictable degree and, like Lorenz's discovery, what the detective is lamenting might be the fact that the system is behaving in such a complicated way that it might as well be random. The disorder that Eco's detective has to contend with on his way to the criminal and the solution of the mystery does not represent the order of a spider web. Eco has written that "the space of conjecture is a rhizome space" (*Postscript* 57), and the fate of his detective's quest seems to bear this out. The text of the crime can be conceived as the signifier of a labyrinth, not a centered one, but rather one whose passageways communicate "rhizomatically":

> Unlike trees or their roots, the rhizome connects any point with any other point, and none of its features necessarily refer to features of the same kind. It puts into play very different regimes of signs and even states of nonsigns. . . . It has neither beginning nor end, but always a middle through which it pushes and overflows. . . . Unlike a structure defined by a set of points and positions . . . the rhizome is made only of lines: lines of segmentation and stratification as dimensions, but also lines of flight. . . . The rhizome proceeds by variation, expansion, conquest, capture, stitching. (Deleuze and Guattari, *On the Line* 47–48)

In Eco's novel, the spiderweb whose order Holmes had been able to deduce from a single strand has become a reason-defying rhizome. In turn, note how the concept of the rhizome is a translation (modification) of a botanical term that has been transformed by critical (and cultural) usage to account for the imprecision of the reading act and for textual indeterminacy.

The Burgos/Moriarty character cannot control the plot in this unstable medium and neither can William of Baskerville, because cause and effect are diffused by accidents and chaos. Having accounted for the crucial difference between source and text, one should repeat that Burgos is also a tracing of Borges. The result of this intertextual operation via Moriarty is the creation of a monster for the purposes of the criminal intrigue that shakes the world represented by the abbey to its very foundations. Of course, "monster" did not always carry the connotation of horror that we hear today in that word. On the contrary, "monstrous" was an adjective applied to the admirable, to the thing or person worthy of contemplation. Lope de Vega, in the sixteenth century, for example, was a "Monster of Nature," according to Cervantes (*Entremeses* 93). As a curious aside, it should be noted that in *Don Quixote*, the "Enchanter," who is the source of all of the protagonist's woes, is described by the ill-fated Quixote in terms similar to the ones used by a fretful Holmes to describe Moriarty. Perhaps a more precise explanation for the Burgos/Borges conjunction would be the textual need for the production of a *monstrum horrendum* for the purposes of the detective plot.

The Minotaur amply justifies its maze. The critic Liberato Santoro considers the presence of a Borges-like character in the novel as "natural": "a labyrinthine library must of course have its blind Jorge" (255). Note that Eco's tracing has organized the sign "Borges" according to its own axes of significance. This result is something that Borges seems to have anticipated, though hardly welcomed, when he invented the alter ego "Borges" in 1960. Perhaps mindful of Berkeley's dictum "to be is to be perceived" and thus to be interpreted, he wrote with certain resignation in "Borges and Myself": "I am fated to become lost once and for all, and only a moment of myself will survive in the other" [estoy destinado a perderme, definitivamente, y sólo algún instante de mí podrá sobrevivir en el otro (*The Aleph* 151; *Obras* 2.186)]. That line conveys the melancholy of a man who has sensed and conjectured the infinite permutations, uncharted and redundant, that time, memory, and forgetfulness have in store for the signifier that is Borges, his given name, and the life it represents. The idea might have come to Borges from a phrase by Thomas Carlyle, which he quotes in *Other Inquisitions*: "Universal history [is] a Sacred Scripture: One that we decipher and write uncertainly, and in which we are also written" (120). Borges explains: "We not only write symbols but are symbols; and we are symbols written by something or someone—we could think of those two words in capital letters to create a greater impression: written by Something or Someone who we will not know, or who we will know only partially sometime" (Borges and Ferrari, *Libro* 130). Once again, the image of Quixote, mortified not because he is a character in fiction but because he has appeared as a character in Avellaneda's "illegitimate" book, recurs in relation to the appropriations of "Borges" that are related in this discussion. The issue that Quixote's lamentations brings to bear is one of falsification. Specifically, Quixote does not mind being a character in Cervantes's fiction, but he laments the falsification of his character in Avellaneda's. The issue also pertains to the appropriating text, whose veracity is called into question by the character's appearance in pages that respond to someone else's parameters and desires. The resulting sense of difference makes that someone else's fictional project clear in the contrast.

Perhaps Don Quixote's mortification is unjustified. He is, after all, a translation of a previous performance in Arabic by Cide Hamete Benegeli, or so we are led to believe by Cervantes. Regardless, he is caught in the web of translations, of interpretations, of difference. What his lament expresses is a nostalgia for the matrix or true source that has been, in the final analysis, denied by Cervantes, the father he recognizes as his own. What Quixote should recognize as the true matrix is language, the sustaining medium of his existence. This recognition is at the heart of Borges's essay on memory and forgetfulness, "Borges and Myself." And perhaps the alter ego "Borges" would feel at home in Eco's Borgesian invention, though the tracing has translated "Borges" into a monstrous image: a Minotaur set loose in the haphazard garden of Eco's novel. This image is true to the law of the text, as we have seen, and may also betray everything else that might be considered true but "outside" the text, if we were to accept that external realm as a tangible reality.

The important consideration for the reader is to recognize the distortion, even if it is an instance of normative fictional deceit. A reader alerted to the nature of the image will interpret the distortion as part of the text's design and pit it against the designs of the reading by referring it to another realm of sense that will reinstitute the created sign into the free play of significance. In his discussion of distorting mirrors, Eco points out that in their projected instance "the image does not give us information about the object, but about the nature of the channel" (*Semiotics and Pholosophy* 219). The image gives information about its object, but it does so in terms of a cartographic projection that must be interpreted back into some corrective configuration. Yet Eco's emphasis is correct: "The semiosis effort actually is between the perceptive surprise . . . and the channel, not between the image and the object" (219). This assertion is not a negative injunction of the image. It is a statement affirming its mimetic power.

In postulating himself as an "other" in "Borges and Myself," Borges was conceiving his self as a sign that is the product of an operation performed by a reader on the author as if he or she were a text. Notice that the configuration of sense that results from the operation is not given by the author himself, but results rather from the intuition and disposition of the reader that enables him or her to incorporate sign and sense. In other words, as Eco reminds us,—"A cat's paw print is motivated by the form of a given cat's paw but it is by convention that a hunter assigns to that expressive shape the content (the abstract notion of) 'cat' " (*Theory* 190). This statement emphasizes that a sign is not self-sufficient, and that it exists in a contingent relation with the reality that it ostensibly represents. This relation depends on a reader who, in fact, defines the correspondence between sign and object, an object that, as Peirce has postulated, is itself another sign. In a literary context, the feline paw-print analogy proves to be a slippery one. One must consider the genre of the text in which the paw print appears, or the figurative function of the print in the transformative ideological context that makes use of it. What at the ground level seems a reference to Borges in such direct clues as blindness, first name, and occupation in the fictional world (the distinct "Borges" signifiers) are merely the foundations of a composite being whose reality is very different from its historical referent's. The case is then one in which the print might be the cat's, but the head is another animal's, as is the torso, and even the tail, if we are to imagine the entire animal.

The norms of Eco's text that brought about the monstrous role for "Borges" and how the author might have arrived at its features, at the contours of the mask, have been the subject of discussion so far. Beyond the indexical relation that the issue of Eco's paw prints brings to our discussion, there is the issue that

signs interpreted to be similar or analogous to their objects,
brings forth: the issue of *iconicity*. Eco explains:

> The iconic sign builds a model of relations homologous to
> the model of perceptive relations that we build when we
> know and remember the object. If the iconic sign has
> properties in common with anything, it is not with the
> object, but with the perceptive model of the object: it is
> constructed and recognized according to the same
> operations that we perform to construct the thing we
> perceive, independently of the matter through which these
> relationships are realized. (Eco in Iser, *Act* 65)

In the case of "Borges" and Burgos, Burgos does not reproduce
the properties of Borges beyond some superficial features of the
author. What the present discussion does reveal is that the
apparently iconic relation of Burgos to "Borges" includes the
category Moriarty and its relation to Doyle's story and the
similarly reproduced context (web to rhizome) at work in Eco's
novel. Further, I suggest that the whole iconic enterprise at work
in Eco's novel is really an act of *code making* on the part of the
author, and that act is, in turn, a proposition to the reader to
complete the correlation. How that correlation is completed by
the reader is not a given, and its validity or ultimate meaning is
open to question.

An examination of the intertextual references to Borges
will reveal that the "Borges" sign signifies ambiguously in
textual composition of *The Name of the Rose*. At one level, the
allusion to Borges is to the creative artist who supplies the
central motifs of the narrative: the mirrors, the labyrinth, the
library, the notion of *ficciones*, and perhaps even the genre that
unifies the pages of the novel. The critic Helen Costiucovich
comments on this aspect of the composition:

> Borgesian motifs are of great importance to the ideological
> system as well as to the setting of the novel. To Borges is
> attributed the layout of the library that is also the universe,
> and the metaphysical identity world = library = mirror =
> book = labyrinth. From Borges come also the more
> detailed thematic elements. The novel uses, for example,
> the parable of Ibn Hakkan, who had built a treacherous
> labyrinth guarded by a black man and a lion and who

waited for his enemy hidden in the center of his spider web. In Eco's novel, the labyrinth has the shape of a web and the central trap is to be found among the LIONS, in the *finis Africae*. . . . Here too the victim is carried towards the trap by his own invincible curiosity. In Borges's tale one can even find "the name of the rose": it is the name of a ship called The Rose of Sharon [Los motivos borgianos son de gran importancia, tanto en el sistema ideológico, como en el escenario de la novela. A Borges se le atribuye el plano de la biblioteca, que es también el universo, y la identidad metafísica mundo = biblioteca = espejo = libro = laberinto. De Borges proceden también elementos temáticos más de detalle. Se utiliza, por ejemplo, la parábola de Abenjacán, que había construido un laberinto trampa custodiado por un negro y un león y esperaba al enemigo escondido en el centro de su tela de araña. En la novela de Eco el laberinto tiene forma de tela de araña y la trampa central se encuentra entre los LEONES, en el *finis Africae*. . . . Aquí también la victima es llevada a la trampa por su propia curiosidad invencible. En el cuento de Borges se puede encontrar también "el nombre de la rosa": es el nombre de un barco llamado La rosa de Sharon]. (Costiucovich in Giovannoli, 95–6)

As has been noted, "Borges" also represents the bad, the negative ethical stance in the novel. In contrast to William of Baskerville, who advocates the many possible readings of a text as the will of a joyful God, Burgos is the closed reader who reminds all that the source of meaning is authority. As the villainous monk who heralds an imminent apocalypse and poisons the desired book, he is "a criminal, a malignant mind brooding for a long time in darkness over a murderous plan" (*Name* 265). By extension, in the closing moments of the novel "Borges" also supplies the grotesque ugliness associated with evil: "His face, in the reddish glow of the lamp, now seemed horrible to us: the features were distorted, a malignant sweat streaked his brow and cheeks, his eyes, usually deathly white, were bloodshot, from his mouth came scraps of parchment, and he looked like a ravening beast . . . the venerable figure of the old man now seemed disgusting and grotesque" (483). Not surprisingly, the detective sees in the librarian's distorted features "the portrait of the Antichrist" (491). And even this portrait, notes Adso, the detective's assistant, would have inspired laughter in different circumstances, the laughter that the grotesque inspires.[2] At this point in the narrative, Eco offers his reader a full view of the malignant Minotaur, full of pride and maddened in his maze.

However, as has been suggested by Costiucovich's compendium of Borges's motifs and textual effects to be found in *The Name of the Rose*, the themes and images of Borges's work play an integral role in the novel. The casting of "Borges" as a villain serves to show the importance of his idea to the plot. Without a villain and his elaborated maneuvers, there would be no mystery, and without Borges and his works, Eco's novel would be an entity very different from the one his readers have known. Eco's conception for the plot of his novel is close to the one deployed by Bustos Domecq in "The Twelve Figures of the World," in which the zodiac provides the order necessary for the resolution of the case (by being revealed to be a *false* pattern). Judged by the standards of the genre, Eco's plot is superior, since Bustos Domecq's figuration needs twelve constituents for completion while Eco's demands only seven, corresponding to the seven trumpets of the Apocalypse according to the Holy Scriptures. In this critical judgment, the economy of William of Occam's formula anticipates the esthetics of the detective story: Entia non sunt multiplicanda praeter necessitatem [Entities should not be multiplied beyond necessity]. Eco's novel, appropriately enough, contains sustained references to Occam, the philosophical mentor of the detective William of Baskerville.

Eco capitalizes on the plot of "Death and the Compass" for the development of his medieval mystery. One might recall that when Lönnrot discovers that Yarmolinsky, a rabbinical scholar, has been murdered, he attempts to explain three mysterious deaths by means of the Cabbala. Lönnrot prefers "a purely rabbinical explanation" over a more mundane one: the confusion of the rabbi's room for the one across the hall, which holds the Tetrarch's valuable sapphires. Instead of considering this possibility, which is the more obvious explanation of the case, Lönnrot wants a solution that is "well suited aesthetically to the nature of the crime" (Boruchoff, 13), and thus the detective seeks to find a pattern in the letters of the name of God, the cardinal points of the compass, and the days of the Hebrew calendar. In the end, the criminal Scharlach admits that he planned the first crime in order to obtain the Tetrarch's sapphires, and that he deliberately made the rest of the crimes appear as if they had been committed in the pattern assumed by Lönnrot.

The Name of the Rose also incorporates the numerical theme that appears in "Death and the Compass." In his short story, Borges misleads the reader by suggesting, through the numerical clues, that there will only be three murders. In the story, one recalls, there are the references to "three years of war," "three thousand years of oppression," and to the third Talmudic conference, among many other threes that appear in relation to the date, the time, and the number of columns that report the incident of the murder. There is even a "three-legged cat" proverb: "No need to look for a three-legged cat here" [No hay que buscarle tres pies al gato] (*The Aleph* 66; *Obras* 500) says the police officer Treviranus, implying that Lönnrot's growing suspicion is overlooking the obvious. Ironically, the reader recognizes the obvious in the allusion. Later on in the story, the numerical clues deviously begin to point to a fourth crime: Lönnrot and Treviranus leave the scene of the last murder at "four o'clock," Lönnrot finds new meaning for the crime in the "Tetragrammaton," the sacred name of God, among many other numerical clues, such as the number of versions of the crime that are being now reported in the newspapers, the number of public establishments that are to be found at the site of the third murder, and so on.

Instead of drawing on Cabbalistic interpretations of sacred Scriptures as Borges does, Eco introduces the related scholastic ponderings on the ideal world of numbers in the Bible. The abbot, whose prestige is derived from having been the man who deposited the body of Thomas Aquinas in his tomb, makes references to numerology in the Bible. In a meeting with the detective where Adso is present, the abbot begins to talk about the virtues of the numbers three and four. The Aedificium, which houses the library and the hall in which the monks carry on their labors of copying, illustrating, and reading the books of the library, has "three stories, because three is the number of the Trinity, three were the angels who visited Abraham" (*Name* 539).

After listing a number of biblical occurrences that stress the importance of the number three, the abbot concludes: "The theological virtues are three, and three are the holy languages, the parts of the soul, the classes of intellectual creatures, angels, men and devils; there are three kinds of voice—vox, flatus, pulsus—and three epochs of human history, before during, and after the law" (444). The abbot goes on to explain, however, that the number four, evident in the square shape of the structure, is also "rich in spiritual lessons" (444). In Eco's mystery, four is a key number, because in deciphering the notes made by Venantius on the contents and the way to find the book hidden in the library, the element missing in William's translation of the cryptic message is "the word four" (556) that is carved over the distorting mirror found in the library. William and Adso must press the letters of this inscription in order to gain access to the *finis Africae*. Eco also includes the number seven, as "three plus four . . . a superlatively mystical number" (445), in the novel. In *The Name of the Rose*, there are seven murders, and the events of the novel take place over seven days. Evidently, Eco takes the numerical patterns that exist in "Death and the Compass" and expands upon them in his medieval mystery.

Eco also expands upon Borges's idea of the religious or mystical pattern to account for murder. The idea is not new. Chesterton's Father Brown series is built precisely on this type of misdirection and rationally explanatory solution. Another source of the "marvelous pattern" solution can be found in Van Dine's *The Bishop Murder Case*, where the murderer apparently uses nursery rhymes as the basis for his crimes; thus, "Johnny Sprigg is shot through the middle of his wig." The important consideration for the detectory reader is that the marvelous pattern must be rejected by the detective, who in turn must offer the reader another, perhaps just as seductive, satisfying product of sober reasoning. Eden Phillpotts's detective John Ringrose explains:

> A crime is not a conjuring trick. . . . It often appears to defy natural laws and argue supernatural interference with reality. But the police never permit any supernatural theory either to challenge or defeat them. We argue that the seemingly impossible means only that the clue, or pass

key, to the mystery is withheld, and we seek steadfastly
and untiringly for that. (Sayers, *Omnibus* 232)

The imminence of a revelation that does not take place is for
Borges "the esthetic fact" ["el hecho estítico" (*Otras inquisiciones*
12]. In "Death and the Compass," Borges's innovation on the marvelous pattern consists in complicating the relation of the rational solution to the expectations of the reader and the detective.

When a third victim turns up in the baths of the abbey in
The Name of the Rose, the monks raise a cry to high heaven:

> Too many dead . . . too many dead. . . . But it was written
> in the second book of the apostle, with the first trumpet
> came the hail, with the second and third part of the sea
> became blood; and you found one body in the hail, the
> other in the blood. . . . The third trumpet warns that a
> burning star will fall in the third part of rivers and
> fountains of water. So I tell you, our third brother has
> disappeared. And fear for the fourth, because the third
> part of the sun will be smitten, and if the moon and the
> stars, so there will be almost complete darkness. (255)

Direct observation of Berengar, the victim, allows the detective
to determine that this fascinating pattern (fascinating to a monk's
mind and adequate to the setting of the abbey) is probably a
veneer superimposed on the crimes. William comes to this
reasoned conclusion because although the third victim was
found submerged in water, the source of his death was clearly
something else. By means of his observations, William suspects
that a single diabolical mind (another detective story convention), using the Apocalypse as guide, is arranging the murders in
a symbolic way.

Like Lönnrot, William of Baskerville is misled, because he
believes that the crimes are being committed and arranged in the
pattern announced in Saint John's Book of the Apocalypse by
this criminal mind. The murders *seem* to follow the apocalyptic
pattern of the scripture: "Hail for [the first dead monk]
Adelmo, . . . blood for Venantius, . . . water for Berengar . . . the
third part of the sky for Severinus . . . and finally scorpions for
Malachi" (*Name* 469–70). The monks' deaths, which seem to
follow the Apocalyptic sequence, are in truth "random acts"
made coherent by the monk Alinardo's fear and fanaticism,

which lead him to prophesy the end of days in the abbey. Jorge of Burgos uses the notion to his advantage in misleading William of Baskerville (and the reader) to believe that the deaths can be explained and forestalled in the terms dictated by the pattern. But finally, like Lönnrot, the detective realizes the nature of the game: "I conceived a false pattern to interpret the moves of the guilty man, and the guilty man fell in with it" (470). Eco, therefore, successfully transplants the plot of Borges's "Death and the Compass" in order to create a mystery with two possible explanations, one of which is unacceptable to the detectory reader: one that is based on observed fact and evidence, but leading to chance and chaos; and another, based on a mystical pattern, and thus attractive to the conventional intellect of the detective. The mystical pattern, as in "Death and the Compass," proves to be incorrect, because the events have no direct motivation other than the monks' desire to read the forbidden text. The divine plan surmised to be at work in the text is revealed in Eco's novel to be the work of desire and personal obsession.

NOTES

1. For a discussion of chaos and strange attractors, see James Gleick, *Chaos: Making a New Science*, 140–44. Also of interest is Ilya Prigogine and Isabelle Stengers's *Order out of Chaos*, a book whose main theme is the "strong interaction of the issues proper to culture as a whole and the internal conceptual problems of science in particular" (19).

2. Is it possible, in reading a book made of quotations such as *The Name of the Rose*, to refrain from linking the image of poison-eating monk to Ben Jonson's assertion—"There be some men are born to suck out the poison of books, *Habeant venenum pro victu; imo, pro deliciis* [To them poison is as a food—nay, as a delicacy]?" (Norman, 70).

Labyrinths and the Detectory Schema

Another of Eco's adaptations of Borges is his use of the labyrinth in *The Name of the Rose*. The labyrinth appears intimately related to the library, an idea that Borges developed in "The Library of Babel." In Borges's story, several librarians guard the library from outsiders who might harm the books. The library is cyclical, unending, and full of "enigmatical volumes":

> The universe (which others call the Library) is composed of an indefinite and perhaps infinite number of hexagonal galleries. . . . On some shelf in some hexagon . . . there must exist a book that is the formula and perfect compendium *of all the rest*: some librarian has gone through it and he is analogous to a god. . . . How could one locate the venerated and secret hexagon which housed Him? Someone proposed a regressive method: To locate book A, consult first a book B which indicates A's position; to locate book B, consult first a book C, and so on to infinity [El universo (que otros llaman la biblioteca) se compone de un número indefinido, y tal vez infinito, de galerías hexagonales. . . . ¿Cómo localizar el venerado hexágono secreto que lo hospedaba? Alguien propuso un metodo regresivo: Para localizar el libro A, consultar previamente el libro B, que indique el sitio del libro A; para localizar el libro B, consultar previamente un libro C, y así hasta lo infinito]. (*Labyrinths* 51–56; *Obras* 1.465–69)

Borges's library contains all the possible combinations of letters and symbols, and therefore represents the universe. The abbey's library, with its various rooms named after the places of the world known to the medieval mind, "reproduces the map of the world" (*Name* 314). In order to understand this world, with its charge of tragedy and finitude, the monks seek the book that is the key to wisdom, represented in Eco's novel by the second part of Aristotle's *Poetics*. This text, in the dangerous terms of comedy, turns the world upside down and liberates the monks from the strictures of a millenarian cult of death.[1]

In *The Name of the Rose*, the library is the key to the mystery because it serves as the obstacle between the monks' wishes and the hiding place of the deadly text. Like a detective story, the labyrinthine library protects the answer and delays Brother William from discovering what he seeks. The concealed book, which is present somewhere in the labyrinth, is comparable to the criminal who is to be found in a detective story. The library, in its configuration, represents the hermeneutic code discussed by Barthes in *S/Z*. The enigma of the abbey is thematized in relation to the library, which by its very structure proves intriguing to the investigator and is the only place that Brother William is not allowed to enter. The prohibition heightens the interest of the reader and the detective, and this interest is increased by the rumors of strange events that take place in the library at night, when dead monks wander its halls and mysterious, inexplicable lights appear reflected in its tower windows.

The enigma is proposed when William realizes the nature of the mystery. Deaths are occurring that are in some way related to a book, as Venatius's notes make evident. There are partial answers about the nature of the book in the monks' scribbled notes, which are written in Greek "in a very fine hand, and yet in a disorderly way" (*Name* 162). When William discovers Venatius's notes there is a commotion in the darkened hall where the monks perform their learned duties, and William's glasses are stolen. He is therefore unable to read or decipher the cryptogram that appears to explain the way to the book. In these events, we see a major device of the hermeneutic code at work; namely, delay. Delay, as Barthes defines it, occurs in different forms: equivocation, snares, jamming, suspended answers, and partial answers (209–10). All delay postpones the revelation and prolongs the story (the novel's library is an embodiment of this device). Promises of an answer are usually followed by some form of delay to avoid revealing the answer too early in the story. The notes written by Venatius, for example, reveal a number of strange images: a shameless stone that rolls over a plain, cicadas that will sing from the ground, and venerable fig trees. From these enigmatic phrases, and in the context of certain conversations and books, William will come to realize that these images were used by Aristotle in the first book of the *Poetics* and also in the *Rhetoric* (*Name* 471). But this revelation does not come until the end of the story. On the way to that answer and to the book, there stands the library and its labyrinthine rooms (Adso asks William, "Is the library, then, an instrument not for distributing the truth but for delaying its appearance?" William is forced to reply that "in this case it is" [286]).

Another of Barthes's forms of delay is the snare, defined by him as "a kind of deliberate evasion of the truth" (75). For example, when William questions Severinus, the herbalist, about the relations among the monks in the abbey, Severinus comments that Adelmo, the first monk to die, was very close to Jorge, Venatius, "and . . . naturally, Berengar" (*Name* 69). There is a suspended answer indicated in the ellipsis that precedes the adverb, but that possibility resolves itself when Severinus names Berengar. Still, Brother William is curious about the qualification of the answer. "And why 'naturally'?" (69) he asks. This is the same question that the detectory reader is prompted to ask in relation to Eco's opening gambit in the preface. The adverb suggests a question about its opposite, "unnaturally," which is warranted both by the ellipsis and by what Eco says in his preface in relation to the preface. Severinus prevaricates further, saying "They were of an age, they had been novices together, it was normal for them to have things to talk about" (69). The suspicious reader will later find out that the relationship between Adelmo and Berengar was "unnatural," not simply because of their sexual involvement but because Berengar had used the lure of the forbidden book in order to obtain Adelmo's favors.

We can detect another snare in the proposal of the enigma, as in the questioning of Aymaro, an Italian monk. "Do improper things take place in the abbey?" asks Brother William of the monk. "A monk is also human," replies Aymaro. "But here they are less human than elsewhere" (*Name* 125). While Aymaro evades the truth, he proposes a riddle that hints, in its suggestion of inhuman behavior, at the possibility of a murderer or group of murderers at large within the confines of the abbey. We detect the snare in Aymaro's subsequent disavowal: "And what I have said: remember that I did not say it" (125).

A snare can also be identified by its practical effects, which are a devious effacing of truth value. Such a snare lurks within the confines of the library. The herbs that burn in a lamp in the library intoxicate and produce visions, a snare in the traditional sense, and also in its effects. The herbs cause Adso to have visions of serpents and female bodies, and to conceive that he is turning into a toad. Adso's visions have some relation to his experiences in the abbey, but they are a distortion of the reality that he has lived alongside his master.

The mirror that is found in the library and the ventilation slits that allow air into the building can be conceived in terms of hermeneutic equivocation. They are also evidence of William's observation on the library: "This place of forbidden knowledge is guarded by many and most cunning devices. Knowledge is used to conceal, rather than to enlighten" (*Name* 176). Adso ventures into a room, holding his lamp, and "[a] giant of threatening dimensions, a swaying and fluttering form came toward me, like a ghost" (172). He flees into William's arms. After a moment's confusion, William realizes that the form is in fact a distorting mirror. The critic D.B. Jewison has noted that "the mirror in Eco's library is clearly intended to create a false impression, and in particular to keep the hidden text secret" (85). The mirror is also an allusion to the one in Borges's "The Library of Babel." Borges's mirror "faithfully duplicates all appearances" [fielmente duplica las apariencias], and its presence in the library has a purpose other than the carnivalesque and frightening one of Eco's: Its polished surfaces "represent and promise the infinite" [figuran y prometen el infinito (*Labyrinths* 51; *Obras* 1.465)]. The second delay by equivocation, the creation of a false impression, is created by the air ventilation slits in the tower rooms. As he makes his way through the labyrinth, Adso recalls, "I felt an invisible hand stroke my cheek, while a groan, not human and not animal, echoed in both that room and the next, as if a ghost were wandering from one to the other" (*Name* 177).

These two devices of the labyrinth, the mirror and the vents, suggest supernatural presences and have to be investigated, causing misdirection and delay on the way to the answer. The fact that they reveal a human agency, however, works to build the anticipation for a rational explanation to the mystery. "Jamming" is Barthes's third category of delay. It occurs repeatedly in the novel in relation to the library, starting with the abbot's denial of the detectives' request for access. Later, the investigators find that the door to the library is locked, which forces them to seek another entrance. Later still, and once inside the place, they find that the *finis Africae* room cannot be entered without some special knowledge that is linked to Venatius's cryptographic note. Once the cryptic message is decoded, William finds that the directions are incomprehensible until Adso hits upon the right interpretation for the riddle of Venatius's note.

The process of partial answers, jammed answers, equivocation, and snares characterizes the hermeneutic code and the process of discernment that is motivated by the detectory schema. Disclosure has two aspects in *The Name of the Rose*. One deals with the way to enter the locked room, which William and Adso are able to do by means of Venatius's notes, hints of the room's existence from some of the monks, and Adso's hunch about the correct way to interpret the key. The second deals with what is to be found in the sought-after book; partial answers to this aspect of the mystery are found in Venatius's Greek notes and other books discovered in the murdered monks' desks. There is a guiding presupposition in both aspects, in both the construction of the labyrinth and the contents of the missing book: They are products of human understanding, and thus accessible to the reasoning mind.

The double disclosure suggests two distinct labyrinths coexisting in *The Name of the Rose*. One is a mannerist maze, described by Eco: "The mannerist maze: if you unravel it, you find in your hands a kind of tree, a structure with roots, with many blind alleys. There is only one exit, but you can get it wrong. You need an Ariadne's thread to keep from getting lost" (*Postscript* 57).

The library is the mannerist maze, and Adso's idea of tying and unraveling a woolen thread as he looks for his master provides the pair with an effective "Ariadne's thread." The figure of the maze also characterizes most of the classic detective stories: A center can be arrived at through reasoned methodology or pathways. The second labyrinth of *The Name of the Rose* has no center, since it represents the space of conjecture. Specifically, the idea of a maze of roots, the rhizomatic labyrinth, is expressed by Adso when he learns that "books speak of other books" (286): the world of books and literature, he has found, is a centerless labyrinth of allusion and citation.

The intertextual maze of allusion and citation is implicit in the holdings of the library, if not in its design. The library has fifty-six rooms set in a symmetrical pattern, with doors placed at different exposures, and not all the rooms connect. But the architecture of the patterns of conjecture are hazy and harder to define. *The Name of the Rose* itself is a case in point. The Bible is well represented in quotations from the Song of Songs and the Book of Apocalypse; the *Coena Cypriani* appears in the context of Adso's revealing dream; the work of the Beato de Liébana, a medieval Spanish commentator on the Bible and of the Apocalypse, is also glossed in the novel; the character of the abbot, who speaks his philosophy of neoplatonism, is a tracing of Abbot Suger of St. Denis; quotations from Marsilius of Padua, François Villon, the *Divine Comedy*, Ludwig Wittgenstein, and Eco himself also appear in the novel. Along with such erudite sources, the reader is also offered a menu of genres with which to make a meal best suited to his or her taste, such as the *bildungsroman*, the treatise, the historical novel, and the allegory.[2] Eco's novel is, then, a pastiche of quotations and allusions that sends its reader in many directions into the universe and tradition of books. The critic can thus choose his own poison, and the reader can easily become the detective, following the clues of multiple quotations in a labyrinth of his or her own making within this book made up largely of other books.

NOTES

1. The regressive method that appears in "The Library of Babel" can be understood as the proposition of semiosis that is found in the work of Charles Peirce and which was elaborated by Eco in his own theoretical works.

2. These references and many others are accounted for in Renato Giovannoli, ed., *Ensayos sobre* El nombre de la rosa.

The Drive toward Resolution
A Case for Conjecture

There is a point in William's investigation where he, Adso, and Severinus view Berengar, the third victim, laid out flat on a table in the infirmary. Berengar is quite dead. Conjecture about symptoms or the physical causes of death assumes a teleology of cause and effect that allows the examiners to formulate the primary causes of the physical change from clues gathered from the discrete system that is the body.[1] Reading the body, then, is an inferential art, which illustrates how the *ground* of a sign is determined. The investigator works to codify the clues on the body, which are all related by contiguity.

In order to arrive at a significant conclusion the examiner must formulate a second term, and add it to an initially observed case, which constitutes a realm of possibilities: "This wound," he or she may note, "does not show any bleeding." With this initial observation, the investigator has made a categorical selection from many possible facts available from the wound, such as its seriousness, the type of tissue damage, or the repeated presence of similar occurrences on the body, and he has focused his attention on the presence or absence of blood. By selecting this characteristic, he or she must use it as a codified index in order to make a determination about some aspect of death. The observation could be used to set forward a hypothesis about the relation of the wound to the moment of death. In the Middle Ages, when blood was believed to flow from a corpse if the murderer touched it, a second term, such as "A wound does not bleed after the heart stops," takes on the air of a small scientific achievement. This hypothesis, tested through observation and experimentation, can then be postulated as a rule for wounds

187

that exhibit this characteristic, and the argument can be stated as follows: "This wound occurred after the heart stopped." In crime fiction, the criminal is not beyond inflicting a wound on the body of the victim in order to mask the real cause of death. The wound, in other words, can be inflicted on the body in order to prompt the investigator into imposing a misleading narrative to account for the facts of death. The temporal fact, that the heart that has stopped before the wound is inflicted, has been arrived at through the inferential process, and may be of significance to a hypothetical criminal case.

But there is no wound on Berengar. One can imagine him on the examination table, like a leather-bound volume which once housed and organized language, but is now a cipher to the world. His current state represents progressive disorder, a gradual loss of information dissipating into chaos. The marks on the parchment that is his body mean nothing without the interpretive activity of William, Severinus, and Adso, readers of the textual body. Their collective work is the recreation of information from disorder; they are the active constituents of sense of the text known as Berengar.

The first order of inductions based on the observation of the victim suggests that he drowned in the balneary. Berengar is found naked at the bottom of a tub, and his features are swollen. At that moment, William remarks that the monk has the face of a drowned man. He has been found in the balneary because of the clue provided by the apocalyptic pattern. Though the detective has reasoned that the first monk had died by his own volition, he takes into account the will of a criminal mind: "The same diabolical or sick mind could have been inspired by Adelmo's death to arrange the other two in a symbolic way. And if this were so, Berengar should be found in a river or a fountain" (*Name* 255). Lacking a river or a fountain near the abbey, Adso hits upon the idea of the balneary as the possible location of Berengar's body. Moments later, Adso's hunch is verified as chillingly correct. In the absence of accessory evidence (such as signs of violence) that ensures their initial conclusion (that Berengar was drowned in the tub) to be correct, the three monks continue their physical examination of the body and find that Berengar's fingers, as well as his tongue, are blackened. A different hypothetical scenario is then produced: that of a poisoned man who seeks relief from the poison in the bath, and is found dead *as if* drowned. A variation is soon suggested, in which the body of the poisoned man could have been carried to the baths by someone intent on impressing upon the others that the deaths follow the pattern of the Book of Apocalypse. This abduction proves much more suggestive to the detective than the initial one, which is ruled both by the victim's "random" action of escaping pain and by being found in the water in accordance with the apocalyptic pattern.

The herbalist then recalls that the second victim, who had been found in a vat of pig's blood, had shown similar marks on his hands, and the connection establishes poison as the channel used by the murderer to carry out his plan. However, William is quick to point out the limits of their discovery:

> We have ventured that Venatius and Berengar touched the same thing, an unquestionably reasonable hypothesis. But when we have imagined a substance that, alone among all substances, causes this result (which is still to be established), we still don't know what it is or where they found it, or why they touched it. And, mind you, we don't even know if it's the substance they touched that brought them to their death. (*Name* 261–62)

Hence, the validity of the reasoning process depends on the way it is used. The case of the murdered monks requires the verification made available by yet another death, which the plot soon generates. Three dead men with blackened fingers is a good indication of a common cause of death. But even this evidence leaves much unanswered in relation to the other terms of the murder equation: How is the poison administered? Who is interested in killing these men? And why? In his review of *Not to Be Taken* by Anthony Berkeley, Borges notes:

> The simple circumstance that a poison can kill a man though the poisoner might be far away, lessens or annuls—in my opinion—its virtue for this genre of fiction. If the instrument is a dagger or a bullet, the instant of the crime is defined; if the instrument is a poison, the instant is magnified and becomes vague [La simple circunstancia de que un veneno puede matar a un hombre aunque el

envenenador esté lejos, aminora o anula—en mi opinión—
su virtud para este género de ficciones. Si el instrumento
es un puñal o un balazo, el instante del crimen es definido;
si el instrumento es un veneno, el instante se agranda y
desdibuja]. (*Textos* 262)

Borges's indictment of the use of poison in detective fiction is
valid for the mystery of *The Name of the Rose*, but the use of
poison suits Eco's argument in relation to the rhizomatic nature
of cause and effect. Poison creates and magnifies the murderous
intent in the novel, and makes it subject to imprecision. As it
circulates in the abbey, poison, the murder weapon, creates a
lethal "space" that has no center or exit until its source can be
found. In fact, many of the monks have poisoned themselves at
will, as it were, since the poison is not added to their food or
drink but rather coats the pages of the book they wish to read.

The pattern of the Apocalypse suggests itself naturally
enough, in the context of the abbey, to monks who believe that
they are experiencing the senility of the world. It is appropriate
that the peculiarities of the deaths suggest the Apocalypse to the
oldest living monk in the Abbey, Alinardo of Grottaferratta.
When Burgos finds out that Baskerville seems intrigued by the
apocalyptic pattern, he, with the devious help of the librarian,
frames the evidence so as to reinforce the pattern that points to a
divine plan. Burgos's ploy is also intended as a warning to
others, who are the potential readers of the text in question.
Ironically, the false pattern puts the detective on the trail of
Burgos by the associations he makes between the Apocalypse
and the many codices produced in Hispania on this subject.
However, William's error lies in expecting consistency in the
course of events. Unlike Lönnrot in "Death and the Compass,"
his mistaken expectations do not prove to be his undoing.
Burgos completes the pattern by becoming the seventh victim of
the poison in the manner prescribed by the Book of John.

Burgos's suicide represents the closure of an intertextual
link between the murders of the abbey and the apocalyptic
prophecy of the Scriptures. The Spaniard's death illustrates that
while Burgos conceives his actions as the end of the line that
makes the prophecy true and final (a triumph of logocentrism,
whose sign is the *centered* labyrinth), his finalizing action merely

indicates a source of interpretation of which he himself is only a particular contrived (and mortal) instance. Burgos's self-inflicted interpretation of the Scriptures is not the ultimate summation of the words inscribed in that text that guides his actions. Saint John's apocalyptic text remains open to other interpretations on the way to the present. The meaning of a text can never be reduced to a final explanatory formulation, since the polysemic, temporal nature of the linguistic sign will invariably yield multiple interpretants to the organizing activity of its reader and allow for creativity and the synthesis of new materials from old. Similarly, Burgos succeeds in destroying Aristotle's book on comedy, but its content had already been traced by William from Venantius's cryptic notes, Adelmo's drawings, and some conversations with Burgos himself. When Jorge finally allows him to read the book on comedy, which William reads while wearing gloves, "[the detective] smiled, as he recognized things he was expecting to find" (*Name* 468). The end of the novel represents a double triumph of intertextuality over prophetic closure and of abductive reasoning, the reasoned practice of shifting, contextual responses to the challenge of mystery (textual and otherwise), over the deductive consciousness that moves in a single direction from general principles.

Conjectural reasoning is the primary tool of the detective in mapping out the many turns and twists of this case. Adso marvels at the fact that William "can know things by looking at them from the outside" (*Name* 218), and William makes an interesting distinction in pointing out the limits of abduction. What William is able to know "from the outside" are "the creations of art, because we retrace in our minds the operations of the artificer. Not the creations of nature, because they are not the work of our minds" (218). What proves sufficient for deciphering the library might not be so for deciphering God's world. And yet William has said, "I work on things of nature." He has despite his protestations exhibited his ability to observe the creations of nature, a performance that has allowed him, much like Voltaire's Zadig before him, to find what is sought by others and is invisible to them. Brother William is an adept reader of the book of the world and has shown the knowledge of the hunter in stalking his prey and following its tracks. Francis

Bacon declared in *Advancement of Learning* that God has offered us two books to forestall error: the Book of Scriptures, which reveals His will, and the volume of His creatures, which reveals His power and is the key to the first one (Borges, *Other Inquisitions* 119).

Francis Bacon's idea was anticipated by Saint Bonaventure in the thirteenth century as *creatura mundi est quasi quidam liber in quo legitur Trinitas*. [creature of the world is like a kind of book in which the Trinity is read] (*Other Inquisitions* 189). This Christian idea is of some importance in showing that abduction and conjectural thinking is a textual discipline not limited to book learning. Marc Bloch notes in relation to the Middle Ages, "The illiterate did read. They read the signs of the visible world: In the eyes of all who were capable of reflection, the material world was scarcely more than a mask, behind which took place all the really important things; it seemed to them also a language, intended to express by signs a more profound reality" (83). The Book of Nature, written by God as the universal key to the Scriptures, like Thomas Browne's elaboration of the theme, which reads: "In brief, all things are artificial; for Nature is the Art of God" is a metaphor that, like Pascal's sphere, has acquired many colorings and has left, as Borges reminds his reader, many a lucid line on the way to the present [Todas las cosas son artificiales, porque la Naturaleza es el Arte de Dios (*Other Inquisitions* 120; *Otras inquisiciones* 114)].

William's reluctance to claim knowledge of the creations of nature is inexplicable. Everything is treated as a sign by man; things of nature are interpreted, and we represent these things for ourselves and translate them into human codes or symbolic systems. We do this even with man—and is not man part of nature? Are we not words or letters of that book? When Jorge says to William, "You would have arrived at the solution no matter what. You know that it suffices to think and to reconstruct in one's mind the thoughts of the other" (*Name* 465), are we to interpret this echo of Poe in relation to Schleiermacher's intersubjective hermeneutics, or as an intertextual statement based on competence and performance of the rules of a game with room for fallibility and uncertainty? Or is Jorge basing his question on the knowledge of universals which precede individuals and make them all variations of Adam, the first man?

In the preceding chapters it has already been seen how Borges adheres to the proposition that our notion of reality is produced by inference. A fundamental semiotic principle underlies this belief: We cannot have direct knowledge of "reality," which can only be conceived as a multiplicity of sign systems. Peirce expresses this idea in the following manner: "If we seek the light of external facts, the only cases of thought that we can find are of thoughts in signs. Plainly, no other thought can be evidenced by external facts" (*Essential Writings* 81). Borges's and Peirce's propositions, and the nominalist thesis of Eco's book (embodied by William's approach to the mystery), lead us to consider that the model of competence represented by the detectory reader and his or her interpretive acts, based on codes of representation assumed to be organizing the mysterious text, provide a positive answer to the novel's central challenge: can truth be arrived at through rational means?

There is another aspect of the detectory reader that must be discussed in relation to the process of conjecture and discovery in the literary text. In his essay "For Bernard Shaw," Borges writes:

> I have said that a book is a dialogue, a form of relation; in dialogue, an interlocutor is not the sum or average of what he says: he may not speak and still reveal that he is intelligent, he may posit intelligent observations and yet reveal stupidity [He dicho que un libro es un diálogo, una forma de relación; en el diálogo, un interlocutor no es la suma o promedio de lo que dice: puede no hablar y traslucir que es inteligente, puede emitir observaciones inteligentes y traslucir estupidez]. (*Otras inquisiciones* 158–59)

This "form of relation," or dialogue, is readily apparent in the course of the detective's investigation, which is based on the principle of complementarity. In line with this tradition in detective fiction, Eco's novel makes clear that the "model reader" proposed by detective fiction does not name a single entity or a single site in language, but at least two. So also in *The Hound of the Baskervilles* Sherlock Holmes, in his characteristic conceited way, recognizes the role Watson has played in the resolution of his mysteries: "I am bound to say that in all the accounts which you have been so good as to give of my own small achievements you have habitually underrated your own abilities. It may be that you yourself are not luminous, but you are a conductor of light" (Doyle, 2.8).

An example from Agatha Christie's work will make clear the "form of relation" that detective fiction proposes in the process of conjecture: "My friend Hastings . . . has helped me— yes, often he has helped me. For he had a knack, that one, of stumbling over the truth unawares—without noticing himself— *bien entendu*. At times he has said something foolish, and behold that foolish remark has revealed the truth to me!" (*Murder* 227). In this lamentation, Hercule Poirot is recognizing the importance of his scribe to the resolution of the mysteries that he records. There is a passive, unconscious understanding represented in these assistants that is sometimes able to condense the loose elements of an investigation into a revealing image.

The conventional presence of the assistant in detective fiction represents how conjecture relates to the truth to be found in equivocation. Poirot's evocation of his friend, and the friend's "foolish statement," makes clear how detective fiction has consistently conceived its "model reader" as a dual entity that defines a space of performance where error clearly plays a role. Sherlock Holmes has noted to his friend Watson that "in noting your fallacies I was occasionally guided toward the truth" (Doyle, 2.9). Similarly, in *The Name of the Rose*, Adso is an expression of this sometimes better half of the detectory reader. Adso doubts at the onset the abilities of his mentor: "I had the impression that William was not at all interested in the truth, which is nothing but the adjustment between the thing and the intellect. On the contrary, he amused himself by imagining how many possibilities were possible" (*Name* 306). And yet Adso's observations, dreams and bumbling revelations prove invaluable to the resolution of the case. William remarks on Adso's surprising ability for enlightening commentary: "My boy, this is the second time today that wisdom has spoken through your mouth, first in dream and now in waking!" (457). At this point in the story, William feels that he has figured out the intriguing circumstances of the abbey, but there remains one thing to be resolved, and that is the way to enter the locked room where the forbidden book is kept. Adso's proper knowledge of Latin and his musings about a certain monk's confusion of the ordinal and the noun form of the number three suggest to Brother William the proper approach to decode Venantius's cryptic instructions that allow them to enter the *finis Africae* room.

Adso narrates the detective's endeavors, often expressing the detectory reader's disorientation, and reestablishes the boundaries of the mystery by the questions that he directs to the detective. The examination of textual content (what have we found so far? what is the meaning of a certain clue?) is a function that Adso shares with Dr. Watson or Dupin's friend in Poe's stories. The fallible Adso, Hastings, and Watson remind one of readers who go for "the point" of a complex narrative structure, leaping over style and form just to get "there," to the self-appointed end. There are also their counterparts in William, Poirot, and Sherlock, who give rhetoric its due, mindful of its problems, thwarting the others' single-minded quests. Together, the detective and the amanuensis arrive at a narrative solution that is usually recorded, not by the site of intertextual competence that is the detective, but by that site of "performativity" that is the often rash assistant.

The rules of genre establish the boundaries within which this dialogue is to take place. A conjectural reader represents the pragmatic production of rules (boundaries) of dialogue and composition. The dialogue maps out a territory that is intertextual and that relies on previous textual tracings that imply the notion of "competence." This process defines (names) and determines the genre of the text (or conversation) in progress. Textual reality is always in progress, in medias res, and subject to change with every event encountered in the investigation. The important fact for the act of reading is that the performance that takes place between these two loci of meaning and the interpretant they produce (their mapmaking) will reveal the rules of interpretation at work, not as a singular anticipated reader would, but as the singular arrangement of Honorio Bustos Domecq has done, in the space of dialogue.

To conclude, the conjectural reader should be understood as a strategy in the face of a text that is suspected of withholding an answer, that is (or is suspected to be) reticent about providing certain information, or whose very composition constitutes an enigma. The author and the reader are both encoded in the genre as equivalent interpretive strategies composing the narrative. Words, like clues, exist in relations of conflict and indeterminacy. In this conflicting environment of contending forces and meanings, the detective must orient the investigation toward the conceptual horizon of the criminal in order to understand the motives that define the other and make the criminal actions intelligible. But we must recall that for Peirce, the self is derived from *error*; that is, "error . . . can be explained only by supposing a *self* that is fallible" (*Essential Writings* 76). Thus, according to Peirce, the existence of a self is derived from inference and hypothesis, which gives it the same status as the signs of the world that can only be known as signs and like any sign "must address itself to some other, must determine some other, since that is the essence of a sign" (*Essential Writings* 81).

The fallible assistant is the necessary complement to the detective's beliefs, and it is the assistant's fallibility that produces the surplus that permits the detective to address himself, and the evidence, in light of the supplementary difference. Error prompts the detectory reader to hold a conversation with him- or herself, in clear evidence of the dialogic nature of reason. By representing an ongoing conversation between detective and helper on the grounds of the detectory schema, the authors studied dramatize the reasoner's decentered self and its importance to the process of structuring a communicated message. As the stand-in for the reader in the text, the assistant also makes evident the reader's active and creative engagement with the fiction. The compositional strategy begun by Poe in 1841 with the Dupin stories suggests that both detective and assistant, reader and writer, are modes of a multifarious process called discovery.

NOTES

1. Reading the body is the art of the coroner. In instances of violent death, the type of wound and its particular characteristics lead to a series of questions aimed at different aspects of the criminal investigation. Different lines of inquiry into the nature of the wound reveal various facts that aid in the identification of the agent and manner of death. The analysis of tissue damage can yield pertinent information about "the absent other" implicated in the criminal act by the traces of his deed. The type of weapon used, the intensity of the assault, and the specific cause and time of death can all be determined from the clues of a single wound, which is part of a tale involving the human community, power, and desire. A forensic report is the explanatory argument resuming the meaning of these clues in a single narrative.

Afterword

We have seen, in relation to Borges's essay "Postulation of Reality," discussed in Part 2 how a text can be constituted with the expectation, or the anticipation, of a reader. Detective fiction is usually designed along these "classic" lines. The detective story is apparently an affirmation of personal intellect, but that intellect has been defined by language in a world of rules made up of interpersonal traditions of interpretation. Intellect, as revealed by detective fiction, is not individual but social. This is so, in part because truth is as multifarious and unpredictable as the meanings and implications found in the experience of reading a literary text. No truth that is socially pertinent can be discovered by the isolated intellect; all truths are socially pertinent and all intellect is social. The codes that the detectory reader appeals to in the search for an answer to a mystery are codes shared by a community.

The experience of detective fiction also shows that the element of truth to be discovered in a text cannot be restricted to a "package," or textual singularity. Elements of truth that are uncovered in a particular text relate to others within the text, and to other texts beyond the permeable boundaries of the book cover. Discovery is, therefore, a public, social event. The revelation that takes place at the end of the detective story is built on the conventions and rules of inquiry that have been developed in the tradition of the genre. To claim that a certain revelation is a Christie truth or a Doyle truth is inappropriate. There are certain milestones in the process: Poe's inventions, Christie's coups in *The Murder of Roger Ackroyd* and in *Murder on the Orient Express*, Bentley's erring detective in *Trent's Last Case*, and Borges's own detective in "Death and the Compass." But these are variations, and even innovations, that take into account a tradition of detective fiction. To claim that a certain author has made a discovery in detective fiction is only to postulate a clearly defined source of authority in relation to the generic text, a move that proves very difficult to sustain without a whole scaffolding of power and the implementation of exclusionary checks and balances which are not quite tenable in the language of a narrative text.

Some texts do try to claim such clear narrative authority by means of the narrator's discourse. They appeal to the authority of a creative or imaginative center at the heart of the narrations. However, fiction will show many discontinuities, digressions, or "breaks" that ultimately require the reader's collaboration to bridge over into a smooth narrative line: "The reader is an accomplice, not of this or that character, but of the discourse itself insofar as it plays on the division of reception, the impurity of communication: the discourse, and not one or another of its characters, is the only *positive* hero of the story" (Barthes, 145). At that point, it is not so clear who is at the center of the work, or what its meaning might be.

Borges summed up the authorial argument succintly in 1936: "Every act of reading implies a collaboration and is almost an act of complicity" [Toda lectura implica una colaboración y casi una complicidad (*Obras* 2.331)]. In this statement, echoed by Barthes, resides the importance of the reader "created" by detective fiction, of his or her skepticism and special resistance to the text. Borges's characterization of the reader recognizes the reader's role in fiction: The golem that the text creates is a "variety of measures" because it represents the opening up (or restricting) of fields of possibility from the text. In reading detective fiction, a reader is forced to acknowledge that it is artificial in nature (recall, for example, Van Dine's *The Bishop Murder Case*, where the pattern of murders is set by nursery rhymes) and that its domain of composition is linguistic and brought into existence by the performative power of words and readers. The sustained effect of the narrative act, finally, depends on the reader's adopting a position as if the text were functioning in accordance with a fictional imperative. This action clearly establishes the pragmatic function of the reader as a semiotic strategy of narrative.

What is the effect of readers on texts other than the ones produced by modern culture, texts whose existence seems indestructible and lasting? The ancient Mayas evidently considered the passing of time when they recorded their history on their temples and on stone obelisks that can still be found in Yucatán and Central America. What do the Mayan *stelae* say to their readers now? Very little; the disorder of their various messages has been progressive, subject to something like a dissipatory physical law, without the sustained organizing activity of their readers. Despite the fact that variants of the language expressed by the inscriptions is still spoken today and although attempts to decipher the *stelae* have been made since the sixteenth century when the glyphs were rediscovered, the Mayan *stelae* are largely mute.

Borges has written, recalling Heraclitus,

> Nobody approaches twice the same river. Nobody approaches twice the same river because the waters change, but the terrifying fact is that we ourselves are no less fluid than the river. Each time we read a book, the book has changed, the connotation of the words is another one [Nadie baja dos veces al mismo río. Nadie baja dos veces al mismo río porque las aguas cambian, pero lo más terrible es que nosotros no somos menos fluidos que el río. Cada vez que leemos un libro, el libro ha cambiado, la connotación de las palabras es otra]. (*Oral* 24)

Without readers and the culture they represent, the text is merely a dissipating structure, moving steadily toward disorganization and meaninglessness. Without the direct apprehension of its signs or the interaction that creates both its sense of order and disorder, what is left of the text? The signs that comprise a text are part of a representational system of relations bound to the historical character of language and readers.

The postulation of signs from signs is the essence of semiosis. Signs representing a rational interpretation were denominated by Peirce as logical interpretants; but, as David Pharies points out (19) "the interpretant is not exactly the *same* sign as the one who motivated it"; the interpretant is, rather, "an

equivalent sign, or perhaps a more developed sign" (Peirce in
Pharies, 19). This Peircian conception has motivated the philosopher Jacques Derrida to develop his idea of *différance* and of
supplementarity. One might say that *différance* represents an
inscription that offers no account of its origin; the act of reading
or interpretation represents surplus insofar as it creates a new
text on the basis of that inscription, "a new writing always open
to other possible writings-readings" (Peretti, 156): "The text can
always remain at the same time open, offered and undecipherable; it might not even be known that it is undecipherable"
(Derrida in Peretti, 155).

For Derrida and Peirce, signification is plural; for Peirce,
however, the indefinite repetition of texts is curtailed by his
"pragmaticist" conception: He postulates an ultimate logical
interpretant. Reality can have no better definition than the final
settled opinion of an indefinite community of investigators:
"Thus, the very origin of the conception of reality shows that this
conception essentially involves the notion of a *community*,
without definite limits, and capable of a definite increase of
knowledge" (Peirce in Pharies, 24). It might do a disservice to
Peirce's notion of a community that agrees on the rules of
inquiry in science to postulate a community of, for example,
Borges's readers as the source of meaning for Borges's texts. But
(keeping in mind Quain's dictum that today everyone is a
potential critic) the notion of a readership or collection of minds
given to the interpretation of Borges is a stabilizing and dynamic
factor for interpretation, with each member of that community
seeking out errors and building on the work of the past.

What one aspect of Borges's work calls into question is
whether meaning and understanding are intrinsically governed
by universal rules. It is clear that there are rules of grammar and
composition, but "Death and the Compass," for example, makes
evident that what reveals the reader of detective fiction is the
disruption of the rules of the genre, which is then transformed
into something new. In Borges's story, language is being used in
a double way—as language about language. "Death and the
Compass" is a textual site where representation occurs and it is
also a model of how representation occurs. The story makes
manifest the degree to which its rules of composition are

historically constituted. In disrupting the norms of detective fiction, it suggests that (unlike universal rules, which are stable), the cultural and historical rules of constitution depend on change and innovation in language. The creative, structural transformations revealed in a work like Borges's assert the importance of the human community in the act of interpretation and foreground the importance of interpretation as a way for the community to redefine itself in novel ways through time.

Borges's and Eco's fictions transform the classic, systematic composition of the detective story by playing with different coexisting forms that mark a return to tradition insofar as it is the referent of the narrative enterprise. But this return to tradition is marked by a certain wistfulness and not a small amount of irony. Both authors utilize the genre as a medium for other concerns and the genre is left at odds with itself in the difference. The play with literary convention is understandable within the current conception that rejects language as the mirror of the world in favor of the self-referentiality of the sign and of representation recognized as the making of fictions. This valorization of the sign recalls Borges's association with the Aristotelians: In *Other Inquisitions*, he recounts the polemic about genres and species—that is, if there are universal models that precede the individual; or if it is in turn the individual, "the imperfect librarian," that construes, a posteriori, the universal concepts.

Both Eco and Borges recognize language as a mediation between the individual and the world. Language is representation, but if signs refer to other signs, as Peirce postulated with his system of triads, and these to other signs of signs, then the detective's role is the task of interpreting signs, not directly from the world, but as if reflected in a mirror or "through a glass, darkly." And in turn, if the image reflected in the mirror is reflected in yet another, and another, then the only object existing for the individual is the one evoked by the name we conceptualize it with and nothing else. This explains the importance of the figure of the detective in Borges's and Eco's fiction and of Peirce's fascination with Poe's games of ratiocination. The possession of a thing by a sign is precarious and suspect.

Eco's indebtedness to Borges is manifest, not just for the purpose of his fictional narrative but for the development of his semiotic theory, which in turn is clearly linked to Peirce's and thus to contemporary critical thought. There is, however, a crucial esthetic difference. If Eco still attempts in his novels the elaborate creation of fictional chronotopes, that is, of sociohistorical contexts for his plots, Borges eschews this practice because, fundamentally, he conceives his fictions (and he never wrote novels) as small instruments of orientation for the concrete reality of reading individuals who, inexorably, bring their own histories (or encyclopedias) to bear on the work.[1] Instead of redundantly falsifying a context for the purpose of creating a world, Borges clearly sees this process at work in his readers and allows it to take its course in the many mirrors confronting his writing.

In taking this position, Borges coincides with the deconstructionist who locates meaning in the structure of difference:

> The deconstruction is not something we have added to the text but it constituted the text in the first place. A literary text simultaneously asserts and denies the authority of its own rhetorical mode, and by reading the text as we did we were only trying to come closer to being as rigorous a reader as the author had to be in order to write the sentence in the first place. (de Man, *Allegories* 17)

The reader's appropriation of discourse is marked by his or her particular social and historical moment. Both authors, Borges and Eco, give dialogism of text and reader its due, but Eco's carefully crafted historical setting is the purest form of history. By means of the fictional reconstruction, Eco asserts the boundaries of a knowable, historical object, a material culture known as the Middle Ages.

For Peirce, a sign exists as a sign because of other signs, because a sign is interpreted by other signs. Peirce, however, is not concerned with a personalist view of interpretation; variability is something that is inherent to the nature of signs. Borges picks up where Peirce left off and exploits the potential for infinite regress that can be derived from Peirce's conception. His fictions illustrate the endless possibilities of representational relations; mindful that every sign *can* generate yet another interpretant, he directs his reader's attention to the intricate web of allusions and echoes found in language. Eco, however, is a linguist, and operates with a system of rules in proposing his theory of semiotics. He is closer to Ferdinand Saussure, for whom a phonemic element is so because of a stable system of language, than Peirce's more radical interpretation.

For Eco, interpretation takes place in the presence of permanent structures; that is to say, stable grids or codes must exist in order for meaning to be produced. Eco's belief is not alien to Peirce's thought. As a scientist, Peirce believed in universals; that is what "thirdness" is in his theory. In contrast to Borges, Peirce denies an infinite regress of signs: Every sign *could* generate an interpretant, Peirce says, but in practice it does not, because there is an object, "that to which the sign refers or points" (Peirce in Pharies, 15), and "thirds" mediate the facts and possibilities derived from the object. In order for science to be scientific, universal laws must be abducted from the phenomena of the world. All signs, according to Peirce, point to some aspect of reality (Pharies, 16). If there were no object to which the sign refers or points, Peirce would not call a sign a sign.

It is in the nature of the sign, as Peirce conceived it, to allow for variation in relation to any causal sequence; a causal relation without the possibility of error or latitude in interpretation is not a sign. Interpretant signs add another feature to the sign relation based on meaning produced from cause and effect dyads, and they dissolve their conception as mechanistic phenomena. What would it take to make a sign operating in a given context neither dyadic nor mechanical? It would take, according to Peirce, first that the interpreter read it as a sign and, second, that the interpreter conceive the sign as built on an amount of variation. Without these actions, no meaning is produced. Thus, Peirce asserts the need for the "interpretant third" in his theory of signs. The detectory reader is a particular realization of Peirce's concept of thirdness and represents an abstraction of the laws that stabilize the form of detective fiction.

In the final analysis, Borges values this detectory reader, who is the product of a literary form centered on a quest for meaning, in that he or she represents a victory for the ordering mind. The arrival at truth and meaning in the detective story represents not a small measure of intellectual fantasy, but this is not a troubling point according to Borges. The important thing is that the interpreter makes something of reality by following certain conventions, which is a process akin to reading and the interpretation of texts. By advocating the process of discovery eminently associated to detective fiction, Borges aims to induce the experience of speculation and possibility in his reader. Borges's invitation to a game of shifting mirrors is not gratuitous —the lifelong process of investigation that it implies has moral and ethical dimensions that will be realized in the interpreter's life. If Borges avoided dealing explicitly with these dimensions in his art, the answer is to be found in that during an age of strong convictions, he limited himself to inducing uncertainty with his writing. In one occasion, Borges spelled out the implications that the reading and writing of fiction held for him by affirming that a narrative's composition is only a point of departure: "The best detective stories are not those with the best plots. . . . work that endures is always capable of an infinite and plastic ambiguity . . . it is a mirror that reflects the reader's own traits and it is also a map of the world" (*Other Inquisitions* 87).

NOTE

1. Leticia Reyes-Tatinclaux has distinguished Eco and Borges in these terms: "Eco opposes a poetics [to Borges's] that assumes the importance of the tellurian, the individual, the socio-historic, the depiction of meaningful detail, for it attempts to recreate the world in a concrete historical context." (9) She also quotes Borges's *Ficciones*: "The composition of vast books is a laborious and impoverishing extravagance . . . A better course of procedure is to pretend that these books already exist, and then to offer a synopsis, a commentary." (9)

Bibliography

Alazraki, Jaime. *Jorge Luis Borges.* New York: Columbia UP, 1971.

———. *La prosa narrativa de Jorge Luis Borges; temas, estilo.* Madrid: Editorial Gredos, 1974.

———. *Versiones, Inversiones, Reversiones: El espejo como modelo estructural en los cuentos de Borges.* Madrid: Editorial Gredos, 1977.

Alifano, Roberto, ed. *Twenty-Four Conversations with Borges,* trans. Nicomedes Suárez Araúz, Willis Barnstone, and Noemi Escandell. Housatonic, MA: Lascaux, 1984.

Anderson, Benedict. *Imagined Communities.* London: Verso, 1983.

Anderson Imbert, Enrique. "Chesterton en Borges." In *El realismo mágico y otros ensayos,* Caracas: Monte Avila Editores, 1976. 53–101.

Aristotle. *The Philosophy of Aristotle,* trans. A.E. Wardman and J.L. Creed. New York: New American Library, 1963.

———. *Poetics.* Trans. Humphry House. London: Rupert Hart-Davis, 1961.

Avellaneda, Andrés. "Borges-Bioy: Modelo para descifrar." In *Homenaje a Ana María Barrenechea,* ed. Lía Schwartz Lerner and Isaías Lerner. Madrid: Castalia, 1984. 37–63.

Ayim, Maryann. "Retroduction: The Rational Instinct." *Transactions of the Charles Sanders Peirce Society* 10.1 (1974): 34–43.

Bakhtin, Mikhail M. *The Dialogic Imagination.* Austin: U of Texas P, 1981.

———. *Rabelais and His World.* Bloomington: Indiana UP, 1981.

Balderston, Daniel. *El precursor velado:* R.L. Stevenson in la obra de Borges. Buenos Aires: Editorial Sudamericana, 1984.

Ball, John, ed. *The Mystery Story.* New York: Penguin Books, 1976.

Bann, Stephen, and John E. Boult. *Russian Formalism.* Edinburgh: Scottish Academy P, 1973.

Barrenechea, Ana María. *Borges: The Labyrinth Maker*. Trans. and ed. Robert Lima. New York: New York UP, 1965.

Barth, John. "Literatura del agotamiento." In *Jorge Luis Borges*, ed. Jaime Alazraki. Madrid: Taurus, 1976. 170–82.

———. "The Literature of Exhaustion." *Atlantic* 220.2 (1967): 30–34.

———. "The Literature of Replenishment: Postmodernist Fiction." *Atlantic* 245.1 (1980): 65–71.

Barthes, Roland. *S/Z*. New York: Hill and Wang, 1974.

Barzun, Jacques, ed. *The Delights of Detection*. New York: Criterion Books, 1961.

Becco, Horacio Jorge. *Jorge Luis Borges: Bibliografía total 1923–1973*. Buenos Aires: Casa Pardo, 1973.

Bedell, Jeanne F. "Borges's Study in Scarlet: 'Death and the Compass' as Detective Fiction and Literary Criticism." *Clues: A Journal of Detection* 6.2 (1985): 109–22.

Bell-Villada, Gene H. *Borges and His Fiction: A Guide*. Chapel Hill: North Carolina UP, 1981.

Bennett, Maurice J. "The Detective Fiction of Poe and Borges." *Comparative Literature* 35.3 (1983): 266–75.

Benoist, Jean Marie. "Le jeu de J.L. Borges." *Critique* 24.254 (1968): 654–73.

Benstock, Bernard, ed. *Art in Crime Writing. Essays on Detective Fiction*. New York: St. Martin's P, 1984.

Bentley, Edmund C. *Trent's Last Case*. New York: Harper and Row, 1978.

Bernstein, Richard J., ed. *Perspectives on Peirce*. New Haven: Yale UP, 1964.

Bilsky, Emily D., ed. *Golem! Danger, Deliverance and Art*. New York: The Jewish Museum, 1988.

Bioy Casares, Adolfo, and Jorge Luis Borges, eds. *Los mejores cuentos policiales*. Madrid: Alianza Emecé.

———, eds. *Los mejores cuentos policiales 2*. Madrid: Alianza Emecé, 1983.

Black, Max. "Induction." In *The Encyclopedia of Philosophy*, ed. Paul Edwards et al. New York: Macmillan and Free P, 1967. 169–81.

Bloch, Marc. *The Historian's Craft*. New York: Knopf, 1953.

Boileau, Pierre, and Thomas Narcejac. *Le Roman policier*. Paris: Payot, 1964.

Books Abroad: The Cardinal Points of Borges and World Literature in Review 45.3 (1971).

Borges, Jorge Luis. *The Aleph and Other Stories, 1933–1969,* Trans. and ed. in collaboration with the author by Norman Thomas di Giovanni. New York: E. P. Dutton, 1970.

———. *El aleph.* Buenos Aires: Editorial Losada, 1949.

———. *Discusión.* (1932). Reprint, Buenos Aires: Emecé Editores, 1964.

———. *Doctor Brodie's Report.* Trans. and ed. in collaboration with the author by Norman Thomas di Giovanni. New York: E.P. Dutton, 1972.

———. *Evaristo Carriego.* Buenos Aires: Emecé Editores, 1955.

———. *Ficciones.* Buenos Aires: Emecé Editores, 1956.

———. *Fictions.* Trans. Anthony Kerrigan. Ed. Alastair Reid. New York: Grove Press, 1962.

———. *Historia universal de la infamia.* Buenos Aires: Emecé Editores, 1954.

———. *El idioma de los argentinos.* Buenos Aires: Gleizer, 1928.

———. *El informe de Brodie.* Buenos Aires: Emecé Editores, 1970.

———. *Inquisiciones.* Buenos Aires: Proa, 1925.

———. *Labyrinths.* Ed. Donald A. Yates and James E. Irby. New York: New Directions, 1964.

———. *Obra poética.* Ed. Carlos V. Frías. Buenos Aires: Emecé Editores, 1977.

———. *Obras completas.* 3 vols. Ed. Carlos V. Frías. Barcelona: Emecé, 1989.

———. *Oral.* Buenos Aires: Emecé Editores/Editorial de Belgrano, 1979.

———. *Other Inquisitions, 1937–1952.* Trans. Ruth C. C. Simms. Austin: U of Texas P, 1964.

———. *Otras inquisiciones.* Buenos Aires: Editorial Sur, 1952.

———. *A Personal Anthology,* ed. Anthony Kerrigan. New York: Grove P, 1967.

———. *Siete noches.* Mexico: Fondo de Cultura Económica, 1986.

———. *El tamaño de mi esperanza.* Buenos Aires: Proa, 1926.

———. *Textos cautivos: Ensayos y reseñas en* El Hogar. Ed. Enrique Saceiro Garí and E. Rodríguez Monegal. Barcelona: Tusquets, 1986.

———. *A Universal History of Infamy*, Trans. and ed. Norman Thomas di Giovanni. New York: E.P. Dutton, 1972.

Borges, Jorge Luis, and Osvaldo Ferrari. *Borges en diálogo*. Buenos Aires: Grijalbo, 1985.

———. *Diálogos últimos*. Buenos Aires: Sudamericana, 1987.

———. *Libro de diálogos*. Buenos Aires: Sudamericana, 1986.

Borges, Jorge Luis, and Margarita Guerrero. *The Book of Imaginary Beings*, trans. Norman Thomas di Giovanni. New York: E.P. Dutton, 1969.

———. *El libro de seres imaginarios*. Buenos Aires: Editorial Kier, 1967.

Boruchoff, David A. "In Pursuit of the Detective Genre: 'La muerte y la brújula' of Jorge Luis Borges." *Inti* 21 (1985): 13–26.

Bottéro, I. "Symptomes, signes, écritures." In *Divination et Rationalité*, ed. J.P. Vernant, et al. Paris: Editions du Seuil, 1974.

Breen, John L., ed. *What about Murder: A Guide to Mystery and Detective Fiction*. Metuchen, N.J.: Scarecrow Press, 1981.

Burgin, Richard. *Conversations with Jorge Luis Borges*. New York: Holt, Rinehart & Winston, 1969.

Bustos Domecq, Honorio [Jorge Luis Borges and Adolfo Bioy Casares]. *Crónicas de Bustos Domecq*. Buenos Aires: Losada, 1967.

———. *Nuevos cuentos de Bustos Domecq*. Buenos Aires: Ediciones Librería La Ciudad, 1977.

———. *Seis problemas para Don Isidro Parodi*. Buenos Aires: Editorial Sur, 1942.

———. *Six Problems for Don Isidro Parodi*. Trans. Norman Thomas di Giovanni. New York: E.P. Dutton, 1981.

Caillois, Roger. "The Detective Novel as Game." In *The Poetics of Murder*, eds. Glenn W. Most and William W. Stowe. New York: Harcourt Brace Jovanovich, 1983. 1–12.

———. *Le Roman policier*. Buenos Aires: Sur, 1941.

Cameron, Alister. *The Identity of Oedipus the King*. New York: New York UP, 1968.

Camurati, Mireya. *Bioy Casares y el alegre trabajo de la inteligencia*. Buenos Aires: Corregidor, 1990.

Canfield, Martha. "El concepto de literatura en Jorge Luis Borges." In *Borges: Obra y personaje*, ed. Jorge Arbeleche. Montevideo: Acali Editor, 1978. 29–47.

Cañizal de la Fuente, Luis. "Universita d'Alessandria." *Insula* 38.22 (1983): 488–89.

Capozzi, Rocco. "Intertextualidad y semiosis: *L'education sémiotique* de Eco." In *Ensayos sobre* El nombre de la rosa, ed. Renato Giovannoli. Barcelona: Lumen, 1985. 187–208.

———. "Palimpsests and Laughter: The Dialogical Pleasure of Unlimited Intertextuality in *The Name of the Rose.*" *Italica* 66 (1989): 412–28.

Caprettini, Gian Paolo. "Peirce, Holmes, Popper." In *The Sign of Three,* ed. Umberto Eco and Thomas A. Sebeok. Bloomington: Indiana UP, 1983. 135–53.

Castañeda Calderón, Héctor Neri. "Philosophical Method and the Theory of Predication and Identity." *Nous* 12 (1978): 189–210.

Catania, Thomas. "What is the Mystery of the Name of the Rose?" *New Catholic World* 228.1363 (1985): 157–61.

Cawelti, John G. *Adventure, Mystery and Romance.* Chicago: Chicago UP, 1976.

Cawelti, John, and Bruce A. Rosenberg. *The Spy Story.* Chicago: U of Chicago P, 1987.

Cervantes Saavedra, Miguel de. *El Ingenioso Hidalgo Don Quijote de la Mancha.* Madrid: Espasa-Calpe, 1967.

———. *Entremeses,* ed. Nicholas Spadaccini. Madrid: Cátedra, 1989.

Champigny, Robert. *What Will Have Happened: A Philosophical and Technical Essay on Mystery Stories.* Bloomington: Indiana UP, 1977.

Chandler, Raymond. "The Simple Art of Murder." In *The Art of the Mystery Story: A Collection of Critical Essays,* ed. Howard Haycraft. New York: Simon and Schuster, 1946. 222–37.

Chappell, Fred. "The Detective Story and the Arrow of Time." *Via* 2 (1977): 29–37.

Chesterton, G.K. "A Defence of Detective Stories." In *The Defendant.* London: R. Brimley Johnson, 1901. 118–23.

———. *The Father Brown Omnibus.* New York: Dodd, Mead , 1933.

———. *Generally Speaking.* New York: Dodd, Mead, 1929.

———. *The Man Who Was Thursday.* New York: Dodd, Mead, 1930.

———. *The Uses of Diversity.* New York: Dodd, Mead, 1921.

Chimera 5.4 (1947).

Christ, Ronald. "The Art of Fiction XXXIX." *Paris Review* 40 (1967): 116–64.

———. *The Narrow Act: Borges's Art of Allusion*. New York: New York UP, 1969.

Christie, Agatha. *Five Complete Hercule Poirot Novels*. New York: Avenell Books, 1989.

———. *The Murder of Roger Ackroyd*. New York: Pocket Books, 1939.

Chumbley, Robert. "Toward Grounding Peirce's Semiotics in a Homologous Architectonic." *SubStance* 13.3–4 (1984): 106–31.

Clausen, Christopher. "Sherlock Holmes, Order, and the Late Victorian Mind." *Georgia Review* 38.1 (1984): 104–23.

Cohen, J.M. *Jorge Luis Borges*. Edinburgh: Oliver and Boyd, 1973.

Coleman, Alexander. "Notes on Borges and American Literature." *Tri Quarterly* 25 (1972): 356–77.

Coletti, Theresa. *Naming the Rose: Eco, Medieval Signs, and Modern Theory*. Ithaca, N.Y.: Cornell UP, 1988.

Collins, Wilkie. *The Moonstone*. London: Penguin Books, 1966.

Colomb, Gregory G. "Semiotics Since Eco: Part I. 'Semiotic Texts'." *Papers on Language and Literature* 16.3 (1980): 329–48.

———. "Semiotics Since Eco: Part II, 'Semiotic Readers'." *Papers on Language and Literature* 16.4 (1980): 443–59.

Copi, Irving M. "The Detective as Scientist." In *Introduction to Logic*. 2nd ed. New York: Macmillan, 1961. 433–51.

Cossío, M.E. "A Parody on Literariness: *Seis problemas para Don Isidro Parodi*." *Dispositio* 5–6.15–16 (1980–1981): 143–53.

Costa, Marithelma and Adelaida López. "Entrevista con Umberto Eco." *Revista de Occidente* 52 (1985): 117–30.

Crispin, Edmund, ed. [Robert Bruce Montgomery]. *Best Detective Stories*. London: Faber and Faber, 1959.

Culler, Jonathan. *On Deconstruction*. Ithaca: Cornell UP, 1982.

———. *The Pursuit of Signs: Semiotics, Literature, Deconstruction*. Ithaca N.Y.: Cornell UP, 1981.

———. *Structuralist Poetics: Structuralism, Linguistics, and the Study of Literature*. Ithaca, N.Y.: Cornell UP, 1981.

Dante Alighieri. *The Portable Dante*, ed. Paolo Milano. New York: Viking P, 1947.

Dauphine, James. "Il nome della rosa ou du labyrinthe culturel." *Revue de Litterature Comparée* 60 (1986): 20.

Dauster, Frank. "Notes on Borges's Labyrinths." *Hispanic Review* 30.2 (1962): 142–48.

Day, Leroy. "Narrative Analysis and 'The Murders in the Rue Morgue': An Exercise in Detecting the Unreal." In *Narrative Transgression and the Foregrounding of Language in Selected Prose Works of Poe, Valéry and Hofmannsthal.* New York: Garland, 1988. 24–65.

Deeley, John N. "The Doctrine of Signs: Taking Form at Last." *Semiotica* 18.2 (1976): 171–93.

De Lauretis, Teresa. *Umberto Eco.* Florence: La Nuova Italia, 1981.

Deleuze, Gilles, and Félix Guattari. *Anti-Oedipus: Capitalism and Schizophrenia,* trans. Robert Hurley, Mark Seem, and Helen R. Lane. New York: Viking P, 1977.

———. "Concrete Rules and Abstract Machines." *SubStance* 13.3–4 (1984): 7–19.

———. *On the Line.* New York: Semiotext(e), 1983.

———. *A Thousand Plateaus: Capitalism and Schizophrenia.* Minneapolis: U of Minnesota P, 1987.

Del Río, Carmen. *Jorge Luis Borges y la ficción: El conocimiento como invención.* Miami: Ediciones Universal, 1983.

de Man, Paul. *Allegories of Reading.* New Haven, Conn.: Yale UP, 1979.

———. *Critical Writings, 1953–1978,* ed. Lindsay Waters. Minneapolis: U of Minnesota P, 1989.

———. *The Resistance to Theory.* Minneapolis: U of Minnesota P, 1986.

Dembo, L.S. "An Interview with Jorge Luis Borges." *Contemporary Literature* 11.3 (1970): 315–23.

De Quincey, Thomas. "On Murder Considered as One of the Fine Arts (1827)." In *Select Writings of Thomas De Quincey,* ed. Philip Van Doren Stern. New York: Random House, 1937. 982–1089.

de Roux, Dominique, ed. *L'Herne: Cahiers Paraissant Deux Fois L'An.* Paris: Editions de L'Herne, 1964.

Derrida, Jacques. "From 'Des Tours de Babel.'" In *A Derrida Reader,* ed. Peggy Kamuf. New York: Columbia UP, 1991. 243–53.

———. *Of Grammatology.* Trans. Gayatri Chakravorti Spivak. Baltimore: Johns Hopkins UP, 1976.

De Vecchi Rocca, Luisa. "Apoteosi e decadenza del romanzo poliziesco d'azione." *Nuova Antologia* 506.2024 (1969): 532–40.

Díaz, César E. *La novela policíaca: síntesis histórica a través de sus autores, sus personajes y sus obras.* Barcelona: Acervo, 1973.

Di Biase, Carmine. *Il nome della rosa ovvero il sortilegio della parola.*" *Studium* 77.3 (1981): 356–64.

di Giovanni, Norman Thomas. "Borges' Infamy: A Chronology and a Guide." *Review* 73 (1973): 6–12.

Doležel, Lubomír. "Eco and His Model Reader." *Poetics Today* 1 (1980): 181–88.

Doyle, Sir Arthur Conan. *Sherlock Holmes: The Complete Novels and Stories.* 2 vols. New York: Bantam Books, 1986.

Durham, Lowell and Ivar Ivask, eds. *The Cardinal Points of Borges.* Norman: Oklahoma UP, 1971.

Dyson, John P. "On Naming in Borges's 'La muerte y la brújula.'" *Comparative Literature* 37.2 (1985): 140–68.

Echavarría, Arturo. "Los arlequines y 'el mundo al revés' en 'La muerte y la brújula' de Jorge Luis Borges." *Nueva Revista de Filología Hispánica* 34.2 (1985): 610–30.

Eco, Umberto. "Horns, Hooves, Insteps: Some Hypotheses on Three Types of Abduction." In *The Sign of Three,* ed. Umberto Eco and Thomas A. Sebeok. Bloomington: Indiana UP, 1983. 198–220.

———. "L'abduction en Uqbar." *Poétique* 67 (1986): 261–68.

———. "Living in the New Middle Ages." In *Travels in Hyper Reality.* New York: Harcourt Brace Jovanovich, 1983. 73–85.

———. *The Name of the Rose.* New York: Harcourt Brace Jovanovich, 1983.

———. *Postscript to* The Name of the Rose. New York: Harcourt Brace Jovanovich, 1984.

———. "Reflections on *The Name of the Rose.*" *Encounter* 64.4 (1985): 7–19.

———. *The Role of the Reader.* Bloomington: Indiana UP, 1979.

———. *Semiotics and the Philosophy of Language.* Bloomington: Indiana UP, 1984.

———. *Sugli specchi e altri saggi.* Milan: Bompiani, 1985.

———. *A Theory of Semiotics.* Bloomington: Indiana UP, 1976.

Eco, Umberto, and Thomas A. Sebeok, eds. *The Sign of Three.* Bloomington: Indiana UP, 1983.

Eden, Rick A. "Detective Fiction as Satire." *Genre* 16 (1983): 279–95.

Eisenstein, Elizabeth L. "Some Conjectures about the Impact of Printing on Western Society and Thought: A Preliminary Report." *Journal of Modern History* 40.1 (1968): 1–56.

Eisenzweig, Uri. "Chaos et Maitruse: Le Discours romanesque de la méthode policière." In *Michigan Romance Studies,* ed. Ross Chambers. Ann Arbor: Michigan UP, 1982. 139–63.

——. "L'instance du policier dans le romanesque: Balzac, Poe et le mystère de la chambre close." *Poétique* 51(1982): 279–302.

Empson, William. *Seven Types of Ambiguity.* Harmondsworth, England: Peregrine, 1961.

Fann, K.T. *Peirce's Theory of Abduction.* The Hague: Martinus Nijhoff, 1970.

Febvre, Lucien, and Henri-Jean Martin. *The Coming of the Book: The Impact of Printing 1450–1800.* London: New Left Books, 1976.

Feibleman, James. *An Introduction to Peirce's Philosophy, Interpreted as a System.* New York: Harper and Bros., 1946.

Flieger, Verlyn. "The Name, the Thing, the Mystery." *Georgia Review* 38.1 (1984): 178–81.

Foucault, Michel. *The Archaeology of Knowledge.* London: Tavistock, 1972.

——. "What Is an Author?" In *Textual Strategies,* ed. Josué V. Harari. Ithaca N.Y.: Cornell UP, 1979. 141–60.

Foster, David William. *A Bibliography of the Works of Jorge Luis Borges.* Tempe: Arizona State UP, 1971.

——. "Borges and Structuralism: Toward an Implied Poetics." *Modern Fiction Studies* 19.3 (1973): 341–351.

——. "Para una caracterización de la *escritura* en los relatos de Borges." *Revista Iberoamericana* 43.100–101 (1977): 337–55.

Galan, F.W. "A Theory of Semiotics." *Canadian Review of Comparative Literature* 18.3 (1977): 354–58.

Gass, William. "Imaginary Borges." *New York Review of Books* 13.9 (November 20, 1969): 6, 8, 10.

Genette, Gérard. "La litterature selon Borges." In *L'Herne: Cahiers Paraissant Deux Fois L'An,* ed. Dominique de Roux. Paris: Editions de L'Herne, 1964. 323–27.

——. "L'utopie littéraire." In *Figures.* Paris: Editions du Seuil, 1966. 123–32.

——. *Narrative Discourse.* Ithaca, N.Y.: Cornell UP, 1980.

Gillespie, Robert. "Detections: Borges and Father Brown." *Novel: A Forum on Fiction* 7.3 (1974): 220–230.

Gilson, Etienne. *La filosofía en la Edad Media.* Trans. Arsenio Palacios and Salvador Caballeros. 2 vols. Madrid: Editorial Gredos, 1958.

Ginzburg, Carlo. "Clues: Morelli, Freud, and Sherlock Holmes." In *The Sign of Three*, ed. Umberto Eco and Thomas A. Sebeok. Bloomington: Indiana UP, 1983. 81–118.

————. "Clues: Roots of a Scientific Paradigm." *Theory and Society* 7.3 (1979): 273–88.

Giovannoli, Renato, ed. *Ensayos sobre* El nombre de la rosa. Madrid: Lumen, 1985.

Gleick, James. *Chaos: Making a New Science*. New York: Penguin, 1987.

Goloboff, Gerardo Mario. "Sueño, memoria, producción del significante en *Ficciones* de Jorge Luis Borges." In *Asedio a Jorge Luis Borges*, ed. Joaquín Marco. Madrid: Ultramar Editores, 1981. 129–159.

Goodhart, Sandor. "Oedipus and Laius' Many Murderers." *Diacritics* 8 (1978): 55–71.

Goudge, Thomas A. *The Thought of C.S. Peirce*. Toronto: Toronto UP, 1950.

Greenlee, Douglas. *Peirce's Concept of a Sign*. The Hague: Mouton, 1973.

Grella, George. "Murder & Manners: The Formal Detective Novel." *Novel: A Forum on Fiction* 4.1 (1970): 30–48.

Grossvogel, David I. *Mystery and Its Fictions: From Oedipus to Agatha Christie*. Baltimore: Johns Hopkins UP, 1979.

Hacking, Ian. *The Emergence of Probability: A Philosophical Study of Early Ideas About Probability, Induction and Statistical Inference*. London: Cambridge UP, 1975.

Hager, Stanton. "Palaces of the Looking Glass: Borges's Deconstruction of Metaphysics." In *The Scope of the Fantastic: Theory, Technique, Major Authors*, ed. Robert A. Collins and Howard D. Pearce. Westport, Conn.: Greenwood, 1985. 231–38.

Hardwick, Charles S., ed. *Semiotics and Significs: The Correspondence Between C.S. Peirce and Victoria Lady Welby*. Bloomington: Indiana UP, 1977.

Harrison, Michael. "A Study in Surmise." *Ellery Queen's Mystery Magazine* 57 (1971): 418–20.

Harrowitz, Nancy. "The Body of the Detective Model: Charles S. Peirce and Edgar Allan Poe." In *The Sign of Three*, ed. Umberto Eco and Thomas A. Sebeok. Bloomington: Indiana UP, 1983. 179–97.

Hart, Thomas R. "The Literary Criticism of Jorge Luis Borges." In *Velocities of Change*, ed. Richard Macksey. Baltimore: Johns Hopkins UP, 1974. 277–291.

Hartman, Geoffrey H. "Literature High and Low: The Case of the Mystery Story." In *The Poetics of Murder*, ed. Glenn W. Most and William W. Stowe. New York: Harcourt Brace Jovanovich, 1983. 210–29.

Hawkes, Terence. "Taking It as Read." *The Yale Review* 69.4 (1980): 560–75.

Haycraft, Howard, ed. *The Art of the Mystery Story: A Collection of Critical Essays.* New York: Simon and Schuster, 1946.

———. *Murder for Pleasure: The Life and Times of the Detective Story.* New York: Appleton-Century, 1941.

Hayes, Ader W., and K. Tolvlyon. "'The Cross and the Compass': Patterns of Order in Chesterton and Borges." *Hispanic Review* 49.4 (1981): 395–405.

Hintikka, Jaakko. *Knowledge and Belief: An Introduction to the Logic of the Two Notions.* Ithaca, N.Y.: Cornell UP, 1962.

———. "Sherlock Holmes Meets Modern Logic: Toward a Theory of Information- Seeking Through Questioning." In *Proceedings of the 1978 Groningen Colloquium*, ed. E.M. Barth and J.L. Martens. Amsterdam: John Benjamins, 1982. 55–76.

Hirsch, David H. "Signs and Wonders." *Sewanee Review* 87.4 (1979): 628–38.

Hirsch, E.D. *The Aims of Interpretation.* Chicago: U of Chicago P, 1976.

Hoffman, Daniel. *Poe Poe Poe Poe Poe Poe Poe.* New York: Doubleday, 1972.

Hogan, James. *A Commentary on the Plays of Sophocles.* Carbondale: Southern Illinois UP, 1991.

Hogan, John, C., and Mortimer D. Schwartz. "The Manly Art of Observation and Deduction." *Journal of Criminal Law: Criminology and Police Science* 55.1 (1964): 157–64.

Holquist, Michael. "Whodunit and Other Questions: Metaphysical Detective Stories in Post-War Fiction." In *The Poetics of Murder*, ed. Glenn W. Most and William W. Stowe. New York: Harcourt Brace Jovanovich, 1983. 149–74.

Hutcheon, Linda. "Modern Parody and Bakhtin." In *Rethinking Bakhtin. Extensions and Challenges*, ed. Gary Saul Morton and Caryl Emerson. Evanston, Ill.: Northwestern UP, 1989. 87–103.

———. *A Theory of Parody: The Teachings of Twentieth-century Art Forms.* New York: Methuen, 1985.

Hutter, Albert D. "Dreams, Transformations and Literature: the Implications of Detective Fiction." *Victorian Studies* 19.2 (1975): 181–209.

Ingarden, Roman. *The Literary Work of Art.* Evanston: Northwestern UP, 1973.

Ionesco, Eugène. *Plays.* Trans. Donald Watson. 12 vols. London: J. Calder, 1958.

Irby, James. "Entrevista con Borges." *Revista de la Universidad de México* 10.16 (1962): 4–10.

Irwin, John T. "A Clew to a Clue: Locked Rooms in Poe and Borges." *Roritan* 10.4 (1991): 40–57.

———. "Mysteries We Reread, Mysteries of Rereading: Poe, Borges and the Analytic Detective Story; also Lacan, Derrida and Johnson." *Modern Language Notes* 101.5 (1986): 1168–1215.

Iser, Wolfgang. *The Act of Reading: A Theory of Aesthetic Response.* Baltimore: Johns Hopkins UP, 1978.

———. *The Implied Reader: Patterns of Communication in Prose Fiction from Bunyan to Beckett.* Baltimore: Johns Hopkins UP, 1974.

———. "Indeterminacy and the Reader's Response in Prose Fiction." In *Aspects of Narrative,* ed. J. Hillis Miller. New York: Columbia UP, 1971. 1–45.

———. "Narrative Strategies as a Means of Communication." In *Interpretation of Narrative,* ed. M.J. Valdés and O.J. Miller. Toronto: Toronto UP, 1978. 100–17.

Jakobson, Roman, and Morris Halle. *Fundamentals of Language.* The Hague: Mouton, 1956.

Jenland-Maynaud, Maryse. "Une Rose pour Talisman." *Revue des Etudes Italiennes* 27 (1981): 251–65.

Jewison, D.B. "The Architecture of Umberto Eco's *The Name of the Rose.*" In *Literature and the Other Arts,* ed. David Hershberg. Louisville, Ky: Kentucky UP, 1987. 83–90.

Jitrik, Noé. "Estructura y significado en *Ficciones* de Jorge Luis Borges." *Casa de las Américas* 9.53 (1969): 50–52.

Johnson, Timothy W., and Julia Johnson, eds. *Crime Fiction Criticism: An Annotated Bibliography.* New York: Garland, 1981.

Kant, Immanuel. *Critique of Judgment.* Trans. J.H. Bernard. New York: Hafner Press, 1951.

Kennedy, J. Gerald. *Poe, Death, and the Life of Writing.* New Haven, Conn.: Yale UP, 1987.

Knight, Stephen. *Form and Ideology in Crime Fiction*. Bloomington: Indiana UP, 1980.

Knox, Bernard. Introduction to *Oedipus the King*. In *The Three Theban Plays*. New York: Viking P, 1982. 115–35.

Krutch, Joseph. W. *Edgar Allan Poe*. London: Alfred A. Knopf, 1926.

Kuhn, Thomas S. *La estructura de las revoluciones científicas*. Mexico: Fondo de Cultura Económica, 1986.

Kushigan, Julia A. "The Detective Genre in Poe and Borges." *Latin American Literature Review* 11.22 (1983): 27–39.

Lacassin, Francis. *Mythologie du Roman Policier*. 2 vols. Paris: Union General d'Editions, 1974.

la Cour, Tage, and Harold Mogensen. *The Murder Book: An Illustrated History of the Detective Story*. London: George Allen and Unwin, 1971.

Landrum, Larry N., Pat Browne, and Ray B. Browne, eds. *Dimensions of Detective Fiction*. Bowling Green, Ky.: Bowling Green UP, 1976.

Laningan, Richard L. "Contemporary Philosophy of Communication." *The Quarterly Journal of Speech* 64.3 (1978): 335–60.

Laura, Ernesto G. *Storia del giallo da Poe a Borges*. Rome: Edizione Studium, 1981.

Lemon, Lee T., and Marion J. Reis, eds. *Russian Formalist Criticism: Four Essays*. Lincoln: Nebraska UP, 1965.

Lepschy, Guilio. "On Content and Form." *Semiotica* 10.2 (1974): 191–203.

Levine, Suzanne J. *Guía de Bioy Casares*. Madrid: Fundamentos, 1982.

Lewald, H.E. "The Labyrinth of Time and Place in Two Stories by Jorge Luis Borges." *Hispania* 45.4 (1962): 630–36.

Lyon, Thomas E. "Borges and the (Somewhat) Personal Narrator." *Modern Fiction Studies* 19.3 (1973): 363–72.

Macdonald, Ross. "The Writer as Detective Hero." In *The Mystery Writer's Art*, ed. Francis M. Nevins, Jr. Bowling Green, Ky.: Bowling Green UP, 1976. 295–305.

Maldrowski, David. "Un enfoque semiótico de la narrativa de Jorge Luis Borges." *Nueva Narrativa Hispanoamericana* 3.2 (1973): 105–20.

Mallac, Guy de. "The Poetics of the Open Form." *Books Abroad* 45.1 (1971): 31–35.

Mandel, Ernest. *Delightful Murder: A Social History of the Crime Story*. Minneapolis: U of Minnesota P, 1986.

McCanles, Michael. "Conventions of the Natural and Naturalness of Conventions." *Diacritics* 7.3 (1977): 54–63.

McGirk, B. J. *Jorge Luis Borges.* New York: Frederic Ungar , 1980.

———."Seminar on Jorge Luis Borges's 'Death and the Compass.'" *Renaissance and Modern Studies* 27 (1983): 47–60.

McGrady, Donald. "Sobre la influencia de Borges en *Il nome della rosa,* de Eco." *Revista Iberoamericana* 14.1 (1987): 787–806.

Melvin, David Skene, and Anne Skene Melvin, eds. *Crime. Detective. Espionage Mystery and Thriller Fiction and Film: A Comprehensive Bibliography of Critical Writing through 1979.* Westport, Conn.: Greenwood, 1980.

Messac, Régis. *La "Detective Novel" et l'influence de la pensée scientifique.* Paris: Librairie Ancienne Honoré Champion, 1929.

Meyer, Nicholas. *The Seven Per Cent Solution.* New York: Ballantine, 1974.

Miller, J. Hillis "Figure in Borges's 'Death and the Compass.'" *Dieciocho* 10.1 (1987): 53–61.

Mira, Juan José. *Biografía de la novela policiaca.* Barcelona: Editorial AHR, 1955.

Mitchell, Sollace. "Semiotics, Codes, and Meanings, or Meanings Are Not Always What They Seem." *PTL* 2 (1977): 385–96.

Modern Fiction Studies Detective and Suspense 29.3 (1983).

Moragas Spa, Miguel. "Umberto Eco y la semiótica italiana." In *Semiótica y comunicación de masa.* Barcelona: Península, 1976. 77–97.

Most, Glenn W., and William W. Stowe, eds. *The Poetics of Murder.* New York: Harcourt Brace Jovanovich, 1983.

Muller, John P., and William J. Richardson, eds. *The Purloined Poe: Lacan, Derrida and Psychoanalytic Reading.* Baltimore: Johns Hopkins UP, 1988.

Murch, A.E. *The Development of the Detective Novel.* London: Peter Owen, 1958.

———. "The Labyrinths of Jorge Luis Borges." *Modern Language Quarterly* 20.30 (1959): 259–66.

Narcejac, Thomas. *Une Machine à Lire: Le Roman Policier.* Paris: Denoël/ Gonthier, 1975.

Navarro, Carlos. "The Endlessness in Borges's Fiction." *Modern Fiction Studies* 19.3 (1973): 362–72.

Norman, Charles, ed. *Poets on Poetry*. New York: Free P, 1965.

O'Brien, M.J., ed. *Twentieth Century Interpretations of* Oedipus Rex. Englewood Cliffs, N.J.: Prentice-Hall, 1968.

Olshewsky, Thomas M., ed. *Problems in the Philosophy of Language*. New York: Holt, Rinehart and Winston, 1969.

Orczy, Baroness Emmuska. *The Old Man in the Corner*. New York: Dover, 1980.

Ossola, Carlo. "La rosa profunda." *Lettere Italiane* 36.4 (1984): 461–83.

Oxford Latin Dictionary, ed. P.G.W. Glare. New York: Oxford UP, 1992.

Palmer, Richard E. *Hermeneutics*. Evanston, Ill.: Northwestern UP, 1969.

Pawling, Christopher, ed. *Popular Fiction and Social Change*. New York: St. Martin's, 1984.

Peirce, Charles Santiago Sanders. *Collected Papers of Charles S. Peirce*, ed. Charles Hawthorne, Paul Weiss, and Arthur W. Burks. 8 vols. Cambridge: Harvard UP, 1935–1966.

———. "Deduction, Induction and Hypothesis." In *Chance, Love and Logic*, ed. Morris R. Cohen. New York: Braziller, 1956. 131–53.

———. *The Essential Writings*, ed. Edward C. Moore. New York: Harper and Row, 1972.

———. "Guessing." *The Hound and Horn* 2 (1929): 267–82.

———. *Philosophical Writings of Peirce*, ed. Justus Buchler. New York: Dover, 1955.

Peretti, Cristina de. *Jacques Derrida: Texto y deconstrucción*. Barcelona: Anthropos, 1989.

Pérez Minik, Domingo. "*El nombre de la rosa*, de Umberto Eco." *Insula* 38.438–39 (1983): 22–24.

Pharies, David A. *Charles S. Peirce and the Linguistic Sign*. Amsterdam: John Benjamins, 1985.

Phillips, Allen W. "Notas sobre Borges y la crítica reciente." *Revista Iberoamericana* 22.43 (1957): 41–59.

Pignatari, Décio. "The Contiguity Illusion." In *Sight, Sound and Sense*, ed. Thomas Sebeok. Bloomington: Indiana UP, 1978. 84–97.

Plato. "Cratylus." In *Collected Dialogues*, ed. Edith Hamilton and H. Cairus. Trans. Benjamin Jowett. New York: Random House, 1961. 421–74.

Poe, Edgar Allan. *Complete Stories and Poems of Edgar Allan Poe*. New York: Doubleday, 1966.

————. *Selected Writings of Edgar Allan Poe*, ed. Edward H. Davidson. Boston: Houghton Mifflin, 1956.

Porter, Dennis. *The Pursuit of Crime: Art and Ideology in Detective Fiction.* New Haven, Conn.: Yale UP, 1981.

Poulet, Georges. "Phenomenology of Reading." *New Literary History* 1 (1969): 53–68.

Prigogine, Ilya, and Isabelle Stengers. *Order out of Chaos.* New York: Bantam, 1984.

Putnam, Hilary. "Is Semantics Possible?" In *Naming, Necessity and Natural Kinds,* ed. Stephen P. Schwartz. Ithaca, N.Y.: Cornell UP, 1977. 102–18.

Rabinowitz, Peter J. *Before Reading: Narrative Conventions and the Politics of Interpretation.* Ithaca, N.Y.: Cornell UP, 1987.

Rabkin, Eric S. *Narrative Suspense.* Ann Arbor: Michigan UP, 1973.

Radzinowicz, Leo. *Crime and Ideology.* New York: Columbia UP, 1966.

Rambelli, Loris. *Storia del 'giallo' italiano.* Milan: Garzanti, 1979.

Random House Dictionary of the English Language, ed. Jess Stein. New York: Random House, 1969.

Randsell, Joseph. "Some Leading Ideas of Peirce's Semiotics." *Semiotica* 19.314 (1977): 157–58.

Reichardt, Paul F. *"The Name of the Rose*: The Sign of the Apocalypse." *Publications of the Missouri Philological Association* 9 (1984): 1–7.

Revzin, I.I. "Notes on the Semiotic Analysis of Detective Novels with Examples from the Novels of Agatha Christie." *New Literary History* 9.2 (1978): 384–88.

Reyes-Tatinclaux, Leticia. "The Face of Evil: Devilish Borges in Eco's *The Name of the Rose.*" *Chasqui* 18.1 (1989): 3–9.

Richards, I.A. *Principles of Literary Criticism.* London: Routledge and Kegan Paul, 1924.

————. *Speculative Instruments.* London: Routledge and Kegan Paul, 1955.

Richter, David H. "Eco's Echoes: Semiotic Theory and Detective Practice in *The Name of the Rose.*" *Studies in Twentieth-Century Literature* 10.2 (1986): 213–26.

Robey, David. "Umberto Eco." In *Writers and Society in Contemporary Italy,* ed. Michael Caesar. New York: St. Martin's, 1984.

Robin, Richard S. *Annotated Catalogue of the Papers of Charles Sanders Peirce.* Amherst: U of Massachusetts P, 1967.

Rodríguez Luis, Julio. "La nueva metáfora de la creación artística en el cuento de Borges." *Insula* 30.340 (1975): 5.

Rodríguez Monegal, Emir. "Borges como crítico literario." *La Palabra y el Hombre* 31 (1964): 411–16.

———. *Jorge Luis Borges. A Literary Biography.* Trans. Homero Alsina Thevenet. New York: E.P. Dutton, 1978.

———. *Jorge Luis Borges: Una biografía literaria.* Mexico: Fondo de Cultura, 1987.

Rodríguez Monegal, Emir, and Alastair Reid, eds. *Borges: A Reader.* New York: E.P. Dutton, 1981.

Rosmarin, Adena. *The Power of Genre.* Minneapolis: U of Minnesota P, 1985.

Rosso, Stefano. "A Correspondence with Umberto Eco," trans. Carolyn Springer. *Boundary* 12.1 (1983): 1–13.

Rousseau, Jean-Jacques. *Ensayo sobre el origen de las lenguas,* trans. Adolfo Castañón. Mexico: Fondo de Cultura Económica, 1984.

Rubin, Nancy F. "Eco's Semiotics: A Classicist's Perspective." *Helios* 6.2 (1978–79): 17–32.

Ruthrof, Horst. *The Reader's Construction of Narrative.* Boston: Routledge and Kegan Paul, 1981.

Saceiro Garí, Enrique. "The Double Intuition of Borges/Wells." *Comparative Literature Studies* 20.3 (1983): 305–16.

Sallis, Steven. "Naming the Rose: Readers and Codes in Umberto Eco's Novel." *The Journal of the Midwest Modern Language Association* 19.2 (1986): 3–12.

Salmon, Wesley C. *The Foundations of Scientific Inference.* Pittsburgh: U of Pittsburgh P, 1966.

Santoro, Liberato. "The Name of the Game the Rose Plays." *Essays on Italian Narrative Literature,* ed. Eric Haywood, and Cormac O. Cuilleanian. Dublin: Irish Academic P, 1989. 254–62.

Sarduy, Severo. "Notas a las notas a las notas . . . A propósito de Manuel Puig." *Revista Iberoamericana* 76 (1971): 555–67.

Sarraute, Nathalie. *L'ere du soupçon.* Paris: Gallimard, 1956.

Savan, David. "An Introduction to C.S. Peirce's Semiotics." *Toronto Semiotic Circle Monograph* 1(1976): 1–35.

Sayers, Dorothy. "Aristotle on Detective Fiction." In *Unpopular Opinions.* New York: Harcourt Brace Jovanovich, 1947. 222–36.

———. *The Omnibus of Crime.* New York: Payson and Clarke, 1929.

Scheglov, Yuri K. "Toward a Description of Detective Story Structure." In *Russian Poetics in Translation 1*, ed. L.M. O'Toole and A. Shukman. Oxford: Holdan Books, 1975. 51–77.

Scheibe, Karl E. *Mirrors, Masks, Lies and Secrets: The Limits of Human Predictability*. New York: Praeger, 1979.

Scholes, Robert. *Fabulation and Metafiction*. Urbana: U of Illinois P, 1977.

———. *Semiotics and Interpretation*. New Haven, Conn.: Yale UP, 1982.

———. *Structuralism in Literature: An Introduction*. New Haven, Conn.: Yale UP, 1974.

———. "A Theory of Semiotics." *Journal of Aesthetics and Art Criticism* 35.4 (1977): 476–78.

Scholes, Robert, and Robert Kellogg. *The Nature of Narration*. New York: Oxford UP, 1966.

Sebeok, Thomas A., ed. *Encyclopedic Dictionary of Semiotics*. 3 vols. New York: Mouton de Gruyter, 1986.

———, ed. *A Perfusion of Signs*. Bloomington: Indiana UP, 1977.

Sebeok, Thomas, and Jean Umiker-Sebeok. "You Know My Method." In *The Sign of Three*, ed. Umberto Eco and Thomas A. Sebeok. Bloomington: Indiana UP, 1983. 11–54.

Seward, Barbara. *The Symbolic Rose*. New York: Columbia UP, 1960.

Shaw, Donald L. *Borges's Ficciones*. London: Grant and Cutler, 1976.

Sheperd, Michael. *Sherlock Holmes and the Case of Dr. Freud*. London: Tavistock, 1985.

Shumway, Nicholas. *The Invention of Argentina*. Berkeley: U of California P, 1991.

Simpson, Amelia Stewart. "Social and Literary Expression in Latin American Detective Fiction." Ph. D. Diss., U Texas at Austin, 1986.

Sklovskij, Viktor. "The Mystery Novel: Dickens's *Little Dorrit*." In *Readings in Russian Poetics*, ed. Ladislaav Matejka and Krystyna Pomorska. Ann Arbor: Michigan Slavic Publications, 1978. 220–26.

Smith, Robert Rutherford. "Semiotics and Communication Theory." *Journal of Communication* 30.1 (1980): 206–10.

Solotorevsky, Mykna. "'La muerte y la brújula': Parodia irónica de una correlación genérica." *Neophilologus* 70.4 (1986): 547–54.

Sophocles. *Oedipus the King*, trans. with a commentary by Thomas Gould. Englewood Cliffs, N.J.: Prentice Hall, 1970.

————. *Oedipus Rex,* trans. Robert Fagles. New York: Viking P, 1982.

Sorrentino, Fernando. *Seven Conversations with Jorge Luis Borges.* Trans. Clark M. Zlotchew. Troy, N.Y.: Whitston, 1982

Spanos, William V. "The Detective and the Boundary: Some Notes on the Post- Modern Literary Imagination." *Boundary* 2.1 (1982): 147–68.

Stabb, Martin. *Jorge Luis Borges.* New York: Twayne, 1970.

Stephens, Walter E. "Ec[h]o in Fabula." *Diacritics* 13.2 (1983): 51–64.

Stornini, Carlos Roberto. *El diccionario de Borges.* Buenos Aires: Editorial Sudamericana, 1986.

Sturrock, John. *Paper Tigers: The Ideal Fiction of Jorge Luis Borges.* Oxford: Oxford UP, 1977.

Suárez Lynch, B. [Jorge Luis Borges and Adolfo Bioy Casares]. *Un modelo para la muerte.* Buenos Aires: Edicom, 1970.

SubStance 47: In Search of Eco's Roses 14.2 (1985).

Sucre, Guillermo. "Borges, una poética de la desposesión." *Revista Iberoamericana* 36.72 (1970): 371–88.

————. "Tendencias de la crítica borgiana." *Revista Iberoamericana* 35.68 (1969): 365–70.

Suleiman, Susan R., and Inge Crossman. *The Reader in the Text: Essays on Audience and Participation.* Princeton: Princeton UP, 1980.

Symons, Julian. *Bloody Murder: From the Detective Story to the Crime Novel: A History.* New York: Penguin, 1985.

————. *The Tell-Tale Heart: The Life and Works of Edgar Allan Poe.* New York: Harper and Row, 1978.

Taibo II, Paco Ignacio. Personal interview, January 21, 1992.

Tamayo, Marcial, and Adolfo Ruiz Díaz. *Borges, enigma y clave.* Buenos Aires: Nuestro Tiempo, 1955.

Tani, Stefano. *The Doomed Detective: The Contribution of the Detective Novel to Postmodern American and Italian Fiction.* Carbondale: Southern Illinois Review P, 1984.

Taylor, Mark C., ed. *Deconstruction in Context.* Chicago: U of Chicago P, 1986.

Thagard, Paul R. "Semiotics and Hypothetic Inference in Charles Sanders Peirce." *VS: quaderni di studi semiotici* 1920 (1978): 163–72.

Thurber, James. "The Macbeth Murder Mystery." In *My World and Welcome to It.* New York: Harcourt Brace, 1942. 13–15.

Todorov, Tzvetan. *The Poetics of Prose*. Ithaca, N.Y.: Cornell UP, 1977.

Tomachevsky, Boris. "Thematics." In *Russian Formalist Criticism: Four Essays*, ed. Lee T. Lemon and Marion J. Reis. Lincoln: U of Nebraska P, 1965. 61–95.

Tompkins, Jane P., ed. *Reader-Response Criticism*. Baltimore: Johns Hopkins UP, 1980.

TriQuarterly: Prose for Borges 25 (1972).

Tuchman, Barbara W. *A Distant Mirror: The Calamitous Fourteenth Century*. New York: Ballantine, 1979.

Updike, John. "The Author as Librarian." *New Yorker* 41.37 (October 30, 1965): 223–46.

Valesio, Paolo. "Toward a Study of the Nature of Signs." *Semiotica* 3.2 (1971): 155–85.

Van Dine, S.S. [Willard Huntington Wright]. *The Benson Murder Case*. New York: C. Scribner's Sons, 1926.

———. *The Bishop Murder Case*. New York: C. Scribner's Sons, 1929.

Vaughan, Larry. "Poe and the Mystery of Things." *SubStance* 13.1 (1983): 95–98.

Vázquez, María Esther. *Everness*. Buenos Aires: Falbo, 1965.

Vernant, Jean-Pierre, and Marcel Detienne. *Cunning Intelligence in Greek Culture and Society*. Trans. Janet Lloyd. Atlantic Highlands, N.J.: Humanities P, 1978.

Vernant, Jean Pierre, and Pierre Vidal-Naquet. *Tragedy and Myth in Ancient Greece*. Trans. Janet Lloyd. Atlantic Highlands, N.J.: Humanities P, 1981.

Villordo, Oscar Hermes. *Genio y figura de Adolfo Bioy Casares*. Buenos Aires: Universitaria, 1983.

Voltaire. *Zadig and Other Romances*. Trans. H.I. Woolf and W.S. Jackson. New York: Dodd, Mead, 1926.

Walsh, F. Michael. "Review of K.T. Fann's *Peirce's Theory of Abduction* (1970)." *Philosophy* 47.182 (1972): 377–79.

Watzlawick, Paul. *How Real is Real?: Confusion, Disinformation, Communication*. New York: Random House, 1976.

Weber, Frances W. "Borges's Stories: Fiction and Philosophy." *Hispanic Review* 36.2 (1968):124–41.

Wheelock, Carter. *Mythmaker: A Study of Motif and Symbol in the Short Stories of Jorge Luis Borges*. Austin: U of Texas P, 1969.

Wilson, Edmund. "Mr. Holmes, They Were the Footprints of a Gigantic Hound!" *New Yorker* 20.49 (February 17, 1945): 73–78.

———. "Who Cares Who Killed Roger Ackroyd? A Second Report on Detective Fiction." *New Yorker* 20.49 (January 20, 1945): 52–58.

———. "Why Do People Read Detective Stories?" *New Yorker* 20.35 (October 14, 1944): 73–75.

Winks, Robin, ed. *Detective Fiction: A Collection of Critical Essays.* Englewood Cliffs, N.J.: Prentice-Hall, 1980.

———. *Historian as Detective: Essays on Evidence.* New York: Harper and Row, 1969.

———. *Modus Operandi: An Excursion into Detective Fiction.* Boston: Godine, 1981.

Yates, Donald A. "The Argentine Detective Story." Ph. D. diss., U of Michigan, 1961.

———. *El cuento policial latinoamericano.* Mexico: Ediciones de Andrea, 1964.

———. "*Six Problems for Don Isidro Parodi* (Review of *Seis problemas para Don Isidro Parodi* by Honorio Bustos Domecq)." *Latin American Literature Review* 11.21 (1982): 58–60.

Yeager, Robert F. "Fear of Writing, or Adso and the Poisoned Text." *SubStance* 14.2 (1985): 40–53.

Zamora, Luis. "Umberto Eco's Revelation: *The Name of the Rose.*" *Humanities in the South* 61 (1985): 3–5.

Zavarzadeh, Mas'ud. "Semiotics of the Foreseen: Contemporary Fiction." *Poetics Today* 6.4 (1985): 607–26.

Zecchini, Giuseppe. "Il medioevo di Eco: Per una Lettura de *Il nome della rosa.*" *Studia Patavina* 31.2 (1984): 325–65.

Zeman, J. Jay. "Peirce's Theory of Signs." In *A Perfusion of Signs,* ed. Thomas A. Sebeok. Bloomington: Indiana UP, 1977. 22–39.

Author Index